plurall

Esta obra está no Plurall.
Baixe o app no seu celular
ou acesse http://plurall.net
e descubra uma nova
forma de estudar!

AASF96WAD

Atenção! Somente serão liberados conteúdos
e serviços relacionados a esta obra.

Ajuda: @plurallnet

SOMOS
EDUCAÇÃO

Organizadora:

Editora Saraiva

Obra coletiva organizada e produzida pela Editora Saraiva

Editor responsável:

Vicente Martínez

Licenciado em Tradução/Interpretação pela
Universidad Pontificia de Comillas (Madrid)
Editor de conteúdos didáticos

Coordenadora:

Gisele Aga

Licenciada em Letras pela FMU - Faculdades Metropolitanas Unidas
Professora de Inglês na rede particular de ensino e em cursos de idiomas
Coordenadora pedagógica em cursos de idiomas
Editora de conteúdos didáticos

TIME TO SHARE

Jornadas 6

Editora Saraiva

DESENVOLVIMENTO DOS CONTEÚDOS:

Adriana Beatriz Saporito
Licenciada em Letras e graduada em Tradução/Interpretação (Inglês-Português) pela Faculdade Ibero-Americana de Letras e Ciências Humanas.
Professora de Português e de Inglês da rede particular de ensino.
Editora de conteúdos didáticos.
Autora de Inglês para os anos iniciais do Ensino Fundamental.

Amini Rassoul
Bacharel e licenciada em Letras (Inglês-Português) pela USP.
Professora em cursos de idiomas e faculdades.

Ana Lúcia Militello
Licenciada em Letras pela Faculdade Ibero-Americana de Letras e Ciências Humanas com habilitação em Tradução/Interpretação.
Editora de conteúdos didáticos.

Carla Maurício Coelho da Silva Vianna
Licenciada em Letras pela UFRJ.
Professora de Inglês da rede particular de ensino.
Editora de conteúdos didáticos.
Autora de Inglês para os anos finais do Ensino Fundamental.

Cristina Gaglianone Pinto Cesar
Bacharel e licenciada em Letras (Língua e Literatura Inglesas) pela PUC-SP.
Mestre em Linguística Aplicada e Estudos de Linguagem pela PUC-SP.
Professora de Inglês em cursos de idiomas e faculdades.
Editora de conteúdos didáticos.

Daniella Bergamo
Graduada em Tradução/Interpretação e licenciada em Inglês e Português pela Faculdade Ibero-Americana de Letras e Ciências Humanas.
Pós-graduada em Educação — Currículo e Prática Educativa — pela PUC-RJ.
Professora de Inglês da rede particular de ensino e em cursos de idiomas.

Lisiane Ott Schulz
Doutoranda em Letras pela Universidade de Caxias do Sul (UCS) em associação com a UniRitter.
Mestre em Educação pela Universidade de Caxias do Sul (UCS).
Bacharel em Letras — Tradução/Interpretação (Português-Inglês) — e licenciada em Letras — Inglês e Literatura — pela UFRGS.
Professora do curso de Letras — Português e Literatura Brasileira — pela UCS.
Professora de Inglês das redes pública e particular de ensino e em cursos de idiomas.

Luciana Santos Pinheiro
Especialista em Estudos Avançados da Língua Inglesa pela PUC-RS.
Mestre em Letras pela Universidade de Caxias do Sul (UCS).
Doutora em Linguística Aplicada pela UFRGS.
Autora e editora de conteúdos didáticos.
Professora universitária e da rede particular de ensino.

Sueli Valente da Silva Caparroz
Graduada e licenciada em Letras pela Universidade Nove de Julho.
Professora de Inglês da rede particular de ensino.
Autora de Inglês para os anos iniciais do Ensino Fundamental.

Time to Share – 6º ano (Ensino Fundamental)

Dados Internacionais de Catalogação na Publicação (CIP)
(Câmara Brasileira do Livro, SP, Brasil)

Jornadas Time to Share, 6º ano / organizadora Editora Saraiva; obra coletiva organizada e produzida pela Editora Saraiva; editor responsável Vicente Martínez; coordenadora Gisele Aga. – 1. ed. – São Paulo : Saraiva, 2016.

Suplementado pelo manual do professor.
Bibliografia.
ISBN 978-85-472-0836-3 (aluno)
ISBN 978-85-472-0837-0 (professor)

1. Inglês (Ensino fundamental) I. Martínez, Vicente. II. Aga, Gisele.

16-02855 CDD-372.652

Índice para catálogo sistemático :

1. Inglês : Ensino fundamental 372.652

CAE: 603688 (LA) / 603986 (PR)
2º Impressão

Gerente editorial M. Esther Nejm
Editor responsável Vicente Martínez
Editores Alice Silvestre, Caroline Zanelli, Myrian Yamamoto, Renata Chimim, Renato Malkov, Vinicius Oliveira, Vivian Viccino
Coordenador de revisão Camila Christi Gazzani
Revisores Diego Carbone, Larissa Vazquez, Patrícia Cordeiro
Produtor editorial Roseli Said
Revisor linguístico Robert Caudle Garner
Coordenador de iconografia Cristina Akisino
Pesquisa iconográfica Fernando Cambetas, Beatriz Micsik, Juliana Prado, Enio Lopes
Licenciamento de textos Ricardo Corridoni, Erica F. Brambila
Gerente de artes Ricardo Borges
Coordenador de artes Narjara Lara
Design Casa Paulistana de Comunicação
Capa Sérgio Cândido com imagem de Dutourdumonde Photography / Shutterstock.com
Diagramação C2 Artes
Assistente Camilla Felix Cianelli
Ilustrações Leo Teixeira, Vicente Mendonça, Zubartez
Tratamento de imagens Emerson de Lima
Produtor gráfico Thais Mendes Petruci Galvão
Impressão e acabamento Corprint

Editora Saraiva
SAC 0800-0117875
De 2ª a 6ª, das 8h às 18h
www.editorasaraiva.com.br/contato
Avenida das Nações Unidas, 7221 – 1º andar – Setor C – Pinheiros – CEP 05425-902

INTRODUCTION

Explorers are we, intrepid and bold,

Out in the wild, amongst wonders untold.

Equipped with our wits, a map, and a snack,

We're searching for fun and we're on the right track!

WATTERSON, Bill. *The Indispensable Calvin and Hobbes.* Kansas: Andrews McMeel Publishing, 1992.

Um novo idioma é uma descoberta que se faz aos poucos e requer uma atitude exploradora. Nesta coleção, você encontrará textos e áudios autênticos, expressões artísticas com diferentes linguagens (música, tirinhas, fotografia, pintura, grafite etc.). Você terá a possibilidade de refletir sobre temas polêmicos e atuais, de pensar sobre sua escola, sua comunidade e sobre seu próprio aprendizado, além de, é claro, realizar atividades linguísticas.

Para que usufrua desse material ao máximo, explore: veja, reveja, leia quantas vezes for necessário os textos e as atividades propostas no livro, pergunte aos amigos e aos professores quando tiver dúvidas, pesquise em livros, revistas, na internet. Quanto mais explorar e buscar a respeito, mais vai descobrir, tanto do idioma quanto de todos os assuntos que são abordados ao longo do livro. Explore e compartilhe suas descobertas.

GET TO KNOW YOUR **BOOK**

The units are organized by sections. Get to know a little bit more about them.

OPENING PAGES

This section presents several artistic manifestations and questions to activate your previous knowledge about the theme you are going to explore throughout the unit.

UNIT 1

Hi! What's your name?

The images on these two pages focus on a project about identity, developed by the year 9 students from Ormiston Bushfield Academy (OBA), in the United Kingdom. We can see that students work on their own images as a way of identifying themselves.

It is natural for us to question who we are every now and then, what our feelings are, which groups we belong to, what we want for our future, that is, our search for identity. These are the questions that move us towards discovery and enable us to recognize our own individuality.

Your learning objectives for this unit are...

- to introduce yourself and give personal information;
- to read and produce presentations in different communicative situations;
- to read and produce profiles.

10 ten

• www.bushfield.co.uk
Ormiston Bushfield Academy official website.

EXCHANGING IDEAS

1. The faces depicted in the images are reconstructed through color and collage. When we observe the facial expressions and colors, is it possible to determine if students see themselves in a positive or negative light? Which elements allow that interpretation?
2. The images are made of many colors, textures and cutouts. What does that tell you about identity formation?

Year 9 students' project. (*Year 9 Identity Project*). 2014. Ormiston Bushfield Academy (OBA). United Kingdom.

eleven 11

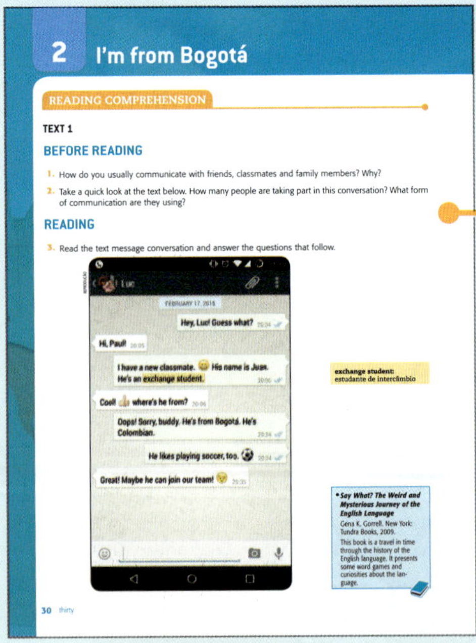
2 I'm from Bogotá

READING COMPREHENSION

TEXT 1

BEFORE READING

1. How do you usually communicate with friends, classmates and family members? Why?
2. Take a quick look at the text below. How many people are taking part in this conversation? What form of communication are they using?

READING

3. Read the text message conversation and answer the questions that follow.

Luc
FEBRUARY 17, 2016
Hey, Luc! Guess what?
Hi, Paul!
I have a new classmate. His name is Juan. He's an exchange student.
Cool! where's he from?
Oops! Sorry, buddy. He's from Bogotá. He's Colombian.
He likes playing soccer, too.
Great! Maybe he can join our team!

exchange student: estudante de intercâmbio

• ***Say What? The Weird and Mysterious Journey of the English Language***
Gena K. Gorrell. New York: Tundra Books, 2009.
This book is a travel in time through the history of the English language. It presents some word games and curiosities about the language.

30 thirty

READING COMPREHENSION

It brings authentic texts about relevant topics in a variety of genres. The texts will help you get prepared for the real use of the language.

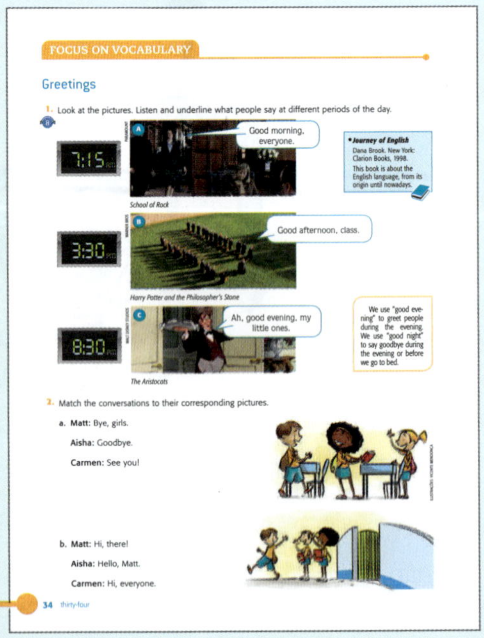
FOCUS ON VOCABULARY

Greetings

1. Look at the pictures. Listen and underline what people say at different periods of the day.

7:15 am — A: Good morning, everyone.
School of Rock

3:30 pm — B: Good afternoon, class.
Harry Potter and the Philosopher's Stone

8:30 pm — C: Ah, good evening, my little ones.
The Aristocats

• ***Journey of English***
Dana Brook. New York: Clarion Books, 1998.
This book is about the English language, from its origin until nowadays.

We use "good evening" to greet people during the evening. We use "good night" to say goodbye during the evening or before we go to bed.

2. Match the conversations to their corresponding pictures.

a. **Matt:** Bye, girls.
Aisha: Goodbye.
Carmen: See you!

b. **Matt:** Hi, there!
Aisha: Hello, Matt.
Carmen: Hi, everyone.

34 thirty-four

FOCUS ON VOCABULARY

Vocabulary practice is contextualized, so it will be easier for you to understand it. You will also have the opportunity to expand the vocabulary related to the topic of the unit.

LANGUAGE IN USE

This section will help you reflect about language in context and practice it with different kinds of activities.

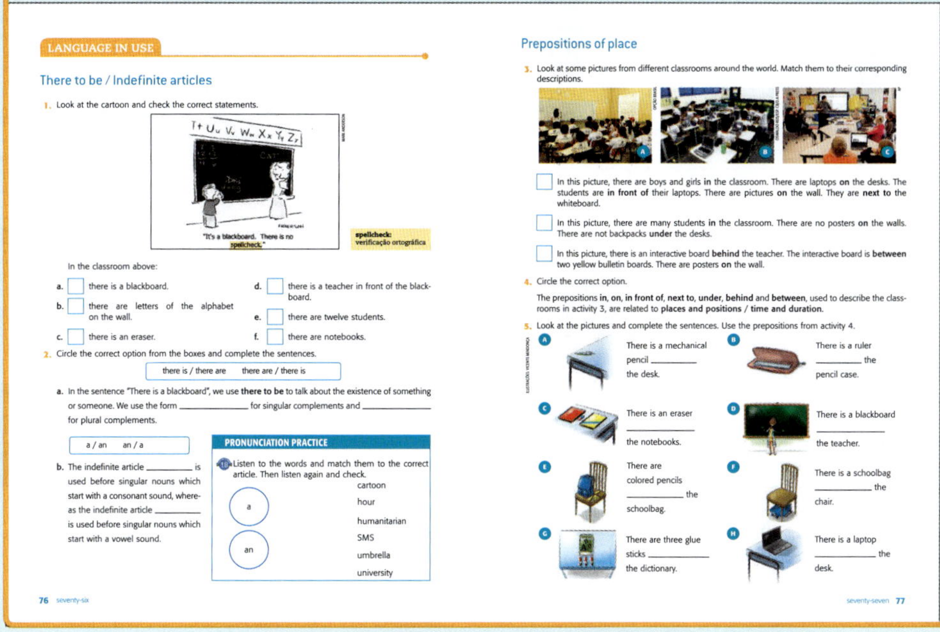

LANGUAGE IN USE

There to be / Indefinite articles

1. Look at the cartoon and check the correct statements.

"It's a blackboard. There is no spellcheck."

spellcheck: verificação ortográfica

In the classroom above:

a. ☐ there is a blackboard.
b. ☐ there are letters of the alphabet on the wall.
c. ☐ there is an eraser.
d. ☐ there is a teacher in front of the blackboard.
e. ☐ there are twelve students.
f. ☐ there are notebooks.

2. Circle the correct option from the boxes and complete the sentences.

there is / there are — there are / there is

a. In the sentence "There is a blackboard", we use **there to be** to talk about the existence of something or someone. We use the form ________ for singular complements and ________ for plural complements.

a / an — an / a

b. The indefinite article ________ is used before singular nouns which start with a consonant sound, whereas the indefinite article ________ is used before singular nouns which start with a vowel sound.

PRONUNCIATION PRACTICE

Listen to the words and match them to the correct article. Then listen again and check.

a — an

cartoon, hour, humanitarian, SMS, umbrella, university

Prepositions of place

3. Look at some pictures from different classrooms around the world. Match them to their corresponding descriptions.

☐ In this picture, there are boys and girls **in** the classroom. There are laptops **on** the desks. The students are **in front of** their laptops. There are pictures **on** the wall. They are **next to** the whiteboard.

☐ In this picture, there are many students **in** the classroom. There are no posters **on** the walls. There are not backpacks **under** the desks.

☐ In this picture, there is an interactive board **behind** the teacher. The interactive board is **between** two yellow bulletin boards. There are posters **on** the wall.

4. Circle the correct option.

The prepositions **in, on, in front of, next to, under, behind** and **between**, used to describe the classrooms in activity 3, are related to **places and positions / time and duration**.

5. Look at the pictures and complete the sentences. Use the prepositions from activity 4.

A There is a mechanical pencil ________ the desk.
B There is a ruler ________ the pencil case.
C There is an eraser ________ the notebooks.
D There is a blackboard ________ the teacher.
E There are colored pencils ________ the schoolbag.
F There is a schoolbag ________ the chair.
G There are three glue sticks ________ the dictionary.
H There is a laptop ________ the desk.

76 seventy-six — seventy-seven 77

LISTENING COMPREHENSION

Presenting different kinds of oral texts with a diversity of language variation, this section aims at helping you fully understand the messages of the texts.

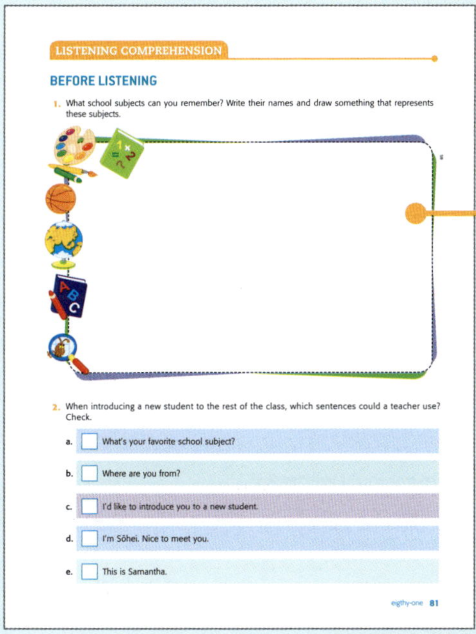

LISTENING COMPREHENSION

BEFORE LISTENING

1. What school subjects can you remember? Write their names and draw something that represents these subjects.

2. When introducing a new student to the rest of the class, which sentences could a teacher use? Check.

a. ☐ What's your favorite school subject?
b. ☐ Where are you from?
c. ☐ I'd like to introduce you to a new student.
d. ☐ I'm Sōhei. Nice to meet you.
e. ☐ This is Samantha.

eigthy-one 81

SPEAKING

Suggestions of contextualized situations for the use of theme-based, communicative and linguistic aspects presented in each unit. The objective of this section is to provide you with an opportunity to use what you learned in other contexts and/or communicative situations.

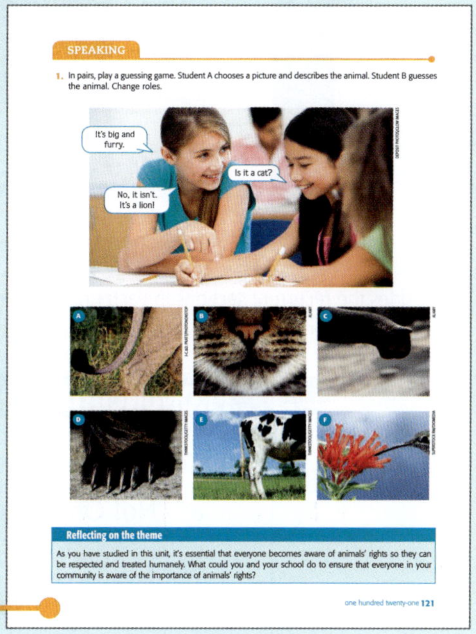

SPEAKING

1. In pairs, play a guessing game. Student A chooses a picture and describes the animal. Student B guesses the animal. Change roles.

It's big and furry.
Is it a cat?
No, it isn't. It's a lion!

Reflecting on the theme

As you have studied in this unit, it's essential that everyone becomes aware of animals' rights so they can be respected and treated humanely. What could you and your school do to ensure that everyone in your community is aware of the importance of animals' rights?

one hundred twenty-one 121

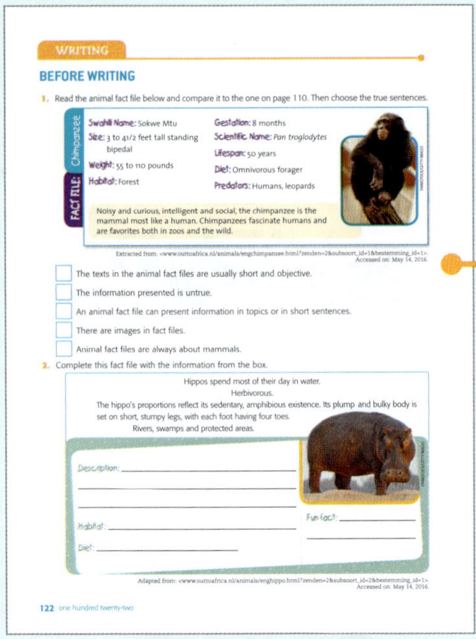
WRITING

BEFORE WRITING

1. Read the animal fact file below and compare it to the one on page 110. Then choose the true sentences.

FACT FILE: Chimpanzee

Swahili Name: Sokwe Mtu
Size: 3 to 4 1/2 feet tall standing bipedal
Weight: 55 to 110 pounds
Habitat: Forest
Gestation: 8 months
Scientific Name: Pan troglodytes
Lifespan: 50 years
Diet: Omnivorous forager
Predators: Humans, leopards

Noisy and curious, intelligent and social, the chimpanzee is the mammal most like a human. Chimpanzees fascinate humans and are favorites both in zoos and the wild.

Extracted from: <www.outtoafrica.nl/animals/engchimpanzee.html?zenden=2&subsoort_id=1&bestemming_id=1>. Accessed on: May 14, 2016.

- [ ] The texts in the animal fact files are usually short and objective.
- [ ] The information presented is untrue.
- [ ] An animal fact file can present information in topics or in short sentences.
- [ ] There are images in fact files.
- [ ] Animal fact files are always about mammals.

2. Complete this fact file with the information from the box.

Hippos spend most of their day in water.
Herbivorous.
The hippo's proportions reflect its sedentary, amphibious existence. Its plump and bulky body is set on short, stumpy legs, with each foot having four toes.
Rivers, swamps and protected areas.

Description: ______
Habitat: ______
Diet: ______
Fun fact: ______

Adapted from: <www.outtoafrica.nl/animals/enghippo.html?zenden=2&subsoort_id=2&bestemming_id=1>. Accessed on: May 14, 2016.

122 one hundred twenty-two

WRITING

This section proposes a writing task based on the theme and genre study of the unit as a closing activity. The task is divided in planning, production, evaluation and review of the work.

SELF-EVALUATION

This last section gives you the opportunity to evaluate your learning by checking your progress and difficulties with the objectives listed in the beginning of the unit.

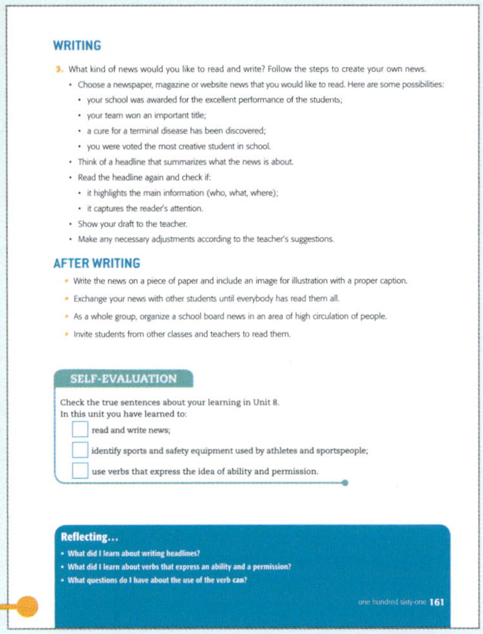
WRITING

3. What kind of news would you like to read and write? Follow the steps to create your own news.
- Choose a newspaper, magazine or website news that you would like to read. Here are some possibilities:
  - your school was awarded for the excellent performance of the students;
  - your team won an important title;
  - a cure for a terminal disease has been discovered;
  - you were voted the most creative student in school.
- Think of a headline that summarizes what the news is about.
- Read the headline again and check if:
  - it highlights the main information (who, what, where);
  - it captures the reader's attention.
- Show your draft to the teacher.
- Make any necessary adjustments according to the teacher's suggestions.

AFTER WRITING
- Write the news on a piece of paper and include an image for illustration with a proper caption.
- Exchange your news with other students until everybody has read them all.
- As a whole group, organize a school board news in an area of high circulation of people.
- Invite students from other classes and teachers to read them.

SELF-EVALUATION

Check the true sentences about your learning in Unit 8.
In this unit you have learned to:
- [ ] read and write news;
- [ ] identify sports and safety equipment used by athletes and sportspeople;
- [ ] use verbs that express the idea of ability and permission.

Reflecting...
- What did I learn about writing headlines?
- What did I learn about verbs that express an ability and a permission?
- What questions do I have about the use of the verb can?

one hundred sixty-one 161

CONNECTIONS

This section presents texts, images and activities related to contents that you have learned in other subjects.

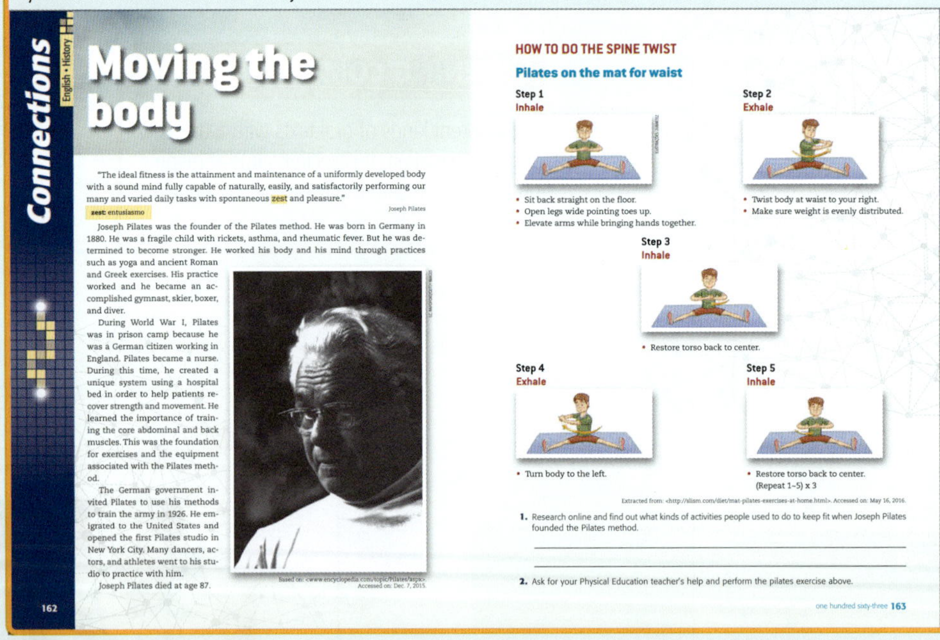
Connections

English • History

Moving the body

"The ideal fitness is the attainment and maintenance of a uniformly developed body with a sound mind fully capable of naturally, easily, and satisfactorily performing our many and varied daily tasks with spontaneous zest and pleasure."

Joseph Pilates

zest: entusiasmo

Joseph Pilates was the founder of the Pilates method. He was born in Germany in 1880. He was a fragile child with rickets, asthma, and rheumatic fever. But he was determined to become stronger. He worked his body and his mind through practices such as yoga and ancient Roman and Greek exercises. His practice worked and he became an accomplished gymnast, skier, boxer, and diver.

During World War I, Pilates was in prison camp because he was a German citizen working in England. Pilates became a nurse. During this time, he created a unique system using a hospital bed in order to help patients recover strength and movement. He learned the importance of training the core abdominal and back muscles. This was the foundation for exercises and the equipment associated with the Pilates method.

The German government invited Pilates to use his methods to train the army in 1926. He emigrated to the United States and opened the first Pilates studio in New York City. Many dancers, actors, and athletes went to his studio to practice with him.

Joseph Pilates died at age 87.

Based on: <www.encyclopedia.com/topic/Pilates.aspx>. Accessed on: Dec. 7, 2015.

162

HOW TO DO THE SPINE TWIST

Pilates on the mat for waist

Step 1 Inhale
- Sit back straight on the floor.
- Open legs wide pointing toes up.
- Elevate arms while bringing hands together.

Step 2 Exhale
- Twist body at waist to your right.
- Make sure weight is evenly distributed.

Step 3 Inhale
- Restore torso back to center.

Step 4 Exhale
- Turn body to the left.

Step 5 Inhale
- Restore torso back to center. (Repeat 1–5) x 3

Extracted from: <http://sliism.com/diet/mat-pilates-exercises-at-home.html>. Accessed on: May 16, 2016.

1. Research online and find out what kinds of activities people used to do to keep fit when Joseph Pilates founded the Pilates method.

2. Ask for your Physical Education teacher's help and perform the pilates exercise above.

one hundred sixty-three 163

Besides the recurrent sections in each unit, the series offer other sections with activities for pronunciation practice, boxes with cultural or linguistic information, extra vocabulary, and reading and/or learning strategies.

11

PRONUNCIATION PRACTICE

Circle the correct options according to what you hear.

a. "No! Oh! Ooh! But, Jane, **they** / **they're** Italian!" – *Tarzan & Jane*

b. "[...] **we're** / **we are** French, and it's dinnertime." – *Ratatouille*

c. "**You're** / **You are** in France, children." – *Anastasia*

This book also contains several appendices which contribute to your learning experience. Read more about them below.

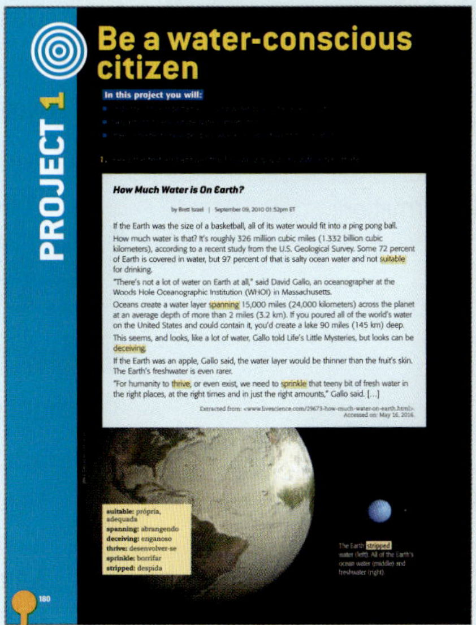

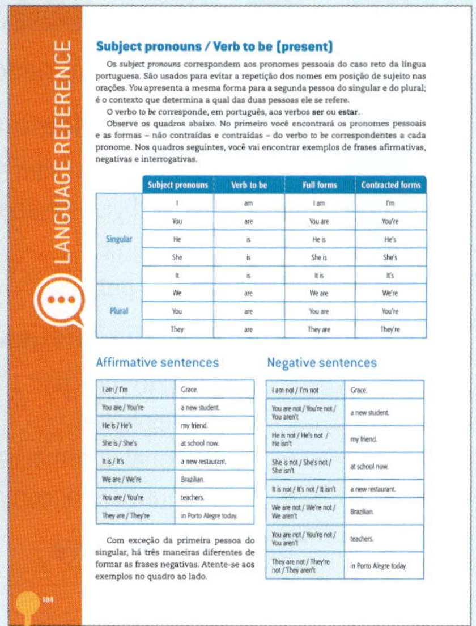

FURTHER PRACTICE

Extra activities covering the unit themes with texts and listening activities that review the most relevant linguistic aspects.

PROJECTS

Each book proposes two interdisciplinary projects with a wider scope. Based on a central theme and aimed at providing a deeper discussion about it, these projects culminate in a group closing activity.

LANGUAGE REFERENCE

A summary of the linguistic aspects presented in the book. It can be used as reference material for studies.

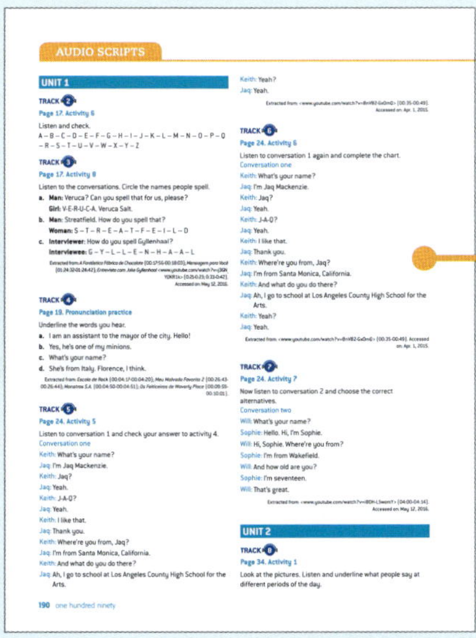

AUDIO SCRIPTS

The transcriptions of the audios used in the "Listening Comprehension" section. They can be helpful while doing some activities or for future reference.

GLOSSARY

A list of the most important words from each volume translated according to the context in which they appear.

CONTENTS

VICENTE MENDONÇA

UNIT

1

Hi! What's your name?

The images on these two pages focus on a project about identity, developed by the year 9 students from Ormiston Bushfield Academy (OBA), in the United Kingdom. We can see that students work on their own images as a way of identifying themselves.

It is natural for us to question who we are every now and then, what our feelings are, which groups we belong to, what we want for our future, that is, our search for identity. These are the questions that move us towards discovery and enable us to recognize our own individuality.

Your learning objectives for this unit are...

- to introduce yourself and give personal information;
- to read and produce presentations in different communicative situations;
- to read and produce profiles.

ORMISTON BUSHFIELD ACADEMY

- **www.bushfield.co.uk**
  Ormiston Bushfield Academy official website.

EXCHANGING IDEAS

1. The faces depicted in the images are reconstructed through color and collage. When we observe the facial expressions and colors, is it possible to determine if students see themselves in a positive or negative light? Which elements allow that interpretation?
2. The images are made of many colors, textures and cutouts. What does that tell you about identity formation?

Year 9 students' project. (*Year 9 Identity Project*). 2014. Ormiston Bushfield Academy (OBA). United Kingdom.

1 Hi! What's your name?

READING COMPREHENSION

TEXT 1

BEFORE READING

The birth certificate is the citizen's first and most important document. With it, a person officially exists to the State and to society.

Translated from: <www.senado.gov.br/noticias/jornal/cidadania/doc/not01.htm>. Accessed on: May 12, 2016.

1. Why is the birth certificate important?
2. What are the essential pieces of information in a Brazilian birth certificate?
3. Look at the document below. What is it?

READING

4. Read the following birth certificate.

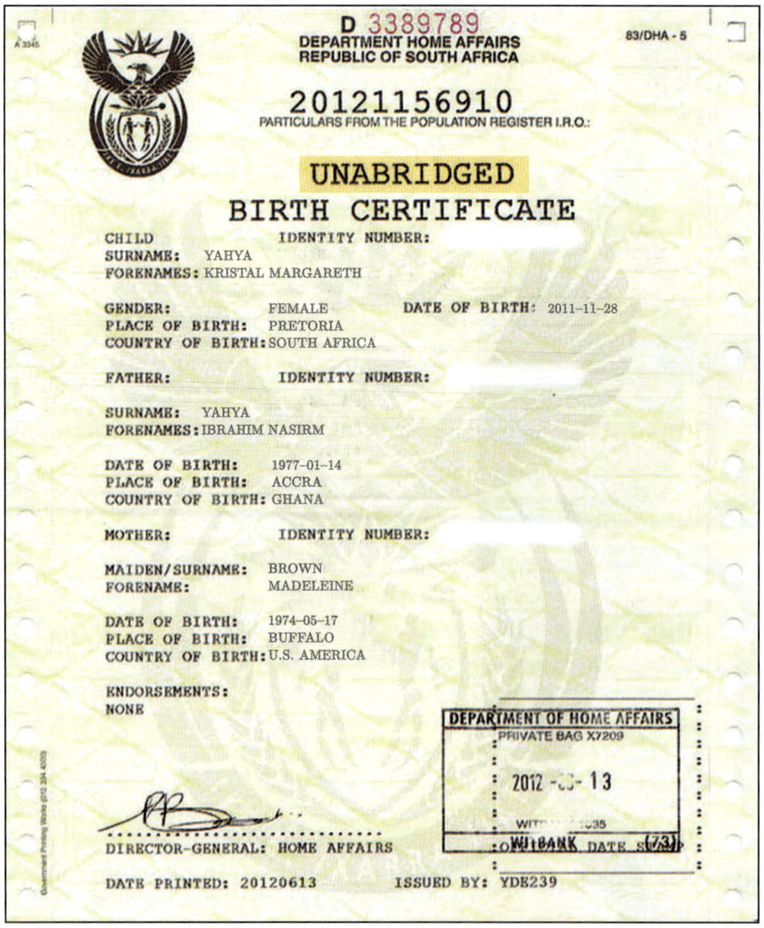

D 3389789
DEPARTMENT HOME AFFAIRS
REPUBLIC OF SOUTH AFRICA
83/DHA - 5

20121156910
PARTICULARS FROM THE POPULATION REGISTER I.R.O.:

UNABRIDGED
BIRTH CERTIFICATE

CHILD IDENTITY NUMBER:
SURNAME: YAHYA
FORENAMES: KRISTAL MARGARETH

GENDER: FEMALE DATE OF BIRTH: 2011-11-28
PLACE OF BIRTH: PRETORIA
COUNTRY OF BIRTH: SOUTH AFRICA

FATHER: IDENTITY NUMBER:

SURNAME: YAHYA
FORENAMES: IBRAHIM NASIRM

DATE OF BIRTH: 1977-01-14
PLACE OF BIRTH: ACCRA
COUNTRY OF BIRTH: GHANA

MOTHER: IDENTITY NUMBER:

MAIDEN/SURNAME: BROWN
FORENAME: MADELEINE

DATE OF BIRTH: 1974-05-17
PLACE OF BIRTH: BUFFALO
COUNTRY OF BIRTH: U.S. AMERICA

ENDORSEMENTS:
NONE

DEPARTMENT OF HOME AFFAIRS
PRIVATE BAG X7209
2012 - [illegible] - 13
WITBANK

DIRECTOR-GENERAL: HOME AFFAIRS

DATE PRINTED: 20120613 ISSUED BY: YDE239

Official document from the Republic of South Africa.

unabridged: completo, integral

There are eleven official languages in South Africa.

5. List the transparent words from the birth certificate.

> There are many words in English that are similar to its equivalent in Portuguese. These words are known as "transparent words". Recognizing them is an important reading skill and it will help you better understand a text.

6. Read the birth certificate again and answer the questions.

a. Which family members are mentioned?

b. What is the child's complete name?

c. Which word identifies the gender of the child?

d. Ibrahim and Krystal were born in the same continent, but in different countries. Which continent is it and which countries are those?

7. Compare the ID card below to the birth certificate on page 12. Read the information and write **BC** (birth certificate) and/or **ID** (identity card).

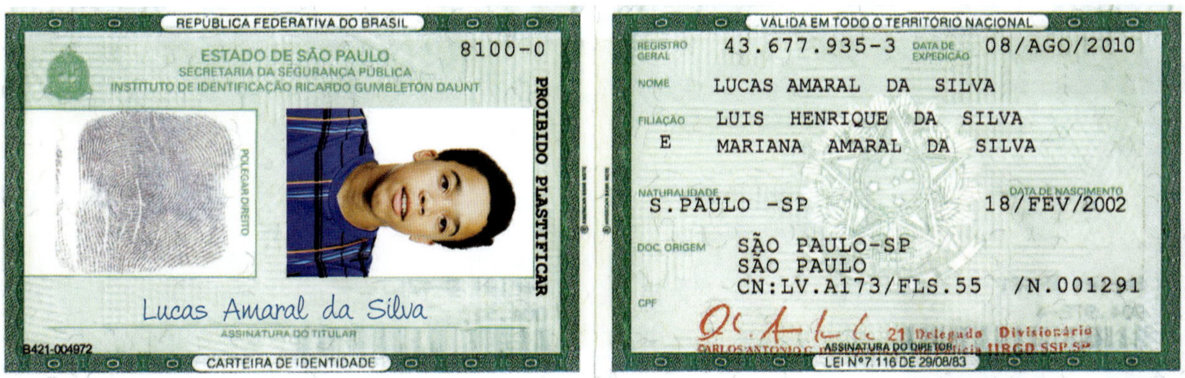

Official document from the Federative Republic of Brazil.

a. ☐ citizen signature

b. ☐ country of birth

c. ☐ parents' names

d. ☐ fingerprint

e. ☐ date of birth

f. ☐ photo

g. ☐ issue date

AFTER READING

- Official documents are used to identify the citizen. When does a person need to use an identification card?
- What official documents do you already have?

> • **www.guiadedireitos.org/index.php?option=com_content&view=article&id=435&Itemid=77**
> Website with information about how to obtain the document Registro Geral (RG) and other rights of a citizen.

TEXT 2

BEFORE READING

1. Look at the texts below. They are:

a. ☐ job ads. b. ☐ personal profiles. c. ☐ e-mails.

2. What do the texts and images show?

READING

3. Read the personal profiles and do the activities.

http://ubelong.org/volunteer-abroad-news

Young Citizens, Great Social Attitudes

FOTOGRAFIAS: UBELONG

Name: Mariely Luz
Age: 21
Hometown: Maranhão
Country: Brazil
Languages spoken: Portuguese, English (advanced), Spanish (beginner)
Volunteer abroad: Building, Renovating and Handywork in Vang Vieng, Laos

Extracted from: <https://ubelong.org/volunteer-abroad-news/volunteer-abroad-laos>. Accessed on: May 12, 2016.

Name: Eduardo Manteca
Age: 27
Hometown: Tempe
Country: United States and Mexico
Languages spoken: English and Spanish
Volunteer abroad: Caring for the elderly in Quito, Ecuador

Extracted from: <https://ubelong.org/volunteer-abroad-news/arizona-state-university-grad-quito-ecuador-caring-for-elderly-volunteer>. Accessed on: May 12, 2016.

Name: Stephen Rousseau
Age: 18
Country: United States
School: Vanguard High School
Languages spoken: English and Spanish (beginner)
Volunteer abroad: Caring for Disabled Children in Cape Town, South Africa

Extracted from: <https://ubelong.org/volunteer-abroad-news/volunteer-vanguard-high-school-grad-florida-cape-town-south-africa>. Accessed on: May 12, 2016.

- **ubelong.org**
Website with opportunities and information about volunteer programmes.

4. Write **M** for Mariely, **E** for Eduardo or **S** for Stephen.

a. ☐ Is the youngest.

b. ☐ Speaks Portuguese.

c. ☐ Does volunteer work with senior citizens.

d. ☐ Is American.

e. ☐ Does volunteer work with children with special needs.

f. ☐ Does volunteer work helping with construction and buildings maintenance.

g. ☐ Has two nationalities.

5. The teens in the text are social activists. What is an activist?

____

____

____

____

____

____

6. Social activists can work in their own country or abroad. Match the names with the countries where they were born or where they work.

a. Mariely

b. Eduardo

c. Stephen

☐ United States

☐ Brazil

☐ South Africa

☐ Ecuador

☐ Laos

AFTER READING

- "To be a citizen is to be aware of your own rights and obligations and make sure they are practiced."

  Translated from: <www.significados.com.br/cidadania>. Accessed on: May 12, 2016.

  The young people mentioned in the texts are very participative citizens. What do you think about their attitudes?
- Is there anyone in your community who does volunteer work? What do they do?
- Would you like to do volunteer work? If so, what are your objectives? If not, justify your answer.
- Which proposals from page 14 could be put into practice in your community? How could you help?

FOCUS ON VOCABULARY

1. Look at the birth certificate on page 12 again. Match the columns.

a. female	☐ date of birth
b. Yahya	☐ surname
c. Pretoria	☐ country of birth
d. Ghana	☐ place of birth
e. Madeleine	☐ gender
f. 2011-11-28	☐ forename

birth date: date of birth
birth place: place of birth

- **www.unhcr.org/pages/49c3646c56.html**
Website with information about Angelina Jolie Pitt's humanitarian work.

2. Complete the paragraph about Angelina Jolie. Use the words from the box.

American actress	humanitarian	June 4

EDWARD PARSONS/AFP

Angelina Jolie Voight, better known as Angelina Jolie, was born on Wednesday, ____________________, 1975. She is a famous ____________________ known worldwide not only for her acting but also for her ____________________ work. [...] She has been awarded by the UN Correspondents Association with "Citizen of the World Award". She is also the recipient of "Global Humanitarian Award" awarded by UNA-USA in 2005.

Extracted from: <www.celebrityfunfacts.com/angelina-jolie/f66m17/>. Accessed on: May 12, 2016.

3. Complete the sentences with information about yourself.

a. My first name is ____________________.

b. My last name is ____________________.

c. My full name is ____________________.

d. My date of birth is ____________________.

e. My place of birth is ____________________.

first name: forename
last name: surname
full name: complete name

Build a glossary in your notebook using some selected words from this lesson. You can translate the words, make a drawing, or write a sentence with the words to help you memorize it.

The alphabet

4. When is spelling important?

5. Do you know the pronunciation of the letters in English?

6. Listen and check.

BIS

In some countries, like India, South Africa, the United Kingdom and in some regions of Canada, the letter "z" is pronounced /zéd/. In American English, it is pronounced /zi/.

7. Read the questions and write **N** for name or **S** for spelling.

- [ ] What's your name?
- [ ] How do you spell it?
- [ ] Can you spell that?
- [ ] What's your last name?
- [ ] Can you spell your name, please?
- [ ] How do you spell "Franklin"?

8. Listen to the conversations. Circle the names people spell.

a. Veruska
Veruca

WARNER BROS

b. Streatfeild
Streetfield

WARNER BROS

c. Gyllenhaal
Gilenhall

REPRODUÇÃO

IT'S YOUR TURN!

Talk to your classmates.
Use the questions below.
Take notes.

What's your first name?
And your last name?
Can you spell that?

	Classmate 1	Classmate 2
first name		
last name		

LANGUAGE IN USE

Verb to be – part I

1. Read the comic strip and answer the questions.

Garfield and Jon were created by the American cartoonist Jim Davis. This is their first comic strip, published on June 19, 1978, in 41 newspapers in the United States.

Garfield by Jim Davis © Paws, Inc. – All Rights Reserved

a. Look at the first panel. What words does Jon use to introduce his name and occupation?

____

b. In "I'm a cartoonist", which word is the verb?

____

c. What is Jon's intention when he says "This is my cat, Garfield."?

____

d. Look at the second panel. Does Garfield introduce himself in the same way as Jon? What does he say?

____

____

e. Garfield also introduces the cartoonist. How does he do that?

____

f. Are the sentences of the strip in the affirmative or negative form?

____

2. Complete the sentences according to activity 1.

a. To introduce yourself, you can say "My name is..." or ______________.

b. You can introduce someone else by saying ______________.

4

PRONUNCIATION PRACTICE

Underline the words you hear.

a. "**I am** / **I'm** an assistant to the mayor of the city. Hello!" – *School of Rock*

b. "Yes, **he is** / **he's** one of my minions." – *Despicable Me 2*

c. "**What is** / **What's** your name?" – *Monsters Inc.*

d. "**She's** / **She is** from Italy. Florence, I think." – *Wizards of Waverly Place*

3. Look at the picture, read the text and do the activities.

Liz Wilson, Garfield's vet, debuted on June 26, 1979.

This is Jon Arbuckle. **He** is a cartoonist.
Garfield is **his** cat.

The girl is **his** girlfriend and **her** name is Liz.
She is a vet.

a. The words in bold are pronouns. Match them with the person they are related to.

he | her | she | his

Liz | Jon

b. Which pronouns express the idea of possession?

____

c. Which form of the verb "to be" is present in all sentences?

____

d. Which pronouns are related to Liz and Jon?

____

4. Complete the chart and write sentences.

I		
	your	
	his	
she		

5. Who are they? Complete the sentences. Use the words from activity 4.

ALESSANDRO SHINODA/ FOLHAPRESS

a. Who is she?

______ name is Ruth Rocha. ______ is a writer.

ADRIAN DENNIS/AFP

b. Who is he?

______ name is Daniel de Faria Dias. ______ is a Paralympic athlete.

FLANIGAN/FILMMAGIC/ GETTY IMAGES

c. Who is she?

______ name is Demi Lovato. ______ is a singer.

GUSTAVO SEREBRENICK/BRAZIL PHOTO PRESS/FOLHAPRESS

d. Who is he?

______ name is Selton Mello. ______ is a Brazilian actor.

BIS

you

e. And you? Who are you?

______ name is ______________. ______ am a student.

6. Rewrite the sentences. Use the contracted form.

a. Jon is a cartoonist. He is very creative.

Jon is a cartoonist. ______________.

b. She is very talented. Her name is Ruth Rocha.

______________. Her name is Ruth Rocha.

c. Garfield is a cat. He is big and fat.

Garfield is a cat. ______________.

d. My name is Mariely. I am a social activist.

My name is Mariely. ______________.

HANDS ON!

Write two sentences about a person you admire. Then share them with a classmate.

____

____

Subject pronouns

THINKSTOCK/GETTY IMAGES

I

THINKSTOCK/GETTY IMAGES

you

KEVIN DODGE/CORBIS/FOTOARENA

he

SHUTTERSTOCK

she

SHUTTERSTOCK

it

THINKSTOCK/GETTY IMAGES

we

MIKE WATSON IMAGES/THINKSTOCK/GETTY IMAGES

you

SHUTTERSTOCK

they

Verb to be – affirmative

Subject pronouns	Verb to be
I	am
you	are
he	is
she	is
it	is
we	are
you	are
they	are

I am a student.

You are a student too.

That is Charlie. **He is** a new student.

That is Marie. **She is** a new student too.

This is my English book. **It is** a good book.

We are students.

You are students.

They are new students.

Full form	Contracted form (subject pronoun + verb to be)
I am	I**'m** (I am)
you are	you**'re** (you are)
he is	he**'s** (he is)
she is	she**'s** (she is)
it is	it**'s** (it is)
we are	we**'re** (we are)
you are	you**'re** (you are)
they are	they**'re** (they are)

I'm Charlie.

You're a student too.

This is Mike. **He's** a new student.

This is Claire. **She's** a new student.

It's good.

We're students.

You're students.

They're new students.

1. Write the correct form of the verb to be in the sentences below.

PHOTOS 12 CINEMA/UN/DIOMEDIA

a. Hello! My name ______ Cara Delevingne. I ______ an actress in the film *Anna Karenina*. I play Princess Sorokina. She ______ a fictional character.

b. My name ______ Jennifer Lawrence and I'______ an actress. And this ______ Josh Hutcherson. He ______ an actor. We ______ in the film *The Hunger Games*. In the film, I ______ Katniss Everdeen and he'______ Peeta Mellark.

PHOTOS 12 CINEMA/UN/DIOMEDIA

KELLEY L. COX/AL MILLIGAN / KLC FOTOS/CORBIS/LATINSTOCK

c. I ______ Chloe Kim. I ______ an American snowboarder. My parents ______ from South Korea. Snowboarding ______ a very popular sport in South Korea.

d. Soccer ______ my favorite sport. My name ______ Martin Odegaard and I ______ a soccer player for Real Madrid. Cristiano Ronaldo and James Rodrígues ______ Real Madrid players too.

REAL MADRID VIA GETTY IMAGES

REUTERS

e. We ______ Sasha Obama and Malia Obama. We ______ sisters. Our father ______ an ex-president of the United States. His name ______ Barack Obama. My mother's name ______ Michelle. They ______ very important people.

2. Look at the picture and complete the sentences with the correct form of the verb to be.

a. They ______ Jon, Garfield and Liz.

b. Jon ______ a cartoonist.

c. Liz ______ a veterinarian. Her last name ______ Wilson.

d. Garfield ______ a funny cat.

e. Jon and Liz ______ boyfriend and girlfriend.

GARFIELD, JIM DAVIS © 1986 PAWS, INC. ALL RIGHTS RESERVED / DIST. UNIVERSAL UCLICK

LISTENING COMPREHENSION

BEFORE LISTENING

1. How do you usually greet people? What do you say when you meet:

    a. a friend at a party?

    b. the principal in the school hallway?

    c. an aunt at the mall?

2. Based on your answer to the previous activity, do you greet everyone in the same way? Why?

____

____

____

3. When do you use a more formal greeting? Make a list of situations.

____

____

____

____

4. Look at the image. In your opinion, what are these people talking about?

FOX

LISTENING

5 **5.** Listen to conversation 1 and check your answer to activity 4.

6. Listen to conversation 1 again and complete the chart.

6

Conversation 1	
First name	____________
Last name	Mackenzie
Hometown	____________, California
School name	____________ County High School for the ____________

7. Now listen to conversation 2 and choose the correct alternatives.

7

a. Her name is...

I. ☐ Sofia. II. ☐ Sophie. III. ☐ Soshi.

b. She is from...

I. ☐ Wakefield. II. ☐ Westfield. III. ☐ Wakelake.

c. She is ... years old.

I. ☐ sixteen II. ☐ seven III. ☐ seventeen

8. Are the conversations formal or informal? How do you know?

____

____

9. Why is the candidate's name spelled in conversation 1? Check the correct option(s).

a. ☐ Because the judge didn't understand her name.

b. ☐ Because her name is spelled in an unusual way.

c. ☐ Because the judge wants to write her name.

10. The judges receive information about the candidates previously to the show. Why did the judges ask the candidate's name again?

____

____

____

____

AFTER LISTENING

- Have you ever had to introduce yourself to many people? What pieces of information did you have to give?
- What is necessary to present yourself effectively in public?
- Mention a situation when you had to introduce yourself at school. When was it? How was it?

SPEAKING

1. Look at the picture and discuss with your classmates.

© HEIDE BENSER/CORBIS

a. What are the people doing?

b. How does the girl probably introduce her friends to one another?

2. Read the sentences below and underline the ones that can be used to introduce people.

a. This is my mother.

b. Jessica, this is my friend Kevin.

c. Hello, Claire.

d. Can you spell your name?

e. Francis, meet my friend Bob.

f. Bye, Paul.

3. In groups of three, introduce one classmate to another. Then, change roles.
Think of the following situations:

- Introducing a new classmate to the teacher.
- Introducing your sister/brother to a friend.
- Introducing your mother/father to the school principal.
- Enrolling at the local sports club.
- Another situation: ____________________________________.

Reflecting on the theme

Do you introduce everyone in the same way, regardless of how close you are? Discuss it with your teacher and classmates.

WRITING

BEFORE WRITING

1. A profile briefly describes some aspects and characteristics of a person. Discuss the following questions with your teacher and classmates.

   a. The texts on page 14 are profiles. Why?

   ____

   b. Which pieces of information can you see in the texts?

   ____

   c. Where do we find profiles?

   ____

2. Complete Malala Yousafzai's profile. Use the information from the box.

MONICA SCHIPPER/GETTY IMAGES

July 12, 1997
Malala Yousafzai
Mingora, Pakistan
Social activist, student
Women's and children's rights to education

- ***I am Malala: The Girl Who Stood Up for Education and Was Shot by the Taliban***
  Malala Yousafzai. USA: Little, Brown and Company, 2013.
  The touching history of Malala Yousafzai, who fought for the right of girls' education.

First name/Forename:	
Last name/Surname:	
Occupation:	
Project:	
Date of Birth/Birth Date:	
Place of Birth/Birth Place:	

3. Based on Malala's information, who would be interested in reading her profile?

____

____

WRITING

4. Follow the steps below and write a profile.
   - Work in pairs and choose a person from school (staff or student) to write a profile about. You can use the profiles from page 14 as models.
   - Explain to the chosen person the objective of the task and ask his/her birth date, birth place, complete name, occupation and if he/she has ever done volunteer work.
   - Write a draft of the profile in your notebook. Ask your teacher for help with vocabulary if needed.
   - Write the final version of the profile.

AFTER WRITING

- Read the profile you created and evaluate if:
  - the information is complete;
  - you checked vocabulary with your teacher.
- Present the person you chose to the class and justify your choice.
- Write the profiles on posters and put them around school so everyone can get to know more about those people. Besides, the people represented in the profiles can see the result of their participation in the project.
- If your school has a blog or website, the texts can be published there too. Ask your teacher for help.

SELF-EVALUATION

Check the true sentences about your learning in Unit 1.
In this unit you have learned to:

- [ ] introduce yourself and give personal information;
- [ ] read and produce presentations in different communicative situations;
- [ ] read and produce profiles.

Reflecting...

- **What did I learn about personal introductions and profiles?**
- **What questions do I still have about making personal introductions and writing profiles in English?**
- **How did I feel presenting something in English?**

UNIT

2

I'm from Bogotá

Oscar Niemeyer (1907-2012) was born in the Laranjeiras district, in Rio de Janeiro, on December 15, 1907. He was responsible for the architectural plan of many buildings in Brasília, the capital of Brazil. He has more than 600 projects around the world and he is considered to be one of the most important modern architects of the 20th century. He is known for exploring reinforced concrete in his projects and also for his unique design.

The sculpture by Oscar Niemeyer on these two pages is called *Mão*. It is located in the Memorial da América Latina, in São Paulo. The Memorial is devoted to promoting the Latin American culture by hosting events like exhibitions, theater, dance, and music performances.

NIEMEYER, Oscar. *Mão*. 1989. Memorial da América Latina. São Paulo, Brazil.

Your learning objectives for this unit are...

- to read text messages and recognize informal language;
- to make questions about people's origins;
- to read, plan and write text messages.

EXCHANGING IDEAS

1. Notice the color red in the sculpture. What does it represent?
2. How is the sculpture related to the space where it is located?

ANTONIO MIOTTO/FOTOARENA

2 I'm from Bogotá

READING COMPREHENSION

TEXT 1

BEFORE READING

1. How do you usually communicate with friends, classmates and family members? Why?
2. Take a quick look at the text below. How many people are taking part in this conversation? What form of communication are they using?

READING

3. Read the text message conversation and answer the questions that follow.

REPRODUÇÃO

exchange student: estudante de intercâmbio

- ***Say What? The Weird and Mysterious Journey of the English Language***
  Gena K. Gorrell. New York: Tundra Books, 2009.
  This book is a travel in time through the history of the English language. It presents some word games and curiosities about the language.

4. What do Luc and Paul talk about?

___

___

___

5. What is Luc's reaction when he hears the news? Justify your answer.

___

___

___

Emoticons (emotion + icon) and **emojis** are very common in text messages and they are used to convey feelings and attitudes. They add fun to messages and make them even more informal.

6. Go back to the text message conversation and identify the missing information.

a. who starts the conversation ___

b. who the message was sent to ___

c. main message ___

d. form of communication ___

7. List the words from the text that show informality.

___

___

8. Check the true sentences about the text message conversation.

a. ☐ Luc and Paul are friends.

b. ☐ The communication started at 8:04 pm.

c. ☐ Luc and Paul are classmates.

d. ☐ Luc and Juan don't know each other.

e. ☐ Luc, Paul and Juan don't like soccer.

We use "am" or "pm" to determine the period of the day. From midnight to 11:59, we use "am" (*ante meridiem*, in Latin) and from midday to 23:59, we use "pm" (*post meridiem*, in Latin).

9. Paul apologizes to Luc by saying "sorry". Why does he do that?

___

___

___

___

___

___

10. Match the countries to their corresponding monuments and maps.

Colombia

THINKSTOCK/GETTY IMAGES

Lincoln Memorial.

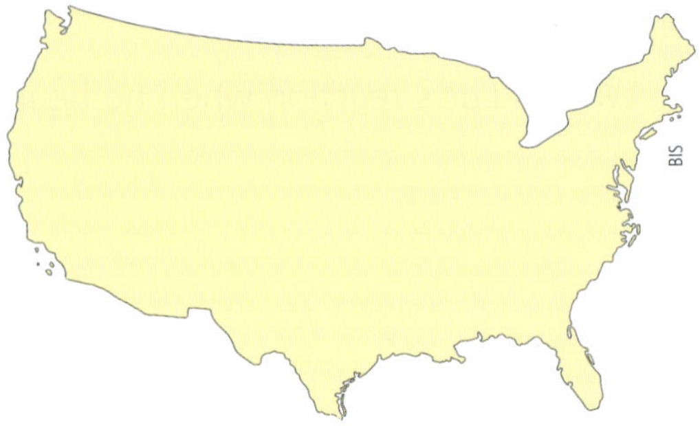
BIS

United States

WWW.GUIARTE3D.COM

Simón Bolívar Statue.

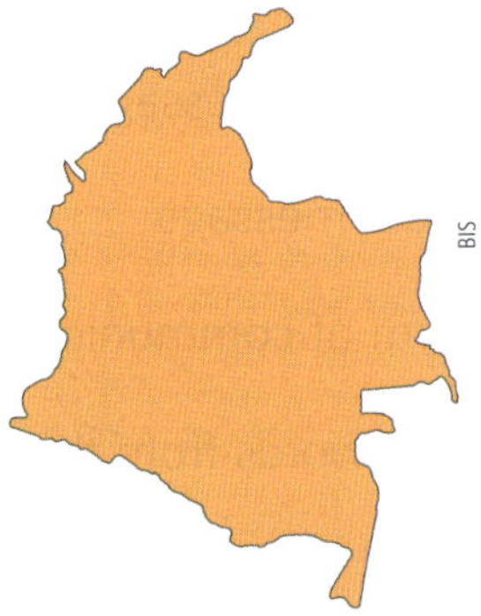
BIS

11. Complete the sentences with words from the box.

the United States	Colombia
American	Colombian

a. Juan is from ____________________. He's ____________________.

b. Paul is from ____________________. He's ____________________.

c. I am from ____________________. I'm ____________________.

AFTER READING

- Although Paul, Luc and Juan are from different countries, they can become close friends because they share a common interest: sport. What other interests can help people from different countries become closer to each other?
- Are there students from different nationalities at your school? What suggestions and tips would you give to them, so they can properly adapt to the school environment and the community?
- What advantages and disadvantages are there in communicating through text messages?

TEXT 2

BEFORE READING

1. Look at the text and choose the correct option.

The text is ☐ a poem. ☐ a recipe.

hi hello namaste! ! !

By Sreelekha Premjit

hi
hello
namaste
the little i knew
i shared boldly
now i feel
there's nothing i know
what's then to share? ? ? ?
So I say again hi hello and namaste! ! !

Extracted from: <www.poemhunter.com/poem/hi-hello-namaste>. Accessed on: May 12, 2016.

TALK TEMPLE

Sreelekha Premjit

Don't interrupt your reading every time you find a word you do not know. Just keep on reading. This strategy will help you understand the text as a whole and expand your vocabulary.

READING

2. Read the poem and choose the correct options.

a. "Hi", "hello" and "*namaste*" are ☐ subject pronouns. ☐ greetings.

b. The three exclamation points in the end of the poem are used to express

☐ doubt. ☐ emphasis.

c. The person in the poem expresses a wish to

☐ be in contact with people. ☐ be away from people.

3. Now answer the questions below.

a. Who's the author of the poem? ____________________

b. Why do you think the author included the word *namaste* in the poem?

____

c. If Juan, the Colombian boy from page 30, were the author of the poem, what greeting would he probably use besides *hi* and *hello*? ____________________

AFTER READING

- We can be friends with people from many different places in the world. Would you like to make new friends from different nationalities? Why?
- What would you like to know about people from other nationalities?

FOCUS ON VOCABULARY

Greetings

1. Look at the pictures. Listen and underline what people say at different periods of the day.

8

PARAMOUNT

School of Rock

> • ***Journey of English***
> Dana Brook. New York: Clarion Books, 1998.
> This book is about the English language, from its origin until nowadays.

WARNER BROS

Harry Potter and the Philosopher's Stone

WALT DISNEY STUDIOS

The Aristocats

> We use "good evening" to greet people during the evening. We use "good night" to say goodbye during the evening or before we go to bed.

2. Match the conversations to their corresponding pictures.

a. **Matt:** Bye, girls.

Aisha: Goodbye.

Carmen: See you!

ILUSTRAÇÕES: VICENTE MENDONÇA

b. **Matt:** Hi, there!

Aisha: Hello, Matt.

Carmen: Hi, everyone.

Countries and nationalities

3. (9) Complete the chart with the words from the box. Then listen to two journalists listing the five coolest countries in the world and number them.

American	Brazil	Jamaican	Mongolian	Singapore

> Nationalities are written with capital letters.

Number	Country	Nationality
______	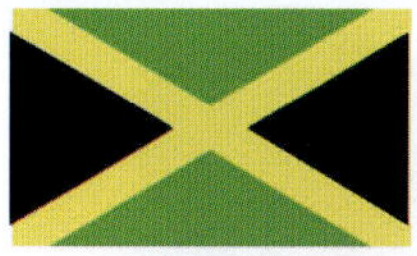 THINKSTOCK/GETTY IMAGES Jamaica	______
______	 THINKSTOCK/GETTY IMAGES Mongolia	______
______	 PALÁCIO DO PLANALTO, BRASÍLIA ______	Brazilian
______	 THINKSTOCK/GETTY IMAGES ______	Singaporean
______	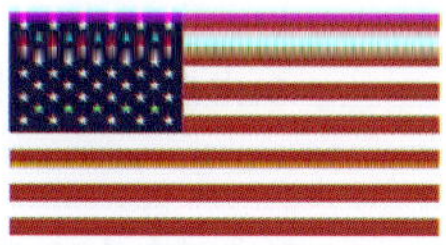 THINKSTOCK/GETTY IMAGES The United States of America	______

- **www.khanacademy.org/partner-content/british-museum/middle-east-bm/ancient-near-east-bm/v/towers-of-babel**
  Video from the British Museum about the Tower of Babel.

(10) PRONUNCIATION PRACTICE

Listen to the nationalities and write them in the correct columm.

-ian	-ese	-ish	-sh
______	______	______	______
______		______	
______		______	
		______	

IT'S YOUR TURN!

In pairs, play a game. Student A says the name of a country and student B says the corresponding nationality. For example, student A says "Canada", student B says "Canadian".

LANGUAGE IN USE

Verb to be – part II

1. List three people you admire the most. Present them to your classmates. Use the text below as an example.

SHUTTERSTOCK

> Hey, guys! My name is Telma. I admire Lionel Messi, J.K. Rowling, and Dira Paes. Dira Paes is an actress and leading member of the Human Rights Watch. She is from Pará, in Brazil, just like me. We are both Brazilian. J.K. Rowling is a writer. She is British. Lionel Messi is a great soccer player. He is Argentinian. They are my heroes.

2. Read the text in activity 1 again and complete the sentences.

a. The pronoun ____________ substitutes the name Lionel Messi, just as the pronoun ____________ substitutes Dira Paes and also the name J.K. Rowling.

b. The pronoun ____________ substitutes the person who is speaking and someone else.

c. The pronoun ____________ substitutes more than one person. This pronoun can be used for men and women.

d. ____________ and ____________ are forms of the verb "to be" which can be used to talk about nationality or origin.

e. The verb form ____________ is used in the third person singular, and ____________ is used in the second person singular and in the first, second and third person plural.

3. Do you know any international celebrities? If so, where are they from? What is their occupation? Write some sentences about them.

____

____

____

PRONUNCIATION PRACTICE

11

Circle the correct options according to what you hear.

a. "No! Oh! Ooh! But, Jane, **they** / **they're** Italian!" – *Tarzan & Jane*

b. "[...] **we're** / **we are** French, and it's dinnertime." – *Ratatouille*

c. "**You're** / **You are** in France, children." – *Anastasia*

We're: We are
You're: You are
They're: They are

4. Complete the dialogue. Use **'m**, **'m not**, **is** or **are**. Then read the statements and write **T** (true) or **F** (false). Correct the false statements.

Akira: Hi, Pablo. This ____________ my friend Claude.

Pablo: Hi, Claude. Where ____________ you from? ____________ you French?

Claude: No, I____________ from France. I'm from Belgium. And you? Are you from Spain?

Pablo: Yes, I am. I____________ from Barcelona.

Claude: Nice to meet you, Pablo. See you later.

Pablo: Nice to meet you, too. Bye!

VICENTE MENDONÇA

a. [ ] We use "where… from" to ask about someone's occupation.

____

b. [ ] In interrogative sentences like "Are you French?", the verb to be comes after the subject.

____

c. [ ] "I'm not from France" is an affirmative sentence.

____

d. [ ] To form the negative, we add **not** after the verb.

____

e. [ ] "Yes, I am" is a short affirmative answer and "No, I'm not" is a short negative answer.

____

5. Read the conversation under picture **a**. Then write sentences about the other pictures.

GETTY IMAGES FOR AFI

A: Brad Pitt? The actor? Is he English?

B: *No, he's American.*

THINKSTOCK/GETTY IMAGES

A: Rodrigo Santoro? The actor? Is he Argentinian?

B: ______________________________

S_BUKLEY/DEPOSIT PHOTOS/GLOW IMAGES

A: J.K. Rowling? The writer? Is she Canadian?

B: ______________________________

D A: What about your teachers? Are they Australian?

B: ______________________________

____

E A: And you and your best friend? Are you Japanese?

B: ______________________________

____

6. Read the cartoon and have fun.

Bizarro

HANDS ON!

Imagine you are a different person, from a different country. You are in Brazil to study. Today is your first class at school. Introduce yourself to a classmate. Change roles.

Verb to be – negative and interrogative

Negative (subject pronoun + verb to be + not)	
full form	contracted form
I am not	I'm not
you are not	you aren't / you're not
he is not	he isn't / he's not
she is not	she isn't / she's not
it is not	it isn't / it's not
we are not	we aren't / we're not
you are not	you aren't / you're not
they are not	they aren't / they're not

Interrogative (verb to be + subject pronoun)	
Am I?	Are we?
Are you?	Are you?
Is he? / Is she? / Is it?	Are they?

Short answers

ANTON GVOZDIKOV/SHUTTERSTOCK

Joan: Am I late?

Julie: No, you aren't.

TOMAS RODRIGUEZ/CORBIS/FOTOARENA

Carrie: Is he French?

Lily: Yes, he is.

AIR IMAGES/SHUTTERSTOCK

Carol: Is he your brother?

Meg: No, he isn't.

THINKSTOCK/GETTY IMAGES

Carl: Are you from Santos?

Mary and Nina: Yes, we are.

1. Complete the questions and answers with the verb to be.

SHUTTERSTOCK

A: __________ from London?

B: No, __________. She's from Paris.

THINKSTOCK/GETTY IMAGES

A: __________ from Mexico?

B: Yes, __________. They are Mexican.

CHRIS SCHMICH/GETTY IMAGES

A: __________ in this class?

B: Yes, __________. Your name is on the list.

THINKSTOCK/GETTY IMAGES

A: __________ classmates?

B: No, __________. We are brothers.

WAVEBREAKMEDIA/SHUTTERSTOCK

A: __________ Colombian?

B: Yes, __________. Colombian coffee is the best!

ISTOCKPHOTO/THINKSTOCK GETTY IMAGES

A: __________ in the white group, too?

B: No, __________. I'm in the blue group.

2. Are these sentences true (**T**) or false (**F**) about you? Rewrite the false sentences to make them true for you.

[F] I'm a teacher. *I'm not a teacher. I'm a student.*

a. [ ] I'm from Recife. __________

b. [ ] My mother is carioca. __________

c. [ ] My best friend is from Portugal. __________

d. [ ] Lionel Messi and J.K. Rowling are my heroes. __________

e. [ ] My favorite school subject is English. __________

f. [ ] My classmates and I are 13 years old. __________

LISTENING COMPREHENSION

BEFORE LISTENING

1. There are approximately 6,912 languages in the world. Which languages do you know? Share your answer with a classmate.

____

____

2. Have you ever talked to someone who speaks a different language? If so, where was this person from? What language did you use to communicate?

____

____

3. Match the pictures to the sentences below. Then listen to the sentences to know how they are pronounced.

12

JOYFULL/SHUTTERSTOCK

ELLEN ROONEY/GETTY IMAGES

THINKSTOCK/GETTY IMAGES

THINKSTOCK/GETTY IMAGES

1 Oh, Gru, se llama Antonio. Me llamo Margo.

2 Je m'appelle Piscine Molitor Patel, dit Pi.

3 Hallo, Philipp. Tag, mein Junge. Willkommen.

4 Ho due sorelle. Una si chiama Viviana e ha ventitré anni, e una si chiama Eleonora, e ne ha tredici.

- **www.ethnologue.com**
  Reference catalog with all languages spoken in the world.

LISTENING

4. Look at the photos and try to complete the sentences with the words from the box. Then listen and check.

13

Brazil	Europe	Iceland	Scotland

_BIRNAH

My name's Birna. I'm an exchange student from ______________________ in the United States, in New York.

ALIS REID

Hi. My name's Alis. I'm 16 years old and I'm from ______________________.

GARRET WHEELER

My name's Matej Kasl and I'm from Czech Republic, in ______________________.

- **cienciahoje.uol.com.br/podcasts/A%20origem%20das%20linguas.mp3/view**
Interview with linguist Carlos Alberto Faraco, from Federal University of Paraná (UFPR), about the origin of the languages.

INTO HIGHER

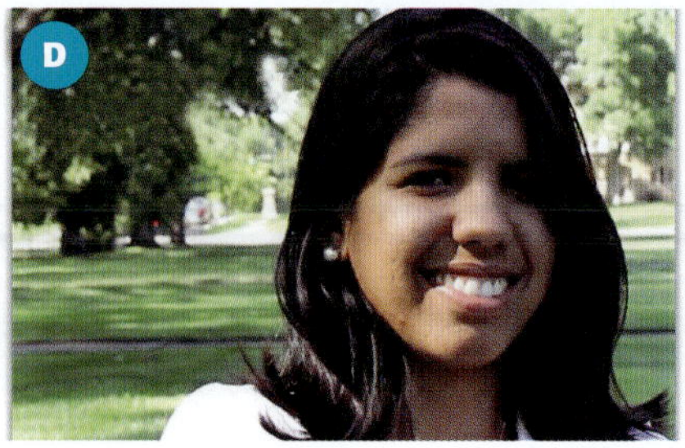

My name is Ellienay Simony. I'm from ______________________, and I am an academic English student.

AFTER LISTENING

- In pairs, interview school staff and students and ask them where they are from (city and state). Follow the steps below.
  - Take notes of their answers.
  - Show the answers to your classmates.
  - Discuss what cultural contributions these people bring to the community they live in.

SPEAKING

1. Look at the picture. Then complete the conversation.

VICENTE MENDONÇA

Ingrid: Hello. What's ____________________?

João Carlos: My ____________________ João Carlos. And your name...?

Ingrid: I'm Ingrid. So, where are you ____________________?

João Carlos: Well, I ____________________ Rio Grande do Sul, Brazil. And you, Ingrid?

Ingrid: I'm from Munich, Germany.

2. Read the conversation above and answer the questions.

a. What question do you use to ask a person's nationality?

____

b. How do you answer that question?

____

c. Which informal question is used to avoid repeating a question?

____

3. In pairs, imagine you are tourists. Introduce yourselves and say where you are from. Think of the situations below.

- A volleyball match.
- At the beach.
- At a school competition.
- Another situation: ____________________.

Reflecting on the theme

If you had the opportunity to talk to people from different states or countries, what would you like to ask them? Why?

BEFORE WRITING

1. In pairs, read the information below. Then do the activities.

Text messaging through SMS (Short Message Service) or Instant Messaging App is one of the most modern forms of communication.

a. Based on the text on page 30, check the characteristics of text messages.

- [ ] Short and objective message.
- [ ] Informal language.
- [ ] No punctuation.
- [ ] Use of emojis.
- [ ] Use of abbreviations and interjections.

b. Do you usually communicate by text messages? If so, describe in which situation and the purpose of it.

2. Look at the abbreviations and read their meanings. Use them to complete the text message conversation.

BFF (best friends forever)

Ily (I love you)

LOL (laughing out loud)

XOXO (hugs and kisses)

GR8 (great)

3. Read the text message conversation again. Then answer the questions about it.

a. Who are the interlocutors?

___

b. How are they related?

___

c. What are they talking about?

___

___

WRITING

4. Write text messages. Follow the steps below.
- Get together with a classmate and build a text message conversation. Talk about something you like.
- Keep in mind the characteristics of a text message and use them in your conversation.
- Write the draft of the conversation on your notebook and show it to your teacher.

AFTER WRITING

Read the conversation you built and evaluate if:
- the message is adequate for this form of communication (text messaging);
- the objective of the communication is clear.

SELF-EVALUATION

Check the true sentences about your learning in Unit 2.
In this unit you have learned to:

- [ ] read text messages and recognize informal language;
- [ ] make questions about people's origins;
- [ ] read, plan and write text messages.

Reflecting...
- **What characteristics of text messages did I learn?**
- **What questions do I still have about writing text messages?**
- **What was most memorable to me about how people introduce themselves in other countries?**
- **Which topic in this unit did I like best?**
- **Which topic in this unit would I like to find out more about?**

Languages around the world

> "As many languages you know, as many times you are a human being."
>
> Czech saying

QUASIMODO/GETTY IMAGES/ISTOCKPHOTO

The languages we speak are a very important part of our identity. That's because they are closely related to our culture, our environment and our outlook on life. Our language shapes the way we view and communicate with the world, but it also influences the choices we make, the values we have and our perspective of time. Besides, we are influenced by the languages we get in contact with: the languages of our immigrant ancestors, the languages we study at school, the languages of the music we listen to, etc. Sometimes our language is influenced by other languages too, for instance, by Native American languages.

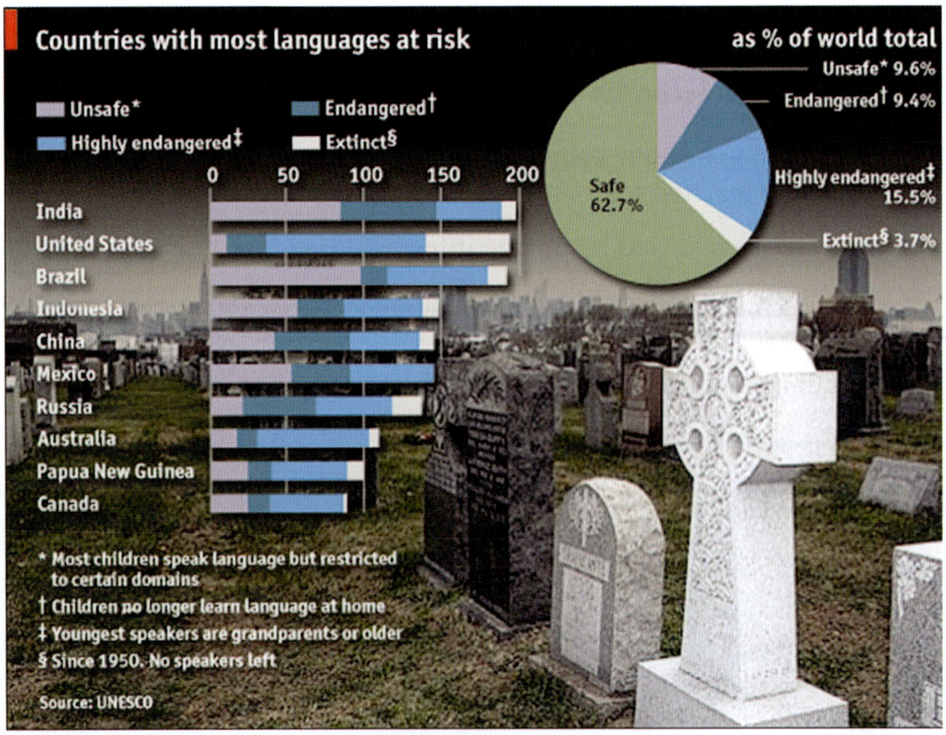

ECONOMIST.COM

Extracted from: <www.economist.com/node/13307780>. Accessed on: Jun. 13, 2016.

But, what happens when your language is endangered? Does part of your identity become endangered too? Did you know that, every two weeks, the last speaker of a language dies? What would you do if you were among the last speakers of your language?

Out of the 6,912 of the world's identified languages, nearly 2,500 are at risk, according to the United Nations Educational, Scientific and Cultural Organization (UNESCO). The reason for this is globalization. The imposition of a colonial language long ago in big countries such as Brazil and USA is still endangering the diversity of native tongues. In the USA, 53 languages have become extinct since 1950, more than in any other country. Also, fewer indigenous languages are now being spoken because of the influence of dominant languages, which are considered to be economically more valuable than minority languages. Nowadays, around a quarter of the world's population speaks just three languages: Mandarin, English and Spanish.

On the map for the Language Hotspots, we see large regions in South America where many languages are critically endangered.

Preservation of the native tongues is very important because, if they become extinct, part of our culture becomes extinct too. Besides, many indigenous communities have in their native tongues vast repositories of information, including centuries of acquired knowledge about medicinal plants, for instance.

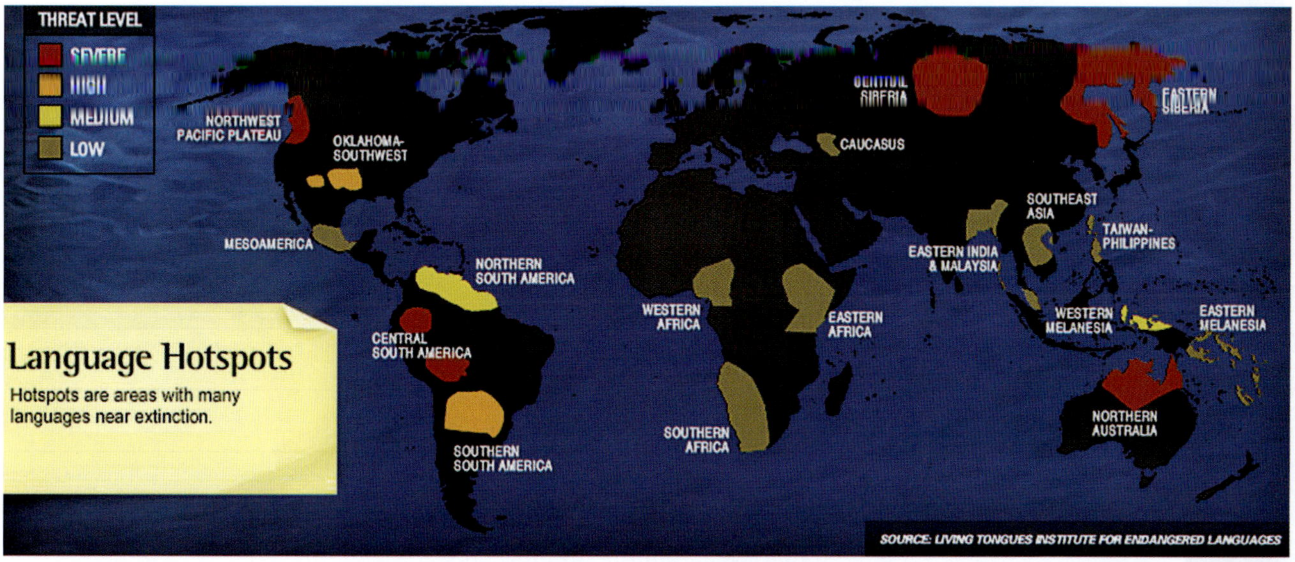

Adapted from: <www.theguardian.com/environment/2014/jun/08/why-we-are-losing-a-world-of-languages>, <livingtongues.wordpress.com/2012/05/21/the-endangered-languages-of-south-america/>, <www.culturechange.org/cms/content/view/363/65/>. Accessed on: May 12, 2016.

1. Based on the graph on page 46, answer the questions below.

a. Which country has more languages at risk?

____

b. Which country has more highly endangered languages?

____

c. Which country has more unsafe languages?

____

d. Which country has less extinct languages?

____

2. Write the correct legend from the box next to the corresponding meaning.

Endangered	Highly endangered
Extinct	Unsafe

a. Since 1950. No speakers left.

____

b. Most children speak language but restricted to certain domains.

____

c. Children no longer learn language at home.

____

d. Youngest speakers are grandparents or older.

____

3. In the Language Hotspots map on page 47, which places of the world have severe threat level of language near extinction?

____

____

____

____

____

____

____

4. Look at the map of languages in South America. How many countries can you name? Can you locate them correctly on the map?

____

____

____

____

____

____

____

____

____

____

____

Extracted from: <www.d-maps.com/>.
Accessed on: Dec. 1, 2015.

5. How many Native American languages are there in Brazil?

____

6. Which European languages are there in South America?

____

____

7. Research about the influence of native tongues in the Portuguese language. Which words did we borrow from indigenous languages?

____

____

____

____

____

8. Discuss with your teacher and classmates: What can we do to help protect endangered languages?

UNIT

3

This is my family

Tarsila do Amaral was a very important modernist painter. Her works depicted Brazilian day-to-day social themes and made use of strong colors and cubist techniques.

AMARAL, Tarsila do. *A família*. 1925. Oil on canvas, 79 cm × 101,5 cm. Museo Nacional Centro de Arte Reina Sofía, Madrid, Spain.

Your learning objectives for this unit are...

- to name family members;
- to indicate possession;
- to read and write notes.

A FAMÍLIA, TARSILA DO AMARAL, 1925

EXCHANGING IDEAS

1. Tarsila do Amaral's work is entitled *A família*. Which elements of the work are related to the title?
2. Which animals are represented in the image?
3. Why were these animals depicted in a piece about a family?
4. Look at the mother. How does she feel about her baby?
5. There are other people in the image. Who do you think they are?

- **tarsiladoamaral.com.br**
  Official website of Tarsila do Amaral, with her biography, works and timeline.

3 This is my family

READING COMPREHENSION

TEXT 1

BEFORE READING

1. According to the Statute of the Child and the Adolescent (ECA), "every child or adolescent has the right to be raised and educated in the midst of his or her family and, exceptionally, in a foster family." In your opinion, what are the requirements for a family to be eligible to adopt a child or adolescent?

READING

2. Scan the book cover below. What do you think the story is about?

> When doing a quick look at the text to get some details and specific ideas, you are using a very important reading strategy called scanning.

3. Look at the book cover again and read the overview about Michael Oher's story. Then check if your prediction is correct.

www.reviewsofbooks.com/blind_side/

Overview

The Blind Side: Evolution of a Game
by Michael Lewis

The Blind Side tells the story of Michael Oher, who was discovered as a football prodigy while in high school. [...] He was incredibly shy, and his high school grade point average was 0.6. He was basically a **homeless** black teenager with a **bleak** future except for his athletic talent. Sean Tuohy [...] and his wife took an interest in Oher, providing him food and clothing, and eventually having him move into their home as one of their family. Michael Lewis explores Michael Oher's story [...] and how the kindness and caring of a family has turned his bleak future into a promising one. [...]

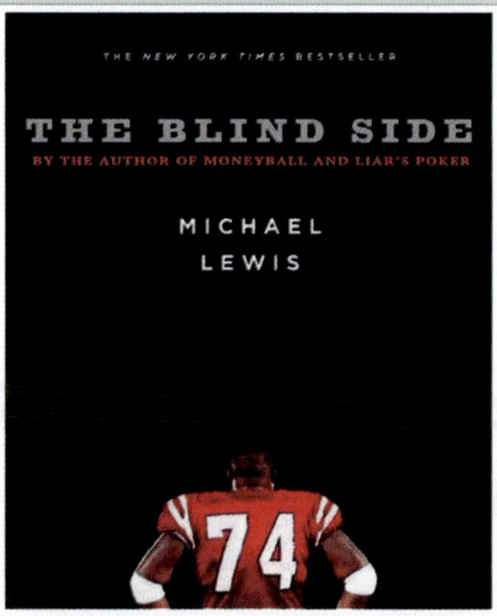

Extracted from: <www.reviewsofbooks.com/blind_side/>. Accessed on: May 14, 2016.

homeless: sem-teto
bleak: sombrio

> In the United States, the word **football** does not refer to the sport practiced in Brazil and in many countries around the world in which the players use their feet to control the ball. Instead, it refers to the most popular sport in the U.S., in which the players use their hands to control the ball.

4. Check the information presented on the book cover.

a. ☐ book title
b. ☐ name of the publishing house
c. ☐ author's name
d. ☐ price tag
e. ☐ appealing sentences
f. ☐ synopsis

5. List the items you checked in activity 4. Then complete with information from the cover.

____
____
____

6. Read the overview again. In Portuguese, write the main idea of the book. Use your own words.

____
____
____

7. Based on the knowledge that it is a true story of a young man from a dysfunctional family who gets a second chance in life after being adopted by the Tuohys, is it possible to say that the title *The Blind Side* is adequate? Why?

____
____
____

8. Read the text again and check what you can infer. Write **T** (true), **F** (false) or **NM** (not mentioned).

a. ☐ Michael Oher's biological family was unstructured.
b. ☐ Michael Oher was dedicated to study.
c. ☐ Although he lived in the streets, sometimes Michael would go to public mass care shelters.
d. ☐ Michael was discovered as a prodigious athlete.
e. ☐ The Tuohy family had a key role to change Michael's life.

9. Michael Oher's life changed enormously. How is he depicted when he was younger?

____

10. What caused the changes in Michael Oher's life?

____

AFTER READING

- Like Michael, who became a gifted football player, people have a lot of aspirations in life. How does having a family help people fulfill their dreams?

TEXT 2

BEFORE READING

WARNER BROS

1. Look at the DVD sleeve. In your opinion, what is the relation between this movie and the book mentioned on page 52?

2. Have you watched this movie? If not, would you like to? Why?

READING

3. Look at the DVD sleeve again and answer the questions.

   a. Which actress is mentioned on the DVD sleeve?

   ____

   b. Only one of the actors and actresses in the movie is mentioned on the DVD sleeve. Why is it so?

   ____

   ____

   ____

   c. The movie tells Michael Oher's story. Which role in the movie may have been played by the actress mentioned before? Justify your answer.

   ____

   ____

   ____

4. Compare the book cover on page 52 to the DVD sleeve. Then write **T** (true) or **F** (false).

   a. ☐ The book cover and the DVD sleeve present the same title.

   b. ☐ There are appealing sentences only on the book cover.

   c. ☐ The book cover and the DVD sleeve present seals of approval.

   d. ☐ The picture on the book cover and on the DVD sleeve is the same.

> • ***The Blind Side (Um sonho possível)***
> Direction: John Lee Hancock. USA: Warner Bros., 2009. 129 min.
> The movie is about a homeless boy who was adopted by a loving family. He sees his life change completly and becomes a famous football player.

AFTER READING

- Michael Oher's story was told in a book and then adapted into a movie. What are the differences between these two formats to present the same story? Which one is your favorite? Why?

FOCUS ON VOCABULARY

Family members

1. This is the real Michael Oher's adoptive family. Match the people in the photo to the words below.

a. ☐ sister
b. ☐ mother
c. ☐ brother
d. ☐ father

ABACAUSA.COM/NEWSCOM

2. Do you know what a family tree is and why it is important? Look at the Simpson's family tree and complete the text with the words from the box.

brother	daughter	grandparents	parents	sisters

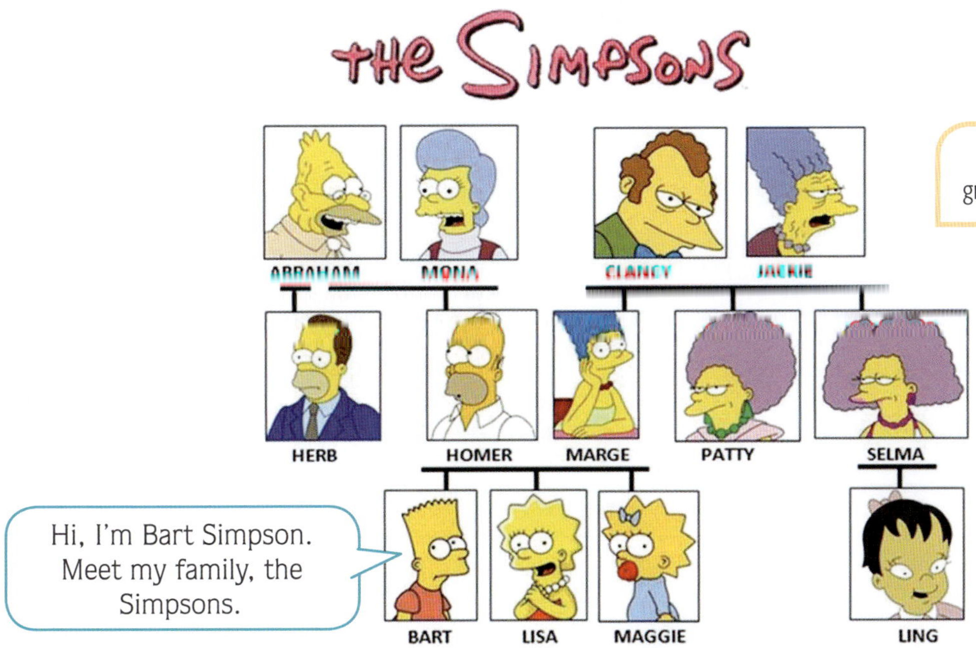

20TH CENTURY FOX FILM CORP.

grandparents: grandfather + grandmother

THE SIMPSONS' FAMILY TREE

Abraham, Mona, Clancy and Jackie are my ____________. I'm the only grandson in this family. Homer and Marge are my ____________. Lisa and Maggie are my ____________. They're Mona's granddaughters. Herb is my uncle. He is my father's ____________. Ling is my cousin. She is my aunt Selma's ____________.

3. Look at the pictures of different types of families. Then join the parts and write sentences.

JAY REITER/GETTY IMAGES

Michele Frost, Mary Helen Walker and their 3-year-old daughter Shea.

NICK OBANK/BARCROFT MEDIA/GETTY IMAGES

Wilco and Keisha van Kleef-Bolton with their children: Jonah, 11 days old; Eva, 4 years old; and Lucas, 6 years old.

TIM GRAHAM/GETTY IMAGES

Chinese family in Beijing.

BARCROFT MEDIA/GETTY IMAGES

Ian Millthorpe's eight children (from left to right): Connor, Jade, Rees, Corey, Ella-Rose, Ryan, Jake and Damon at home in Barnsley, England. His wife died of a cancer.

Ian Millthorpe is
Wilco has
Shea's family consists of
This Chinese couple has

two moms and herself.
a single father.
a wife and three children.
only one son.

a. Ian Millthorpe is ______________________________.

b. Wilco has ______________________________.

c. Shea's family consists of ______________________________.

d. This Chinese couple has ______________________________.

IT'S YOUR TURN!

Choose two important people for you and write about them. Then report to your classmates.

• ***How Artists See Families: Mother, Father, Sister, Brother***

Carroll Colleen. New York: Abbeville Press, 1999.

This book shows how families are depicted in works of art from different places and periods of time.

LANGUAGE IN USE

Possessive adjectives / Genitive case

grant: doação
purchase: comprar

1. Read Kristen's note and answer the questions.

> Dear ISF donor
>
> Thank you! With a grant she received from ISF, my child's kindergarten teacher was able to purchase books that really pushed the emerging readers and challenged those already reading. In one year, my child went from knowing her letters and a few letter sounds to reading at a second grade level. When ISF partners with amazing teachers, great things happen!
>
> Thank you!
>
> Kristen

Extracted from: <grants2011.issaquahschoolsfoundation.org/ThankYouSamples.php>. Accessed on: May 14, 2016.

a. Why did Kristen write this note?

____

b. Which noun does the word **my** (line 2) refer to?

____

c. Note the example of the use of **'s** in the note. What do you think **'s** represents?

____

2. Go back to Kristen's note. Match the parts of the sentences properly.

a. The word **my** (line 6) ☐ indicates possession.

b. The use of **'s** ☐ refers to the noun **child**.

3. Circle the possessive adjectives and underline the words they modify.

www.myblog.com/coolmary/celebs

Celebs!

Cool Mary

REED KAESTNER/CORBIS

Posted on Nov. 28, 2014 – 4:27 pm

My sister and I love American movies.
This is our favorite American actress.
Her name is Sandra Bullock. This is
her adopted son. His name is Louis
Bardo Bullock. One of their homes is
in Austin, Texas. Sandra loves dogs.
She also adopted three special dogs,
Poppy, Ruby and Bebe.
What about your favorite actors, guys?

ZUMAPRESS.COM

4. Participate in Cool Mary's forum. Write about your favorite actor or actress.

Demonstrative pronouns

5. Look at the pictures and underline the correct words.

a. The words **this and that** / **our and my** are used to show the relative distance between the speaker and someone or something else.

b. The demonstrative pronoun **this** / **that** is used to indicate that someone or something is close to the speaker. The demonstrative pronoun **this** / **that** is used to indicate that someone or something is far from the speaker.

c. The pronouns **this** and **that** refer to **a single person or thing** / **more than one person or thing**, so they are followed by a **singular** / **plural** noun.

6. Complete the conversations with the words from the box.

's	that	this	who

a. A: Liza, ________________ is my Italian friend, Giovanni.

B: Nice to meet you, Giovanni.

b. A: ________________ is that girl?

B: ________________ is my friend's daughter, Rachel.

c. A: Whose dog is this?

B: This is my baby sister________________ dog.

HANDS ON!

Talk to a classmate about the position of objects and people in your classroom. Change roles.

Possessive adjectives

They are used to indicate possession.

Personal pronouns	Possessive adjectives
I	my
you	your
he	his
she	her
it	its
we	our
you	your
they	their

DIEGO CERVO/SHUTTERSTOCK

This isn't **my** book. This is **your** book.

THINKSTOCK/GETTY IMAGES/FUSE

Their mother is a beautiful woman.

THINKSTOCK/GETTY IMAGES/FUSE

Her brother is a teacher. **His** name is Claus.

SHUTTERSTOCK

This is **our** classroom.

Genitive case

It is used to indicate that a noun possesses another noun.

THINKSTOCK/GETTY IMAGES

Maria is my aunt. She is my father**'s** sister.

THINKSTOCK/GETTY IMAGES

These are my grand-parents. They are my mother**'s** parents.

ALEX BOECKERT/THINKSTOCK/GETTY IMAGES

This is not my cat. This is my sister**'s** cat.

Demonstrative pronouns (singular)

They are used to refer to something or someone that is near (this) or far (that) from the speaker.

THINKSTOCK/GETTY IMAGES/FUSE

This is my bike.

THINKSTOCK/GETTY IMAGES/FUSE

That is my bike.

1. Complete the conversation with possessive adjectives.

A: Who's that?

B: That's ________________ mother.

A: What's ________________ name?

B: Mary Helen. And this is my little brother, isn't he cute? ________________ name is Johnny.

A: Very cute! You have two cats, right?

B: Yes, Lola and Niki. Look! This is ________________ favorite toy.

A: Great photo! Here's a photo of ________________ dog.

B: Wow! That's a big dog! Is it male or female?

A: Male. ________________ name is Gregory.

B: Is that ________________ sister with Gregory?

A: Yes, they are best friends!

THINKSTOCK/GETTY IMAGES

2. Follow the example and complete the sentences.

My mother's *mother* is my grandmother.

a. My ________________'s brother is my uncle.

b. My mother's ________________ is my aunt.

c. My aunt's ________________ are my cousins.

d. My ________________' daughter is my mother.

e. My ________________'s son is my grandson.

f. My parents' ________________ are my sisters.

3. Underline the correct word to complete the conversations.

FUSE/THINKSTOCK/GETTY IMAGES/FUSE

a. A: Who's **that** / **this** man by the school window?

B: **That** / **This** is my teacher, Mr. Cardozo.

YELLOW DOG PRODUCTIONS/GETTY IMAGES

b. A: **That** / **This** is my uncle, Mark.

B: Nice to meet you, Mark. I'm Jennifer and **that** / **this** is my sister Luiza.

LISTENING COMPREHENSION

BEFORE LISTENING

1. Read the sentences below. Check the ones that refer to family members.

a. ☐ Hi, I am from Curitiba, Paraná.

b. ☐ My father's name is Donald.

c. ☐ Rihanna is a famous pop singer.

d. ☐ I have a brother. His name is Matt.

e. ☐ I have a twin sister. Her name's Andrea.

- **www.youtube.com/watch?v=rZLbUIa7exE**
The song "Daughters", by John Mayer, presents the importance of a good relationship among parents and children.

twin sister: irmã gêmea

2. Match the picture that corresponds to the conversation below.

Mandy: Look, Emma. This is a picture of my family. This is my sister Pamela.

Emma: Wow, she's gorgeous!

Mandy: Oh, yes, she is.

Emma: And who is this man?

Mandy: Oh, this is my father, Joe.

Emma: Really? What a handsome man! Whose cat is this?

Mandy: This is Phoenix, Pamela's cat.

A

B

ILUSTRAÇÕES: VICENTE MENDONÇA

LISTENING

3. (14) Listen to Homer Simpson introducing his family. Check the alternatives that best complete the sentences.

20TH CENTURY FOX FILM CORP.

a. Marge is Homer's

☐ wife. ☐ daughter. ☐ grandmother.

b. Bart and Lisa are Homer's

☐ friends. ☐ parents. ☐ children.

4. (15) Listen to Homer again and answer the questions.

a. How many children does Homer have?

____

b. How is Lisa related to Bart?

____

c. Homer mentioned "IQ 156". Who was he referring to?

IQ = INTELLIGENCE QUOTIENT

____

AFTER LISTENING

- In the diagrams below, write the words that correspond to each group. Use the words from the conversations in activities 1 to 3.

MALE ♂	♀ FEMALE

SPEAKING

1. Go back to activity 2 on page 55. Draw a similar family tree. Use your own family or create a new one.

BIS

2. Show the family tree you created to a classmate and talk about it.

Reflecting on the theme

"The love of family and the admiration of friends is much more important than wealth and privilege." (Charles Kuralt)

Extracted from: <www.brainyquote.com/quotes/quotes/c/charleskur364308.html>. Accessed on: May 14, 2016.

Do you agree with this quote? Justify your answer.

WRITING

BEFORE WRITING

The abbreviated form **Mr.** is used to address men and it is equivalent to *Sr.* in Portuguese. Mr. is used before a man's last name.

1. Read the text and do the activities that follow.

BIS

> Dear Mr. Kennedy,
>
> Please stop the Russians from bombing the North Pole because they will kill Santa Claus. I am 8 years old. I am in the third grade at Holy Cross School.
>
> Yours truly,
>
> Michelle Rochon

Extracted from: <www.lettersofnote.com/2013/09/you-must-not-worry-about-santa.html>. Accessed on: May 14, 2016.

2. Compare the text above to the one on page 57. What do they have in common?

a. ☐ Both texts are notes.

b. ☐ The messages are long and complex.

c. ☐ The recipient is mentioned.

d. ☐ Both texts are formal.

e. ☐ The sender in both texts is known.

3. The note above was exchanged between which two people?

____

____

4. What is the objective of the note presented in activity 1?

a. ☐ Entertain the recipient.

b. ☐ Give the recipient a message.

c. ☐ Tell a story.

d. ☐ Identify objects.

5. Michelle complains about something to the president of the United States. What does she ask him to do?

6. Why does she ask that?

7. What are the parts of a note? Write their names in the correct place.

addressee	body message	closing	greeting	sender

Dear Annika, ____________ ____________

Happy birthday! ____________

Have a special day, sweetie!

Love, ❤ ____________

Mom ____________

8. Write **G** for greetings and **C** for closings.

a. ☐ Bye

b. ☐ Hello

c. ☐ Hi

d. ☐ Love

e. ☐ See you later

f. ☐ What's up?

WRITING

9. In pairs, write an answer to the note on page 65.
   - Read the indicated note again.
   - Have in mind that the note to the president of the United States was written by an 8-year-old girl.
   - Write an answer to the note in your notebook.
   - The note must present a solution for the problem mentioned by Michelle.
   - You have to write an answer to Michelle as if you were the president of the United States.
   - Write a draft and show it to your teacher.

AFTER WRITING

- In pairs, exchange your notes and evaluate them based on the following questions.
  - Does the note answer Michelle's question?
  - Are the recipient and the sender indicated in the note?
- After your classmate's evaluation, do the necessary corrections and write the final text on the next page.
- You can illustrate your note by drawing small illustrations and using colored pens.

BIS

SELF-EVALUATION

Check the true sentences about your learning in Unit 3.
In this unit you have learned to:

- [ ] name family members;
- [ ] indicate possession;
- [ ] read and write notes.

Reflecting...

- **What did I learn about showing possession?**
- **What did I learn about writing notes in English?**
- **What questions do I have about what I've learned in this unit?**

UNIT

4

Our school is awesome!

Greater Latrobe Junior High School in Pennsylvania, in the USA.

Libras teacher and interpreter at Municipal School Professora Edna Umbelina de Sant'Anna da Silva, in Rio de Janeiro.

Riverside School, in Ahmedabad, in India.

Your learning objectives for this unit are...

- **to name school objects and subjects;**
- **to say the numbers from 0 to 20;**
- **to understand and act out a dialogue;**
- **to describe places;**
- **to make a cartoon.**

EXCHANGING IDEAS

1. The schools on these two pages represent different places in the world. Which school places are shown in the pictures?
2. What do the schools have in common?
3. Choose an element shown in the pictures that you would like to have in your school. Justify your choice.
4. How do you imagine that a classroom will be like in 20 years? Will it look like your present classroom?
5. What innovative objects will there be in the schools of the future?

PEDRO KIRILOS/AGÊNCIA O GLOBO

ROSA GAUDITANO/STUDIO R

Municipal School E. Waro Biatpu in Jacareacanga, in Pará.

LEONARDO WEN/FOLHAPRESS

State School Desembargador Amorim Lima, in São Paulo.

- ***Pro dia nascer feliz***

  Direction: João Jardim. Brazil: Flávio Tambellini Produções Cinematográficas, 2006. 88 min.

  This documentary shows the daily life of adolescents of four different public schools in Pernambuco, São Paulo, Duque de Caxias and Rio de Janeiro, besides a private school in São Paulo.

- **www.youtube.com/watch?v=HX6P6P3x1Qg**

  Quando sinto que já sei

  Direction: Antonio Sagrado; Raul Perez; Anderson Lima. Brazil: Despertar Filmes, 2014. 78 min.

  The documentary shows schools that do not follow the traditional school system and are investing in a new relationship between the students and the teachers and also in innovation.

4 Our school is awesome!

READING COMPREHENSION

TEXT 1

BEFORE READING

1. What do you know about natural phenomena? What makes a natural phenomenon become a natural disaster?
2. Take a quick look at the title and the image of the text below. What natural disaster affected the population?

READING

3. Read the text and check if your prediction in activity 2 is correct.

www.nytimes.com/2013/07/01/world/asia/floating-schools-in-bangladesh.html?_r=0

'Floating Schools' Bring Classrooms to Stranded Students

By AMY YEE June 30, 2013

[...]

In Bangladesh, annual flooding can disrupt school for hundreds of thousands of students. In some areas, roads are impassable during the rainy season from July to October, when rivers rise as much as 4 meters, or 12 feet. In 1998, the same year Shidhulai was founded, flooding inundated two-thirds of the country, killing 700 people and leaving 21 million homeless.

ALLISON JOYCE/GETTY IMAGES

The inside of a boat carrying a "floating school" operated by Shidhulai Swanirvar Sangstha, a nonprofit organization in Bangladesh.

[...]

Mohammed Rezwan, Shidhulai's founder and executive director, grew up in the country's northwest, where his organization operates.

[...]

'Many friends and relatives were denied access to education,' he said.
'I thought, if the children cannot come to school because of floods, then the school should go to them by boat.'

[...]

The organization now has 20 schools – mostly for the young children of landless families – 10 libraries and 7 adult education centers, all on boats. There are also five floating health clinics that help transport medical staff to remote areas.

Mr. Rezwan plans to add 100 more boats in the next five years to reach an additional 100,000 people.

'Our floating schools are combination of school bus and school house,' he said.

[...]

Extracted from: <www.nytimes.com/2013/07/01/world/asia/floating-schools-in-bangladesh.html>. Accessed on: May 11, 2016.

disrupt: interromper **nonprofit:** sem fins lucrativos

Bangladesh is a country in Asia, near India and Myanmar. There are floating schools in this country for children and adults and they offer courses about sustainable agriculture, women's rights, marketing, nutrition and climate change adaptation.

4. Read the sentences below and write **T** (true), **F** (false) or **NM** (not mentioned).

a. ☐ The NGO has more than 200 staff members and 300 volunteers.

b. ☐ The rainy season in Bangladesh is from July to October.

c. ☐ There are annual floods in Bangladesh.

d. ☐ There aren't classes during the floods.

- ***Être et avoir (Ser e ter)***

Direction: Nicolas Philibert. France: Maïa Films, 2002. 104 min.

This documentary tells a story about a school in France that has only one classroom. All children study together, transferring the familiar universe to an environment where individuality counts and without any generalizations.

5. Go back to the text and answer the questions in Portuguese.

a. Who is Mohammed Rezwan?

____

____

____

b. What is the goal of this organization?

____

____

____

6. Check what we can infer from the text.

a. ☐ Mohammed Rezwan cares about the victims' suffering.

b. ☐ The NGO Shidhulai Swanirvar Sangstha promotes events to raise project funds.

c. ☐ Mohammed Rezwan, founder of the NGO, has experienced the tragedies caused by the floods.

AFTER READING

- What are the advantages of having floating schools during the rainy season in Bangladesh?
- The floating schools offer different kinds of courses to the population. What courses could be taught at your school, in order to improve the students' well-being? Justify your answer.
- In the official site of Shidhulai Swanirvar Sangstha, it is stated that "Shidhulai realized that the rivers do not have to be barriers to information, they can be communication channels." Based on that sentence, what is your opinion about the way the NGO faces the floods problem? Justify your answer.

TEXT 2

BEFORE READING

1. Look at the texts below and check the correct option. The texts are:

   a. ☐ editorial cartoons. b. ☐ comic strips.

2. What do you think the characters are talking about in the texts?

READING

3. Read the comic strips and check if your prediction in activity 2 was correct.

A

B

guesses: palpites
doomed: condenado

In the American and British school systems, students go to summer school as a form of remedial education. When students don't achieve the expected competences in specific academic skills, they can take classes during the summer to avoid failing the grade.

4. Read the comic strips again. Then write the missing information.

a. name of a country ______________________________

b. a school subject ______________________________

c. a number ______________________________

d. a grammar point ______________________________

e. school term ______________________________

f. an invertebrate marine animal ______________________________

5. Answer the questions below.

a. In the first comic strip, why does the boy give many answers?

____

____

b. The boy in the first comic strip doesn't seem to know which subject he is studying. Write the sentence that supports this argument.

____

____

c. What did George Santayana, Spanish poet, essayist and philosopher, meant by his quote mentioned in the second comic strip? What did the boy understand?

____

____

____

____

____

6. What are some characteristics of comic strips? Check the correct ones.

a. ☐ speech balloon

b. ☐ formal language

c. ☐ illustrations

d. ☐ humor

e. ☐ title and paragraphs

f. ☐ long text

AFTER READING

- Comic strips can be found in newspapers, magazines, websites. What is the reader's objective when reading a comic strip?
- Both comic strips on page 72 talk about a common situation that happens to students. What is it?

FOCUS ON VOCABULARY

1. Read the text on page 70 again and check the words or expressions that correspond to the definitions.

a. Places to borrow books or make researches.

☐ bookstores ☐ libraries

b. Period of the year with a lot of rainfalls.

☐ flood ☐ rainy season

c. Inundations of a land that is normally dry.

☐ boats ☐ floods

Numbers 0-20

2. Look at the list of numbers below and write the missing ones. Then listen and check.

16

0 ____________
1 one
2 ____________
3 three
4 four
5 five

6 ____________
7 seven
8 eight
9 nine
10 ten
11 ____________

12 twelve
13 thirteen
14 fourteen
15 fifteen
16 sixteen
17 ____________

18 eighteen
19 ____________
20 twenty

School supplies and subjects

3. These are some of the school supplies students use the most. Listen and write their names. Then check the ones you use.

17

THINKSTOCK/GETTY IMAGES

____

DIOMEDIA / UIG EDUCATION / MEDIA FOR MEDICAL

____

THINKSTOCK/GETTY IMAGES

____

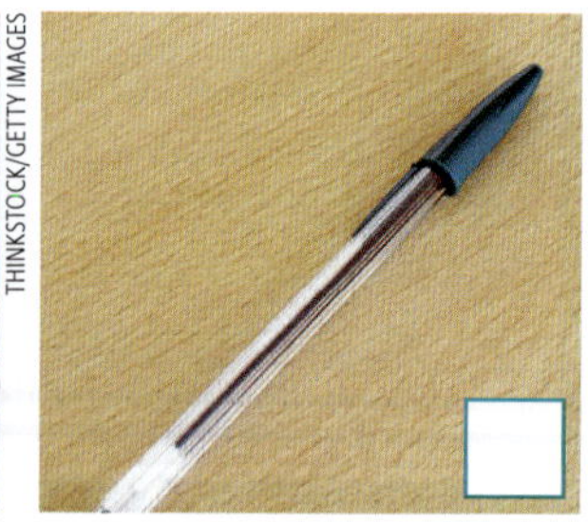
ALAMY

____

THINKSTOCK/GETTY IMAGES

____

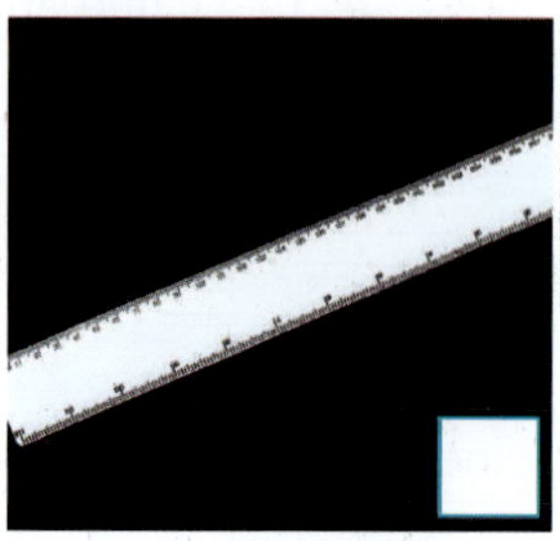
THINKSTOCK/GETTY IMAGES

____

THINKSTOCK/GETTY IMAGES

____

THINKSTOCK/GETTY IMAGES

____

4. Look at the images below. Then write the quantity and the name of the school objects.

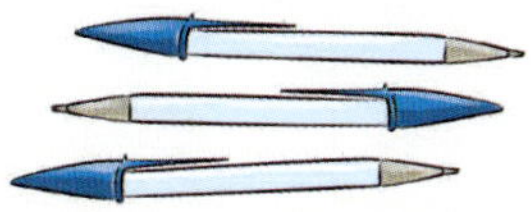

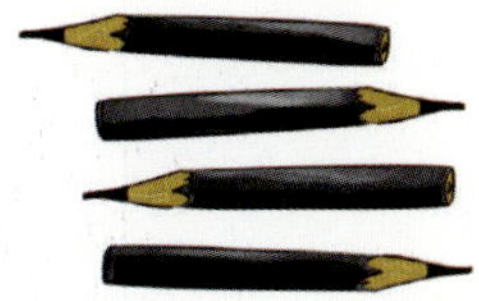

5. Look at the icons that represent the school subjects. Find the names of the school subjects in the word search.

P	H	Y	S	I	C	A	L	E	D	U	C	A	T	I	O	N	J	N	W
C	W	C	N	I	N	L	S	W	Q	Y	E	H	K	S	N	F	I	L	G
R	C	L	H	I	S	T	O	R	Y	K	H	N	V	U	Z	S	V	M	O
U	E	C	X	X	C	F	U	W	W	R	N	G	X	I	M	S	X	Z	F
P	N	G	H	V	Z	J	Z	L	A	D	Y	E	G	E	G	C	N	D	H
C	G	I	P	V	G	E	O	G	R	A	P	H	Y	U	K	I	P	P	M
O	L	Y	R	B	J	S	L	F	A	Q	R	A	R	O	D	E	U	P	I
N	I	L	G	A	M	A	T	H	K	Z	X	S	H	B	K	N	K	O	B
V	S	Q	O	F	Z	L	A	R	T	S	Z	U	I	D	A	C	P	A	G
F	H	Z	M	K	X	T	Z	Q	A	U	S	X	D	F	K	E	X	E	U
D	Q	G	U	E	A	U	E	K	Y	O	S	P	S	O	W	R	X	K	V
P	C	K	B	M	K	O	J	L	S	E	L	X	B	A	E	S	W	K	Z

Math

Science

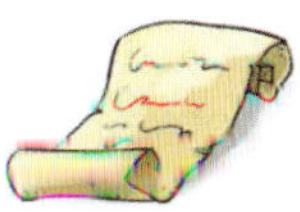
History

Geography

English

Physical Education

Art

IT'S YOUR TURN!

Walk around the classroom and ask your classmates about their favorite school subjects. Use: *What's your favorite school subject?* Then create a graph using the results. You can say: *"Eleven students like Math."*

American English: Math, Art
British English: Maths, Arts

LANGUAGE IN USE

There to be / Indefinite articles

1. Look at the cartoon and check the correct statements.

"It's a blackboard. There is no spellcheck."

MARK ANDERSON

spellcheck: verificação ortográfica

In the classroom above:

a. [ ] there is a blackboard.

b. [ ] there are letters of the alphabet on the wall.

c. [ ] there is an eraser.

d. [ ] there is a teacher in front of the blackboard.

e. [ ] there are twelve students.

f. [ ] there are notebooks.

2. Circle the correct option from the boxes and complete the sentences.

there is / there are   there are / there is

a. In the sentence "There is a blackboard", we use **there to be** to talk about the existence of something or someone. We use the form ______________ for singular complements and ______________ for plural complements.

a / an   an / a

b. The indefinite article __________ is used before singular nouns which start with a consonant sound, whereas the indefinite article __________ is used before singular nouns which start with a vowel sound.

PRONUNCIATION PRACTICE

18 Listen to the words and match them to the correct article. Then listen again and check.

a

an

cartoon
hour
humanitarian
SMS
umbrella
university

Prepositions of place

3. Look at some pictures from different classrooms around the world. Match them to their corresponding descriptions.

OPÇÃO BRASIL

OSWALDO REIS/ESP. CB/D.A PRESS

AP

☐ In this picture, there are boys and girls **in** the classroom. There are laptops **on** the desks. The students are **in front of** their laptops. There are pictures **on** the wall. They are **next to** the whiteboard.

☐ In this picture, there are many students **in** the classroom. There are no posters **on** the walls. There are not backpacks **under** the desks.

☐ In this picture, there is an interactive board **behind** the teacher. The interactive board is **between** two yellow bulletin boards. There are posters **on** the wall.

4. Circle the correct option.

The prepositions **in**, **on**, **in front of**, **next to**, **under**, **behind** and **between**, used to describe the classrooms in activity 3, are related to **places and positions** / **time and duration**.

5. Look at the pictures and complete the sentences. Use the prepositions from activity 4.

ILUSTRAÇÕES: VICENTE MENDONÇA

A

There is a mechanical pencil ____________ the desk.

B

There is a ruler ____________ the pencil case.

C

There is an eraser ____________ the notebooks.

D

There is a blackboard ____________ the teacher.

E

There are colored pencils ____________ the schoolbag.

F

There is a schoolbag ____________ the chair.

G

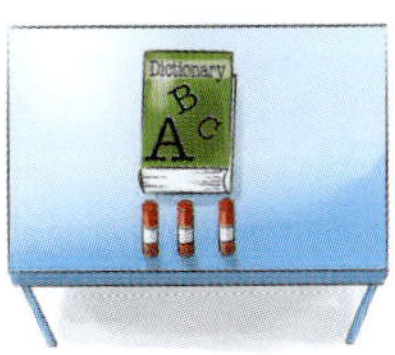

There are three glue sticks ____________ the dictionary.

H

There is a laptop ____________ the desk.

6. Look at the picture and write **T** (true) or **F** (false).

ILUSTRAÇÕES: VICENTE MENDONÇA

a. ☐ There is a globe behind the teacher's desk.

b. ☐ There is a calculator between the books and the globe.

c. ☐ The teacher is next to the desk.

d. ☐ There is a big schoolbag on the chair.

e. ☐ There are books on the teacher's desk.

7. Complete the text with the words or expressions from the box. Then choose the picture that best describes Rosa's classroom.

a	an	next to	on	there are	there is

I'm Rosa and this is my English classroom. There are six desks and one window next to the door. There is ______________ air conditioner. It's very hot here in Barcelona. ______________ a school calendar ______________ the door.

______________ posters on the wall and ______________ blackboard, too. The teacher's tablet is ______________ her desk, next to the stereo set.

THINKSTOCK/GETTY IMAGES

 ☐

 ☐

HANDS ON!

Imagine your ideal classroom and describe it to a classmate. Ask him/her to draw it in his/her notebook. Then change roles.

There to be

We use **there to be** to say that something exists or does not exist.

Affirmative	
There is + **singular** noun	**There is** a **book** on the table
There are + **plural** noun	**There are books** on the table.

Negative	
There is + **not** + **singular** noun	**There isn't** a **book** on the table.
There are + **not** + **plural** noun	**There aren't books** on the table.

We use **indefinite articles** to refer to an undetermined person or thing. There are two indefinite articles: **a** and **an**.

Indefinite articles	
We use **a** when the next word starts with a consonant sound.	**A book**.
We use **a** before words that start with a vowel, but sound like a consonant, such as "European", "euro", "university", "unit".	I live in **a European** country. I have **a euro**. I study in **a university** in Brazil. It's **a unit** in the book.
We use **an** when the next word starts with a vowel sound.	**An apple**.
We use **an** before words that start with a consonant, but sound like a vowel, such as "hour", "F", "honor".	I have a class in **an hour**. There isn't **an F** in my name! It's **an honor** to me.

Prepositions of place

We use **prepositions of place** to indicate the position of something or someone.

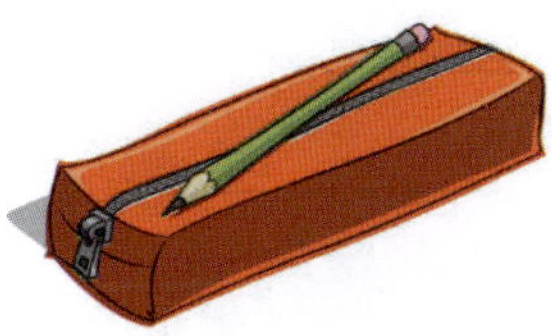
on

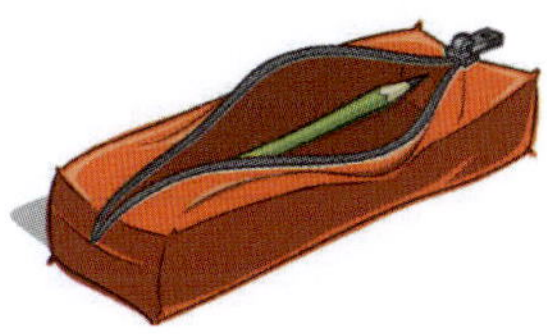
in

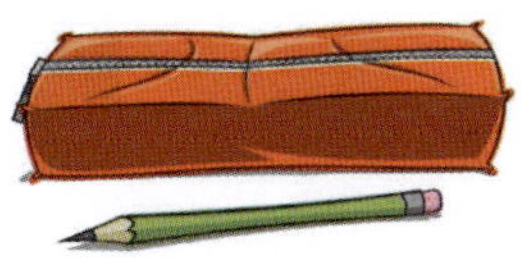
in front of

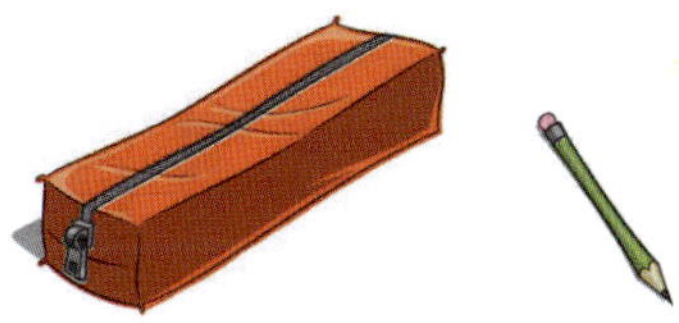
next to

ILUSTRAÇÕES: ZUBARTEZ

near

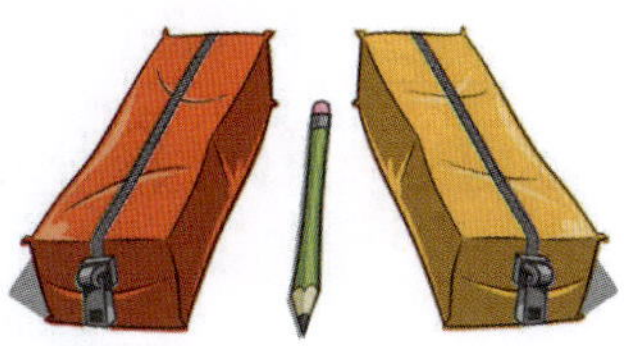
between

behind

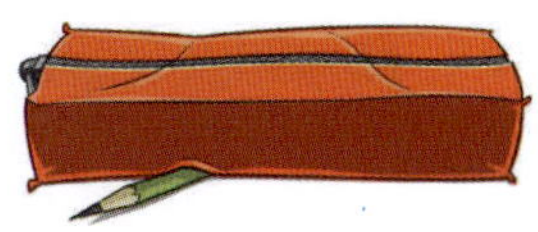
under

1. Add **a**, **an** or leave a blank space before the words below.

a. __________ mechanical pencil
b. __________ pencil cases
c. __________ eraser
d. __________ library
e. __________ flood
f. __________ 8
g. __________ art class
h. __________ yellow pencils
i. __________ old book
j. __________ umbrellas

2. Use the words from activity 1 to complete the sentences below.

a. There is __________________ alert for my area.
b. There are two __________________ next to the door.
c. There aren't __________________ on my desk. They are under the chair.
d. There isn't __________________ in my pencil case but there are many pencils.
e. There is __________________ in the library.
f. There is __________________ in my school.
g. There is __________________ in room 21 now.
h. There aren't __________________ in my pencil case but there are other colors.
i. There is __________________ in my pencil case but it's not my eraser.
j. There isn't __________________ on my telephone number.

3. Look at the image and write **T** (true) or **F** (false) for the sentences below.

a. ☐ There are two rulers in the backpack.
b. ☐ There is an apple on the books.
c. ☐ The calculator is on the pencils.
d. ☐ The pencils are next to the calculator.
e. ☐ The books are under the apple.

SEREZNIY/THINKSTOCK/GETTY IMAGES

LISTENING COMPREHENSION

BEFORE LISTENING

1. What school subjects can you remember? Write their names and draw something that represents these subjects.

BIS

2. When introducing a new student to the rest of the class, which sentences could a teacher use? Check.

a. ☐ What's your favorite school subject?

b. ☐ Where are you from?

c. ☐ I'd like to introduce you to a new student.

d. ☐ I'm Sōhei. Nice to meet you.

e. ☐ This is Samantha.

LISTENING

3. Listen to the conversations. Then answer the questions.

19

a. What are the new students' names?

____

b. Who mentions where he/she is from?

____

c. Where is he/she from?

____

4. In pairs, read and number the sentences. Write **1** for the first conversation and **2** for the second conversation.

RED OM FILMS

Samantha, an American Girl Holiday

NIPPON TELEVISION NETWORK (NTV)

Wolf Children

☐ Go ahead. Introduce yourself.

• **www.juliangermain.com/projects/classrooms.php**
Official website of the photographer Julian Germain. He shot classrooms in different countries around the world.

☐ All right, class. Listen up! We're getting a new student today.

☐ Samantha Parkington who comes for us from Mount Bedford, New York.

☐ I'd like to introduce a new student.

☐ Make him feel at home.

☐ It's nice to meet you.

☐ Maybe you would like to tell us a little about your life in Mount Bedford.

AFTER LISTENING

- Are there any new students in your class? What do you know about them?
- In small groups, act out a situation where one of you is a new student and has to introduce yourself.

SPEAKING

1. Choose one of the topics below and inform your choice to a classmate. Your classmate should create a sentence using words related to the topic you chose. Change roles and don't use the same words used by your classmate.

A

family members

B

school subjects

ILUSTRAÇÕES: VICENTE MENDONÇA

C

numbers

D

school supplies

E

countries and nationalities

2. Work in pairs. Student A is from another country. Student B asks him/her personal questions. You can ask about name, nationality and favorite school subjects. Change roles.

Reflecting on the theme

It's important to have a study routine at school and also at home. How do you get organized to study? Describe your routine. What can you do to improve your conditions for studying at home?

WRITING

BEFORE WRITING

1. Discuss the questions below with a classmate.

   a. What are cartoons?

   b. Do you read cartoons? If so, why?

   c. What are your favorite cartoons?

   d. Where can you find cartoons?

2. Look at the cartoon and answer the questions.

"There aren't any icons to click. It's a **chalk** board."

chalk: giz

   a. Who are the characters in the comic strip and where are they?

   ____

   b. How does the kid seem to be feeling? Why?

   ____

   ____

3. Go back to activity 1 on page 76 and read the cartoon again. Compare it to the cartoon above. Join the parts and find out the characteristics the cartoons have.

a. The written text is	☐	captions.
b. There are	☐	short, but it has strong impact.
c. The cartoons	☐	visual impact in the cartoon.
d. They have one	☐	panel.
e. There is	☐	are humorous.

WRITING

4. In pairs, follow the steps and create your own cartoon.
   - Choose a topic about which you would like to make a commentary or criticism in a cartoon; for instance, someone's funny habit or behavior, funny situations that usually happen at home or school, the overuse of technology, etc.
   - Research images that can illustrate the topic in the cartoon.
   - In your notebook, write a draft of the cartoon about the topic you chose.
   - Use the images you selected and relate them to the text.
   - Show the draft to your teacher.

AFTER WRITING

- Read the cartoon you created and evaluate if:
  - there's a connection between image and text;
  - it makes a commentary or criticism.
- Make the necessary changes to the cartoon.
- Get together with your classmates and make a comic book using all the cartoons created by the group.
- Create the book cover with a title and the authors' names.
- Donate the book to the school library so that everyone in the school can read the cartoons you created.

SELF-EVALUATION

Check the true sentences about your learning in Unit 4.
In this unit you have learned to:

- [ ] name school objects and subjects;
- [ ] say the numbers from 0 to 20;
- [ ] understand and act out a dialogue;
- [ ] describe places;
- [ ] make a cartoon.

Reflecting...

- **Which words related to school did I learn?**
- **What did I learn about cartoons?**
- **What questions do I still have about writing cartoons?**

Connections

English • Math

American and Brazilian Population

BETTMANN/CORBIS/LATINSTOCK

JACK HOLLIQWORTH/THINKSTOCK/GETTY IMAGES

The number of children younger than 18 in the United States in 2013 was about 74 million. It is a small number in relation to the total population because adults live longer and there are less births nowadays.

It is important to know the number of children today and predict the number of children in the future. It determines the investments in many areas of life, such as health and safety, education and training, recreation and social development, and other services for children and their families.

During the 1950s, the number of children increased by over a third, reaching 64.5 million in 1960.

In the 1980s, the number of children actually fell.

But in the 1990s, the number of children started to increase again. Most people who were born in the 1950s had children, and there was more immigration.

The number of children in the total national population gets smaller every year. The percentage of children was 36 percent in 1960 and 26 percent in 1990. This is the result of declining birth rates and also because the population lives longer. In 2010 children represented 24 percent of the population. The prediction for 2050 is 20.1 percent.

People believe the number of children in the United States will continue to increase.

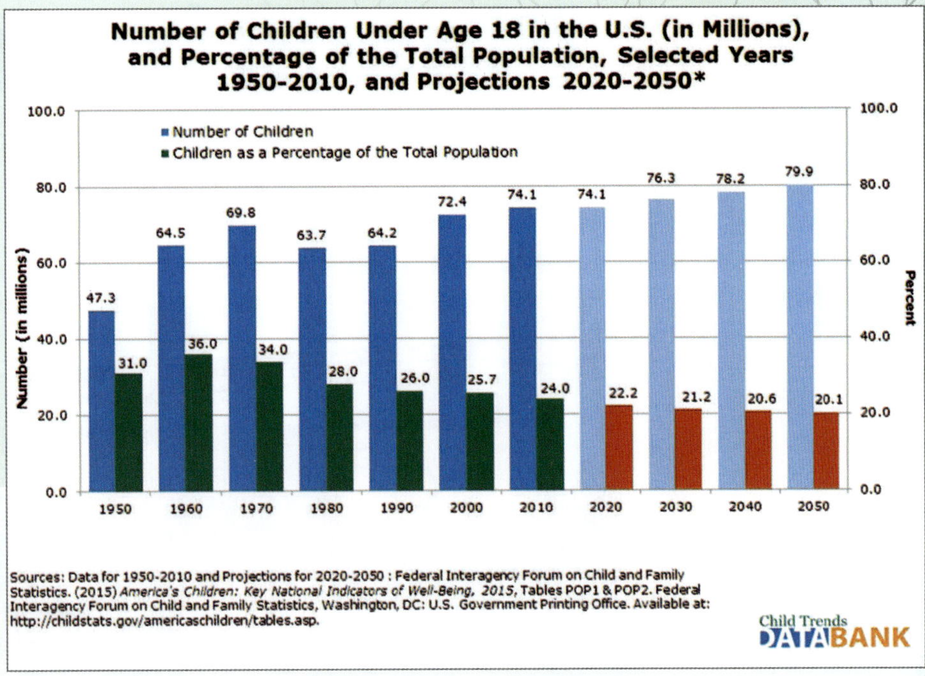

HTTP://WWW.CHILDTRENDS.ORG/

Adapted from: <www.childtrends.org/?indicators=number-of-children>. Accessed on: Dec. 3, 2015.

The number of children under age 18 in the United States in 1950 was 47.3 million.
The number of children under age 18 in the United States in 2010 was 74.1 million.

1. Look at the graph above and answer: what will probably be the percentage of children in 2050?

____

2. Look at the graph below. It refers to Brazilian population. Now compare it to the graph above. Do they present the same children's age group? Justify your answer.

____

3. Look at the graph beside again. What is approximately the percentage of children in the Brazilian population in the 2010s?

____

____

____

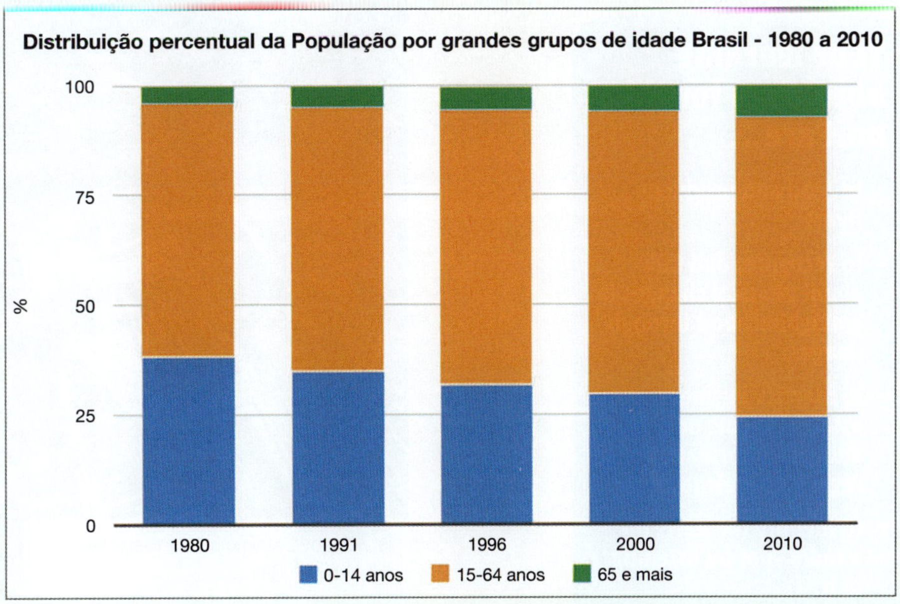

Extracted from: <http://7a12.ibge.gov.br/vamos-conhecer-o-brasil/nosso-povo/caracteristicas-da-população.html>. Acessed on: Dec. 15, 2015.

UNIT

5

Places in town

- **www.osgemeos.com.br/pt**
  Official website of the Brazilian artists OSGEMEOS. It includes a biography and their projects around the world.
- **www.huffingtonpost.com/2014/04/17/best-street-art-cities_n_5155653.html**
  Website that presents a list of the 26 best cities in the world to appreciate street art, including some examples of each mentioned city.

OSGEMEOS

Graffiti art by OSGEMEOS on six gigantic concrete silos alongside the famous Public Market, Emily Carr University and False Creek in Vancouver (Canada), in 2014.

MANNY CRISOSTOMO/GETTY IMAGES

Jazz-themed wall painting in San Francisco (USA) by Bill Weber.

Your learning objectives for this unit are...

- to read and produce flyers;
- to recognize and talk about physical changes in a neighborhood through images;
- to identify business establishments on a map and give information regarding their location;
- to identify the parts of a radio spot by listening to it.

Graffiti art on a storm drain by SÃO and Delafuente on a street in São Paulo.

6EMEIA

Mural in Bialystok city (Poland) by Natalia Rak.

NATALIA RAK

EXCHANGING IDEAS

1. Graffiti art is present in many cities around the world. Look at the photos on the left. What was used as the basis for the graffiti art?
2. Which images are represented in the graffiti arts?
3. Graffiti art is produced for different purposes: to criticize, to embellish a public space, to expose an artist's work, etc. What is the importance of graffiti art for cities?
4. Pay close attention to the mural in Poland. What is the relation between the graffiti art and the building?
5. Imagine that you are going to draw a graffiti somewhere in your school. Consider the people who usually use this space and choose a theme which can captivate all visitors.

- ***Cidade cinza***

Direction: Marcelo Mesquita; Guilherme Valiengo. Brazil: Espaço Filmes, 2013. 85 min.

This documentary takes place in the year 2008 and shows the street art in the city of São Paulo. It presents OSGEMEOS, Nunca and Nina Pandolfo working in a 700-meter wall.

5 Places in town

READING COMPREHENSION

TEXT 1

BEFORE READING

1. Are there any events such as parties and community-based actions that stimulate the residents and the community as a whole in your neighborhood? If so, what are they? If not, which ones should be created? Why?
2. Scan the text below and check.

a. The text is a:

- [ ] book cover.
- [ ] flyer.

b. The objective of the text is to:

- [ ] promote a bookstore.
- [ ] describe a bookstore.

READING

3. Read the flyer and check if your predictions in activity 2 are correct.

BINDINGS BOOKSTORE

Homeschooling is the education of children and young adults of school age at home. It is very common in countries such as the United States, Canada, Australia, New Zealand and Belgium. The students in this type of education system are called **homeschoolers**.

4. Match the parts of the sentences to form questions. Then answer the questions.

a. How much is the discount for ☐ name of the bookstore?

b. Who can have ☐ used books?

c. What is the ☐ a 15% discount?

a. ______________________________

b. ______________________________

c. ______________________________

5. Extract from the flyer on page 90 the sentences that correspond to the pictures below.

A

B

C

ILUSTRAÇÕES: LEO TEIXEIRA

______________ ______________ ______________

6. Go back to the flyer on page 90. Write what this information is about.

a. Oct 23 – 10 am-4 pm

____

____

b. Drawing Room Studio

____

____

c. 10:30-12:30

____

____

AFTER READING

- The flyer announces several events and discounts on the opening day. Why was this information given?

TEXT 2

BEFORE READING

1. Look at the photos below. What do they show?
2. Why is the first photo in black and white?

- **www.laparola.com.br/31-fotografias-antigas-de-grandes-cidades**
  Website with ancient pictures of big Brazilian cities.

- ***Cities and Nature – A Handbook for Renewal***
  Roger L. Kemp. North Carolina: McFarland & Company, 2005.
  This book presents proposals of American cities that made every possible effort to revitalize and increase green spaces.

READING

3. Look at the photos and read the captions. Then do the activities that follow.

BIS

Leo

My Place

CITY OF VANCOUVER ARCHIVES

Granville Street, Vancouver.

In 1910

This calm and beautiful place is my neighborhood in the past. All my relatives have lived here.

REPRODUÇÃO

Granville Street, Vancouver.

Nowadays

This is my neighborhood nowadays! Just like my ancestors, I live on Granville Street. It's a place I love to live in.

4. Check the places or things you can see in the photos on page 92.

	1910	Nowadays
a larger street		
a street car		
a bicycle		
trees		
buildings		
a skyscraper		
stores		

5. Based on the photos and the captions, answer the questions.

a. Does Leo like to live in Granville Street? Which sentence from the text supports that answer?

____

____

____

b. Which changes in the photos were surprising to you?

____

____

____

____

c. Why have these changes happened in the neighborhood since 1910?

____

____

____

____

AFTER READING

- Why is it important to know the history of the place where you live?
- Have there been changes in your neighborhood and in the local business establishments recently? If so, which ones? Why? If not, do you think there is a need for changes? Justify your answer.
- What would you like to do in order to keep your neighborhood well cared for and meet the needs of its residents? Who could join you in performing these actions?

FOCUS ON VOCABULARY

1. Match the abbreviations to the corresponding words.

a. St. ☐ Road

b. Ave. ☐ Avenue

c. Rd. ☐ Street

2. Match the words from activity 1 to the definitions below.

a. A public road, paved or not. It is usually surrounded by houses, buildings and business establisments on one or both sides. ______________________

b. A wide and long urban road. It is more common to be surrounded by parks and business establishments on one or both sides. ______________________

c. A high-speed urban transportation route. ______________________

3. Match the places and things to the corresponding pictures.

a. ☐ stores

b. ☐ trees

c. ☐ a skyscraper

d. ☐ a church

e. ☐ a bookstore

f. ☐ a bus

g. ☐ bicycles

1

OPÇÃO BRASIL

2

THINKSTOCK/GETTY IMAGES

3

SPACES IMAGES/GETTY IMAGES

4

THINKSTOCK/GETTY IMAGES

5

THINKSTOCK/GETTY IMAGES

6

FÁBIO VIEIRA/FOTOARENA

7

JOÃO PRUDENTE/PULSAR IMAGENS

Numbers 21-100

4. Complete with the missing numbers. Then listen and check.

20

21	twenty-one	30	thirty
______	twenty-two	31	______________
23	twenty-__________	40	forty
______	twenty-four	______	fifty
25	______________	60	sixty
______	twenty-six	70	______________
27	______________	______	eighty
28	twenty-eight	90	______________
29	______________	100	one hundred (or a hundred)

5. Use the numbers from units 4 and 5 to complete the sentences below.

a. There are __________ students in my classroom.

b. There are __________ boys and __________ girls.

c. There are __________ teachers in my school.

IT'S YOUR TURN!

Draw a map of your neighborhood. Write sentences to describe it. Use: **There is/are... on my street**. Then tell a classmate.

____

____

____

____

____

LANGUAGE IN USE

There to be / Prepositions of place

1. Look at the invitation and choose the correct answers.

valet provided: com serviço de manobrista

The acronym RSVP stands for "please reply" (from the French expression "*répondez, s'il vous plaît*"). The expression comes from the court of Louis XIV, who kept strict etiquette rules. Nowadays, RSVP is a common request confirmation of attendance in formal invitations. It is used in many languages, including Portuguese and English.

a. Is there a map of the location?

☐ Yes, there is. ☐ No, there isn't.

b. Is there the address of the new Sweet E's Bake Shop?

☐ Yes, there is. ☐ No, there isn't.

c. Are there pictures of the cupcakes?

☐ Yes, there are. ☐ No, there aren't.

d. Are there prices of the products on the invitation?

☐ Yes, there are. ☐ No, there aren't.

2. Complete the questions with **is there** or **are there**. Then look at the map and give short answers.

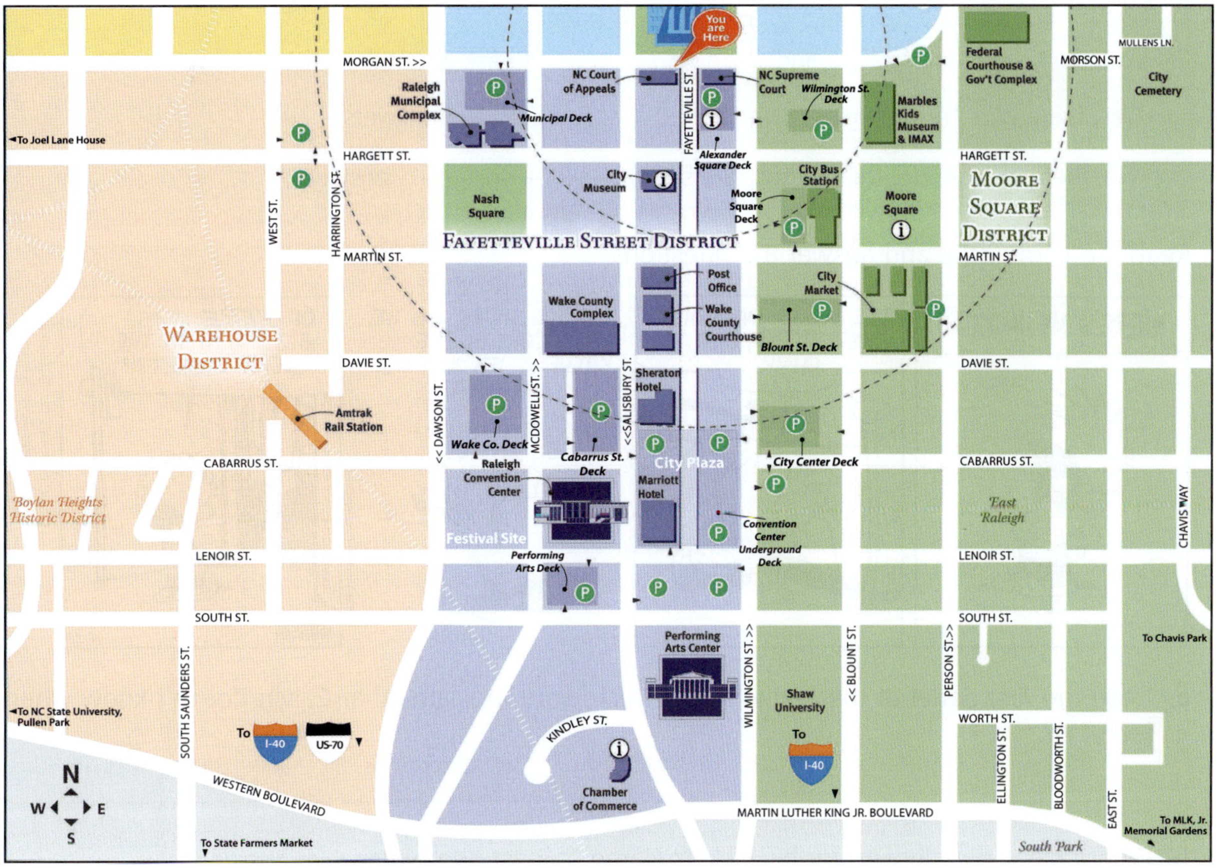

Source: <raleighconvention.com/assets/files/3/downtown-raleigh-map.pdf>. Accessed on: May 29, 2015.

a. ______________ a train station nearby? ______________

b. ______________ a post office near the university? ______________

c. ______________ museums on Dawson Street? ______________

d. ______________ hotels on Salisbury Street? ______________

3. Choose the correct picture for the following conversation.

A: Where is the bakery, Sophia?

B: Well, there is a bakery between the supermarket and the bank.

A: OK, thank you.

☐

☐

4. Based on the previous activities, complete the text.

We use ____________ and ____________ to ask about the existence of something.

"Yes, there is" / "Yes, there are" are short ____________ answers.

"No, there isn't" / "No, there aren't" are short ____________ answers.

5. Read the comic strip and answer the questions.

a. Read the first panel of the comic strip. Which word indicates that Calvin doesn't know where his jacket is?

____

b. Where has Calvin looked for his jacket? Name at least two places.

____

____

c. Which elements in the story produce humor?

____

____

____

HANDS ON!

In pairs, play a game. Student A asks five questions to find out what there is in Student B's schoolbag. Student B answers Student A's questions. Then change roles.

Use:

Student A

Is there a mechanical pencil?

Are there rulers?

Student B

Yes, there is. / No, there isn't.

Yes, there are. / No, there aren't.

There to be

Interrogative	
Is there + **singular** noun	**Is there** a **book** on the table?
Are there + **plural** noun	**Are there books** on the table?

Short answers

BAX WALKER / ALAMY/FOTOARENA

A: Is there a drugstore on Palm Street?

B: Yes, there is.

SHUTTERSTOCK

A: Are there many people on the street?

B: Yes, there are.

KEN TANNENBAUM/SHUTTERSTOCK

A: Is there a cell phone in the box?

B: No, there isn't.

THINKSTOCK/GETTY IMAGES

A: Are there cookies in the bakery?

B: No, there aren't.

Prepositions of place

We use prepositions of place to talk about location.

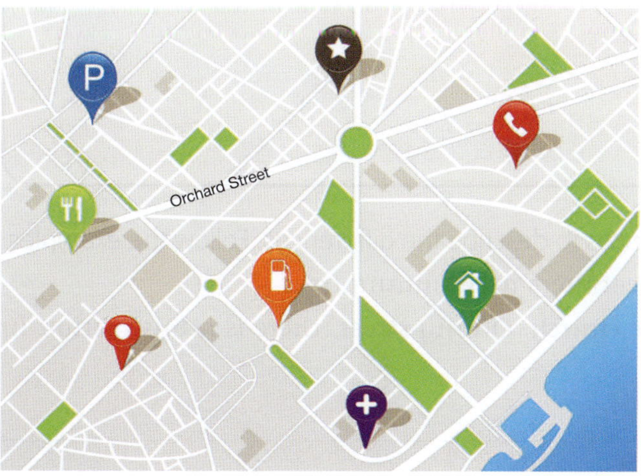

GIORGOS245/THINKSTOCK/GETTY IMAGES

— Is there a drugstore **near** the restaurant?

— No, there isn't.

— Where is the parking lot?

— It's **between** the gas station and the restaurant.

— Is the restaurant **next to** the gas station?

— No, it isn't. It's **next to** the parking lot.

— Is the restaurant **on** Orchard Street?

— Yes, it is.

1. Complete the questions and answer them with real information.

a. ______________ a shopping mall in your neighborhood?

____

b. ______________ restaurants near your school?

____

c. ______________ toy stores in your neighborhood?

____

d. ______________ a skyscraper next to your school?

____

e. ______________ many trees in your neighborhood?

____

f. ______________ a bus stop near your school?

____

2. Follow Luis' description and make a drawing of his street.

THINKSTOCK/GETTY IMAGES

I live on Treasure Street. There aren't many houses on my street but there are many trees. On one side of the street, there is a church between a small park and a bus station. On the other side of the street, there is a bookstore. Next to the bookstore, there is a bike shop. There isn't a drugstore or a shopping mall in my street.

3. Is Luis' street similar to your street? Write three sentences to describe the differences. Follow the examples.

On Luis' street there are many trees. On my street there aren't many trees.

On Luis' street there is a bus station next to the church. On my street, there is a bus station in front of a house.

____

____

____

LISTENING COMPREHENSION

BEFORE LISTENING

1. You and your family are visiting a neighborhood you want to live in. You see these places as you walk by. Look at the pictures and underline the correct alternatives.

A

KONSTANTIN L/SHUTTERSTOCK

school / supermarket

B

LYNN WATSON/SHUTTERSTOCK

bank / department store

C

GETTY IMAGES

park / bookstore

2. Read the information on the banners and identify the places. Use the words from the box.

bookstore	department store	school

A

NORDSTROM

____

B

BOLINAS-STINSON SCHOOL

____

C

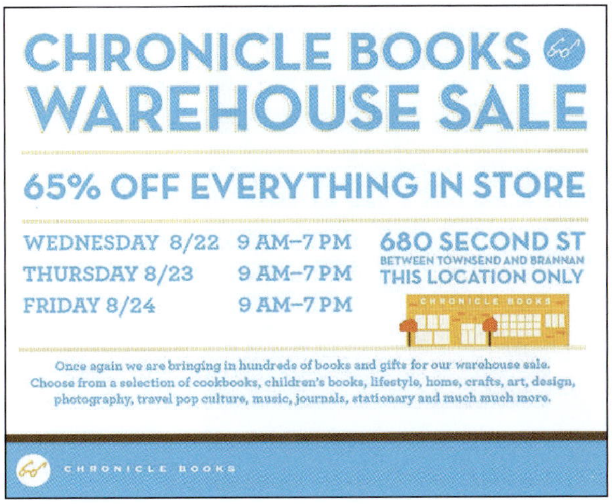

CHRONICLE BOOKS

____

LISTENING

3. Listen to a department store commercial and check the correct answers.

21

a. What is the commercial about?

- [ ] It's about a new product.
- [ ] It's about an opening sale.

b. Where is it?

- [ ] It's in New York.
- [ ] It's in Chicago.

c. When is the event?

- [ ] It's on Saturday.
- [ ] It's on Sunday.

4. Listen to the commercial again and order the parts. Then listen once more and check.

22

a. [ ] Just about to start in every Zayre store. It starts 10 am Sunday.

b. [ ] Just in time for spring.

c. [ ] We're celebrating the opening of our new store at 115th Street and South Austin Street and every Zayre store in Chicago land is joining in. A great grand opening sale just when you need it.

d. [ ] It's about to happen! Zayre is stocking up for a grand opening sale you won't wanna miss. Setting up special brand opening bargains everywhere you look.

AFTER LISTENING

- What is the best way to promote an opening sale in a neighborhood? Choose the best alternatives. Explain your choices to your classmates and report to the class.

- [ ] Radio ad.
- [ ] Local newspapers ads.
- [ ] Distribution of flyers in the neighborhood.
- [ ] Banners throughout the city.
- [ ] TV commercials.
- [ ] Loudspeaker ads.
- [ ] Social network ads.
- [ ] Word of mouth advertising.

BIS

SPEAKING

1. In pairs, give instructions to your classmate to draw an imaginary neighborhood. Follow the steps below.

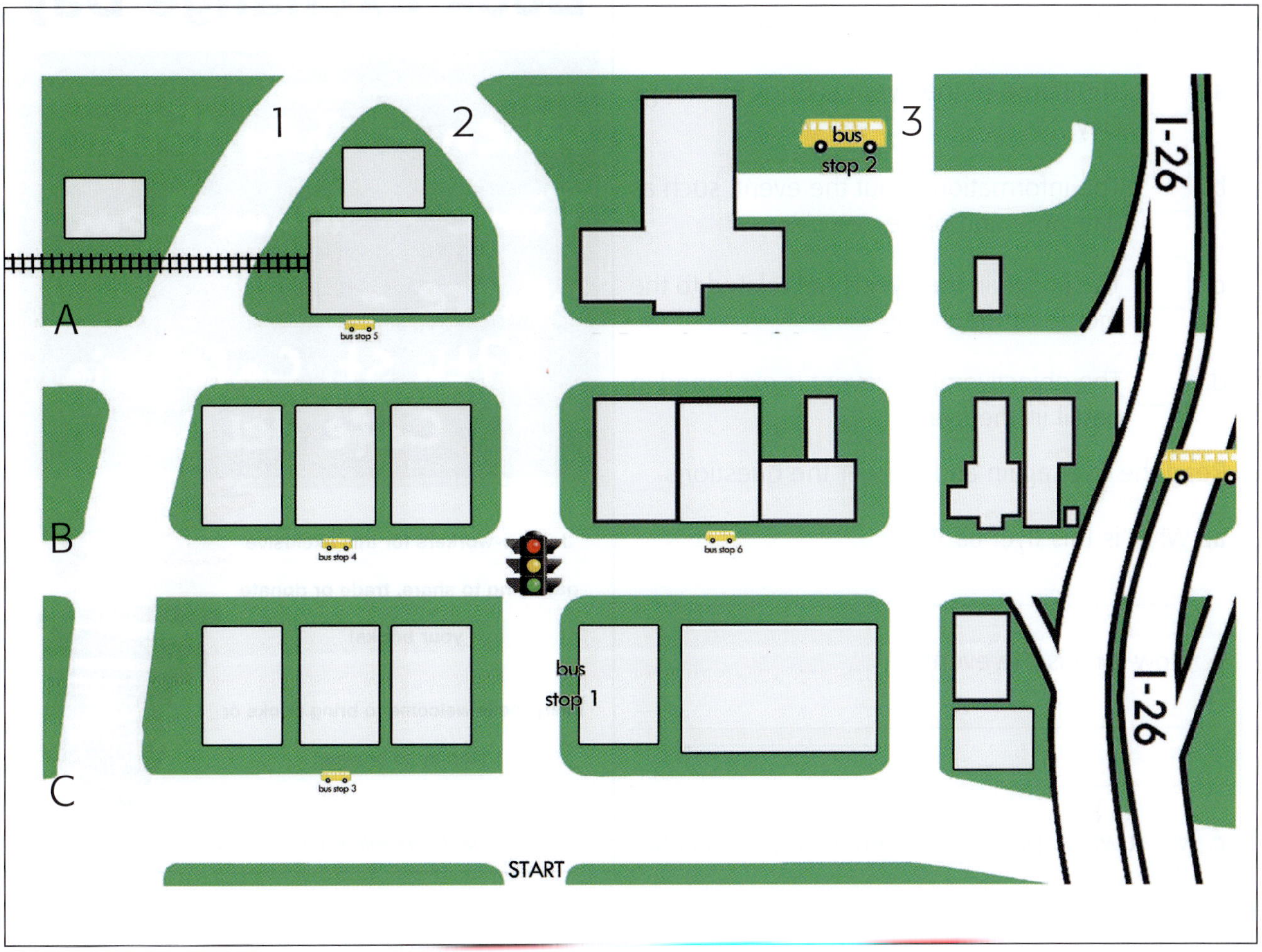

- Name the streets on the map. Use similar sentences, "A is St. Paul's Avenue
- Decide the places you want your classmate to draw.
- Give instructions to him or her. Use similar sentences: "There is a bookstore next to the bakery on St. Paul's Avenue."
- After giving all the instructions, check your classmate's drawing.
- Change roles.

Reflecting on the theme

Are the stores in your neighborhood far from your house?

What are the positive and negative aspects in relation to shopping and services in your neighborhood?

What kind of store or service provider would you like to be available in your neighborhood? Why?

WRITING

BEFORE WRITING

1. Read the flyer and check the true statements.

   a. ☐ The name of the event is Book Exchange Day.

   b. ☐ The information about the event, such as day, time and place, are clear.

   c. ☐ The image in the flyer is not related to the theme of the event.

   d. ☐ The objective of the event is explained in detail in the flyer.

2. Read the flyer again and answer the questions.

   a. What is this flyer about?

   ____

   b. How long is the event?

   ____

   ____

   c. What will happen to the remaining books after the event?

   ____

3. Compare this flyer to the one on page 90. Then answer the questions.

   a. Do they have similar characteristics?

   ____

   ____

   ____

   ____

   b. Where are they probably distributed?

   ____

   ____

   ____

   ____

WRITING

4. Create your own flyer. Follow the steps below.
   - Choose an event for a flyer that you will produce: book donation collection for the school or community library; clothes, shoes and toys collection for charity; or school event promotion.
   - Prepare a draft of your flyer. Remember to include the necessary information in the flyer: event name, place, day and time and also an appropriate image.
   - Show the draft to your teacher. Discuss the teacher's suggestions and make the necessary adjustments.

AFTER WRITING

- In groups of three students, read the flyers of the group and decide if:
  - the information about the event are complete;
  - the image is adequate for promoting the event;
  - the image catches the attention of the target audience;
  - the flyer and font sizes are adequate for promotion.
- Make the necessary adjustments and use an A4 sheet of paper to make the flyer.
- Each group will choose one of the flyers to present to the other students.
- The selected flyers will be displayed on a message board.

SELF-EVALUATION

Check the true sentences about your learning in Unit 5.
In this unit you have learned to:

- [ ] read and produce flyers;
- [ ] recognize and talk about physical changes in a neighborhood through images;
- [ ] identify business establishments on a map and give information regarding their location;
- [ ] identify the parts of a radio spot by listening to it.

Reflecting...

- **What did I learn about the characteristics of a flyer?**
- **What did I learn about talking about location?**
- **Which questions do I have about the characteristics of a flyer?**

UNIT

6

Be kind to the innocent

CHILD WITH CAT (JULIE MANET), PIERRE-AUGUSTE RENOIR, 1887.

RENOIR, Pierre-Auguste. *Child with Cat*. 1887. Oil on canvas, 54 cm × 65 cm. Musée d'Orsay, Paris, France.

Renoir was one of the most important figures of the impressionist movement and one of the most famous French painters of all times. His work is characterized by a richness of feeling and the pleasant combination of light and colors.

Your learning objectives for this unit are...

- to read and write fact files about animals;
- to name some animals;
- to use adjectives in descriptions;
- to describe animals.

EXCHANGING IDEAS

1. Describe the elements that are part of the painting on these two pages.
2. Notice the colors used in the painting. Which colors are there and what do they refer to?
3. How does the color contrast in the painting impact the viewer?
4. How do you think the cat in the painting is feeling? Justify your answer.

- **www.nationalgallery.org.uk/artists/pierre-auguste-renoir**
  Renoir's short biography available at London National Gallery website.
- **www.musee-orsay.fr/en/collections/works-in-focus/painting/commentaire_id/julie-manet-10652.html?tx_commentaire_pi1%5BpidLi%5D=509&tx_commentaire_pi1%5Bfrom%5D=841&cHash=bd914f9a0e**
  Explanation of the painting *Child with Cat* provided by Museu d'Orsay.

6 Be kind to the innocent

READING COMPREHENSION

TEXT 1

BEFORE READING

1. The animals were born free in nature, but some species are used by people as working animals. In which situations are animals used to help people?

READING

2. Pay attention to the subheadings in bold in the article below and infer what it is about.
3. Read the text and check your answer in activity 2.

are afraid of: têm medo de
mistreatment: maus-tratos
dazzle: deslumbram

www.peta.org/issues/animals-in-entertainment/circuses/#ixzz3LL0DOBeb

Circuses

Bears, elephants, tigers, and other animals do not voluntarily ride bicycles, stand on their heads, balance on balls, or jump through rings of fire. They don't perform these and other difficult tricks because they want to; they perform them because they're afraid of what will happen if they don't.

[...]

Constant Confinement

Constant travel means that animals are confined to boxcars, trailers, or trucks for days at a time in extremely hot and cold weather, often without access to basic necessities such as food, water, and veterinary care.

[...]

Circus Bans

Because of concerns about animal mistreatment and public safety, a growing number of communities are banning or restricting the use of animals in circuses.

Animal-Free Circuses

[...]

We applaud trapeze artists, jugglers, clowns, tightrope walkers, and acrobats, but let's leave animals in peace. The Latest Shows on Earth – Cirque du Soleil, the New Pickle Family Circus, Cirque Éloize, and others – are exciting and innovative circuses that dazzle audiences without animal acts.

[...]

Extracted from: <www.peta.org/issues/animals-in-entertainment/circuses/#ixzz3LL0DOBeb>. Accessed on: May.14, 2016.

4. Number the information according to the order it appears in the text.

a. ☐ There are circuses that perform beautiful shows without the use of animals.

b. ☐ Animals are confined in inadequate spaces where they don't have access to their basic needs.

c. ☐ Animals perform in circuses because they are afraid of the consequences in case they don't do what they are told to.

d. ☐ Circus artists must be admired for their talent. However, animal exploitation must not be tolerated.

5. Go back to the text and find the words below. Then circle what they refer to.

a. their (line 1)	b. these (line 2)	c. We (line 9)
bicycles / animals	tricks / circuses	audience / communities

6. Match the questions to their corresponding answers.

a. What are the basic necessities of the animals?

b. What performances can animals do in circuses?

c. What are some communities doing in favor of the animals?

d. What is different about the circuses mentioned in the end of the text?

☐ Ride bicycles, stand on their heads, balance on balls, or jump through rings of fire.

☐ They are creative and do not present animal performances.

☐ Food, water, and veterinary care.

☐ They are banning or restricting animals in circuses.

AFTER READING

- The text on the previous page was taken from a website that belongs to Peta, which is the biggest animal rights organization in the world. Peta fights against all kinds of animal abuse, including the use of animals for tests in labs and working animals. Why are organizations like Peta important for animal rights?
- What is your opinion about circuses that feature animal acts? Justify your answer.
- If a circus that features animal acts came to your city, how should people react?
- What is your opinion about other shows that feature animals, like the ones at aquariums and zoos?

TEXT 2

BEFORE READING

1. Look at the fact file published on the London zoo website about a type of penguin. What kind of information would you like to know about this animal?

> • ***SOS Animals***
> Liani Moraes. São Paulo: Atual, 1996.
> Book about how animals from around the world live. Some of them are endangered species.

READING

2. Read the fact file. Then do the activities that follow.

Penguin (Humboldt)

THINKSTOCK/GETTY IMAGES

LACZ, GERARD/ANIMALS ANIMALS/KEYSTONE BRASIL

What they look like

Humboldts are medium-sized penguins. They have black heads with a white stripe on either side and pink skin around their eyes and base of the bill.

Animal facts

These penguins need to lose heat, rather than conserve it. [...] Humboldt penguins swallow their fish head first and can reach up to 30 miles per hour in the water in order to catch prey.

What they eat

Small fish and crustaceans.

Habitat

At sea, but nests on rocky coasts, burrowing holes in guano and also using scrape nests or caves.

Where they live

Coastal Peru and Chile.

Threats

Numbers in the wild are declining. They are at risk from disturbance of colonies by Guano harvesting. Guano (penguin droppings) is a valuable fertiliser and is harvested periodically from many colonies. They are also threatened by pollution from oil spills, overfishing, and habitat loss. Humboldt penguins are hunted by seals, sealions and sharks.

Conservation Status	Vulnerable (VU)
Population	2,500-9,999 (1999 IUCN)
Order	Sphenisciformes
Family	Spheniscidae

Extracted from: <www.zsl.org/zsl-london-zoo/humboldt-penguin>. Accessed on: May 14, 2016.

3. Check the true sentences about the fact file.

a. ☐ Penguins eat big fish and crustaceans.

b. ☐ They live in two countries.

c. ☐ They live and nest only on rocky coasts.

d. ☐ There isn't any information about the penguins' physical characteristics.

e. ☐ Penguins are threatened by pollution.

f. ☐ Humboldt penguins are hunted by seals, sealions and sharks.

4. Answer the questions below.

a. Where do the Humboldt penguins live?

____

b. Which of the following threats are mentioned in the text: pollution, overfishing, climate change, too many predators?

____

____

c. What does a "vulnerable" conservation status mean?

____

____

d. How is the penguin excrement used?

____

5. Check the best option to answer the question:

Who usually reads animal fact files?

a. ☐ People who like animals and read about them.

b. ☐ People who want to have information about scientific experiments on animals.

AFTER READING

- Research online and find out which animals are endangered and where they live.
- What must we do in order to prevent animals from going extinct?

- ***Horses – Mr Carter's Plan***

  Kerry Powell. Oxford, UK: Macmillan, 2014.

  Book about human and horses relationship through history.

FOCUS ON VOCABULARY

1. Unscramble the letters and form names of animals. Then listen and check.

23

THINKSTOCK/GETTY IMAGES

B A E R

____

THINKSTOCK/GETTY IMAGES

W O C

____

THINKSTOCK/GETTY IMAGES

P H A E L E N T

____

© MARGARET LARYS

E S R O H

____

THINKSTOCK/GETTY IMAGES

N O I L

____

THINKSTOCK/GETTY IMAGES

E R G I T

____

THINKSTOCK/GETTY IMAGES

G M B R I D M H U N I

____

THINKSTOCK/GETTY IMAGES

C I A D C A

____

2. Check the sentences that are true according to the text on page 108.

a. ☐ Animals jump through rings of fire because they are punished if they don't.

☐ Animals jump through rings of fire voluntarily.

b. ☐ Bears, elephants and tigers aren't the only animals exploited in circuses.

☐ Only big, wild animals are explored in circuses.

c. ☐ People go to circuses just to watch animal performances.

☐ Trapeze artists, jugglers, clowns, tightrope walkers, and acrobats are examples of artists who perform in circuses.

- ***Madagascar***
  Direction: Eric Darnell. USA: Dreamworks Animation, 2005. 86 min.
  Alex (a lion) and his friends escaped from a zoo in New York to discover what is outside the walls.

Descriptive adjectives

3. Read the sentences and look at the pictures. Then circle the words and expressions that describe these animals.

THINKSTOCK/GETTY IMAGES

Lions are easily recognized by their manes. Larger and darker mane suggests that lion is very strong and other lions often avoid him. [...] Until they reach 2 years, lions can't roar. Once they learn how to vocalize, their roars can be heard on the distance of up to 5 miles.

SHUTTERSTOCK

Rhino is a fast running animal. It can run up to 40 miles per hour.

> • **zoo.sandiegozoo.org**
> You find information about animals in this website.

THINKSTOCK/GETTY IMAGES

Penguins are flightless birds. Instead of regular wings, penguins have flippers. [...] Penguins are excellent swimmers. They can swim 15-20 miles per hour. They can keep their breath for 20 minutes and can dive deeper than any other bird.

ANDRZEJ KUBIK/SHUTTERSTOCK

Ostriches are large, non-flying birds that live in Africa. [...] Ostriches are the fastest running bird. They can run faster than lions or leopards.

Extracted from: <www.softschools.com/facts/animals/lion_facts/2/>; <www.softschools.com/facts/animals/rhinoceros_facts/1/>; <www.softschools.com/facts/animals/penguin_facts/7/>; <www.softschools.com/facts/animals/ostrich_facts/17/>. Accessed on: Mar. 31, 2015.

4. What verbs mentioned in activity 3 are related to these animals abilities?

____

____

____

IT'S YOUR TURN!

Choose an animal from activity 1 and describe it to a classmate. Remember to use descriptive adjectives. You can use a dictionary to help you. Example: *I like elephants. They're big and strong. They can swim.*

LANGUAGE IN USE

Definite article

1. Look at the picture and answer the questions.

a. Does the girl like dogs? Which sentence from the text supports your answer?

____

b. Does the father let the girl adopt a dog? Justify your answer.

____

c. In the sentence "How about the white cat?" which word expresses the fact that we refer to a specific white cat?

____

2. Use the words from the box to complete the text below.

identify	plural	singular

Based on the questions "Can we adopt one of the dogs, Dad?" and "How about the white cat?", we can infer that the article **the** is used to ______________ nouns in the ______________ and ______________.

PRONUNCIATION PRACTICE

24 Listen to the pronunciation of the words below. Then choose the best answer to the question that follows.

the ant – the elephant – the tiger – the lion

Is there any difference in the pronunciation of the word **the**?

a. [ ] Yes, there is. The pronunciation of **the** before words that start with vowels is /ði/ (**thee**) and before words that start with consonants is /ðə/ (**thuh**).

b. [ ] No, there isn't. The pronunciation of **the** is the same in all cases.

To have, to like (simple present – affirmative form)

3. Read the conversation between two friends, Laura and Justin. Pay attention to the words in bold. Then match the parts and form complete sentences.

VICENTE MENDONÇA

Laura: Hey, Justin! Look at the birds! Aren't they beautiful?

Justin: Oh, yeah. I **like** birds, too. Look how beautiful the canaries and the parrots are!

Laura: I really **like** birds! I don't **have** any birds at home, though. I **have** a puppy, Otto. In fact, I love dogs.

Justin: Let's check the dogs, then!

Laura: Sure, let's go.

a. The verb **have** in "I have a puppy, Otto."	[ ]	expresses preference or enjoyment.
b. The verb **like** in "I like birds, too."	[ ]	expresses possession.

4. Complete the sentences with the animals you like and the animals you have. Then talk to a classmate.

I like ______________________.

I have ______________________.

Plural nouns

5. Complete the chart with the words from the box.

Singular	Plural
one lion	two ___
one monkey	four ___
one aviary	two ___
one ___	three ostriches
one wolf	five ___
one ___	four deer

aviaries
deer
lions
monkeys
ostrich
wolves

6. Read the rules for forming the plural of some nouns. Then go back to activity 5 and find some examples.

a. We usually add "-s" at the end of the noun:

___

b. For nouns ending in "ch", "x", "s", "sh", we usually add "-es" at the end of them:

___

c. When a noun ends in "y" and it is preceded by a consonant, we change the "y" to "i". Then we add "-es" at the end of it:

___

d. When a noun ends in "f" or "fe", we usually change it to "-ves":

___

e. Some nouns don't change in the plural form:

___

7. Write the plural form of these animals' names in the correct column. Then listen and check.

25

butterfly

canary

fox

ILUSTRAÇÕES: VICENTE MENDONÇA

frog

platypus

monkey

-s	-es	-ies

HANDS ON!

Choose an animal from this unit. Say the name of this animal to a classmate. He/She has 10 seconds to give you the plural form of this word. Change roles.

Definite article

We use the definite article **the** to refer to **specific** people (male and female) or things.

We use the definite article with singular and plural nouns.

The black cat is the mother.

Remember: we use **a/an** to refer to **undetermined** people or things.

THINKSTOCK/GETTY IMAGES

THINKSTOCK/GETTY IMAGES/IS

A: I want to adopt **a calm cat**.

B: The cat on the right is very calm.

To have, to like (simple present)

We use **have** to express possession and **like** to express we enjoy something or someone.

We use the base form of the verb with the pronouns **I**, **you**, **we** and **they**.

Affirmative form	
subject + verb + complement	I **like** birds. You **have** a dog. They **like** black cats.

Plural nouns

For most nouns, you add **-s**.	bird – **birds**
For most nouns ending in **ch**, **x**, **s**, **sh**, you add **-es**.	ostrich – **ostriches** fox – **foxes** hippopotamus – **hippopotamuses** fish – **fishes**
Eliminate **-y** and add **-ies** to nouns ending in **-y** preceded by a consonant.	canary – **canaries**
Sometimes we eliminate **-f** or **-fe** and add **-ves** to nouns ending in **-f** or **-fe**. Consult a dictionary if you are not sure.	wolf – **wolves**
Some nouns do not change in the plural form.	deer – **deer**
Some nouns have irregular plural forms. Consult a dictionary if you are not sure.	goose – **geese**

1. Complete the sentences below with **a**, **an**, or **the**.

a. I want to see ________ white lion at ________ zoo.

b. I want to adopt ________ pet. I want ________ cat and ________ dog.

c. ________ monkeys at ________ zoo are very funny!

d. I want to see ________ platypus at ________ aquarium!

e. They have five dogs. Rex is ________ white dog.

f. We want to play with one of ________ cats at ________ shelter.

2. Circle the correct verb that completes each sentence.

a. I **have** / **like** birds but I **have** / **like** a cat.

b. I love dogs. I **have** / **like** 10 dogs at home!

c. My friends Karen and William **have** / **like** two cats. I **have** / **like** Chess, the black cat.

3. Choose the correct plural form for each sentence below.

a. We have an English class in an hour.

- [ ] We have English classies in two hours.
- [ ] We have English classes in two hours.

b. There is a university in my city.

- [ ] There are universitys in my city.
- [ ] There are universities in my city.

c. The church is between the bank and the school.

- [ ] The churches are between the banks and the schools.
- [ ] The churchs are between the banks and the schools.

d. There is a bus in front of the school.

- [ ] There are buses in front of the school.
- [ ] There are busoes in front of the school.

e. The school patio is big.

- [ ] The school patios are big.
- [ ] The school patioes are big.

LISTENING COMPREHENSION

BEFORE LISTENING

1. Read some of the animal rights declared by UNESCO. Then match the articles to the words/expressions that summarize them.

> **Article 1**
> All animals have equal rights to exist within the context of biological equilibrium. [...]
> **Article 2**
> All animal life has the right to be respected.
> [...]
> **Article 4**
> 1º Wild animals have the right to live and to reproduce in freedom in their own natural environment.
> [...]
> **Article 5**
> 1º Any animal which is dependent on man has the right to proper sustenance and care.
> [...]

Extracted from: <www.la.utexas.edu/users/bump/Universal%20Declaration%20of%20Animal%20Rights.htm>. Accessed on: May 14, 2016.

a. reproductive rights: ____________________

b. proper sustenance guarantee: ____________________

c. maintenance of biological balance: ____________________

d. respect: ____________________

> The United Nations Educational, Scientific and Cultural Organization (UNESCO), which was founded in 1945, promotes international collaboration through education, science, and culture to ensure universal respect for justice, laws protection and human rights.

2. Check the pictures that show violations of animal rights.

THINKSTOCK/GETTY IMAGES

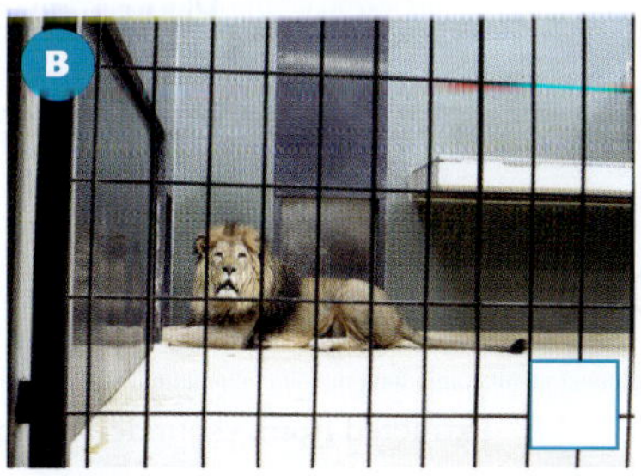

DIOMEDIA/PLAINPICTURE RM/CHRISTOPH EBERLE

THINKSTOCK/GETTY IMAGES

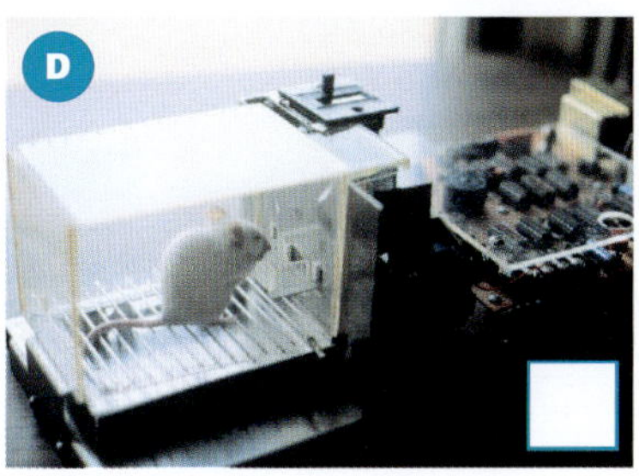

© MIMI FORSYTH

DIOMEDIA/BRUCE COLEMAN INTERNATIONAL

© PHOTOSINDIA.COM

LISTENING

3. Listen to the song below and complete the verses. Use the words from the box.

26

chance	free	heart	love	pet	right

Be Kind to the Innocent – A Song for the Animal Rights

Dabbicco Simone

Please give me the ______________
just to be free
To grow up normally
To grow up happily
Please give me the choice just to live
____

A voice unspoken
is talking straight to your heart
to your ______________ (x 3)

Cramped up in cages
cryin' pain for ages
while the dawn is gone
the kill of life is done

Give it a ______________
eyes full of revenge
savage and cold
Now it's time to evolve (x 2)

Set me free (x 4)

I will never see the sunrise
I will never see it set
Never feel a kind touch
I will never be a ______________

I will never feel ______________
For I will not be loved
As I'm led to my end
I wonder who would care...

Please give me the right just to be free
To grow up normally
To grow up happily
Please give me the choice just to live free
Please give me the right just to be free (x 5)

Extracted from: <soundcloud.com/simon-dabbicco/be-kind-to-the-innocent-simon>. Accessed on: May 14, 2016.

AFTER LISTENING

- Check the best alternative to complete the sentence below.
  The feelings in the song are expressed by ______________.

☐ a human being

☐ an animal

SPEAKING

1. In pairs, play a guessing game. Student A chooses a picture and describes the animal. Student B guesses the animal. Change roles.

DEPOSIT PHOTOS/GLOW IMAGES

J-C.&D. PRATT/PHOTONONSTOP

ALAMY

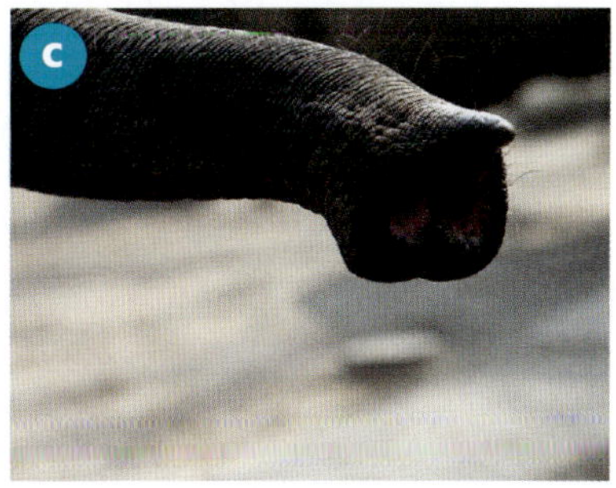

ALAMY

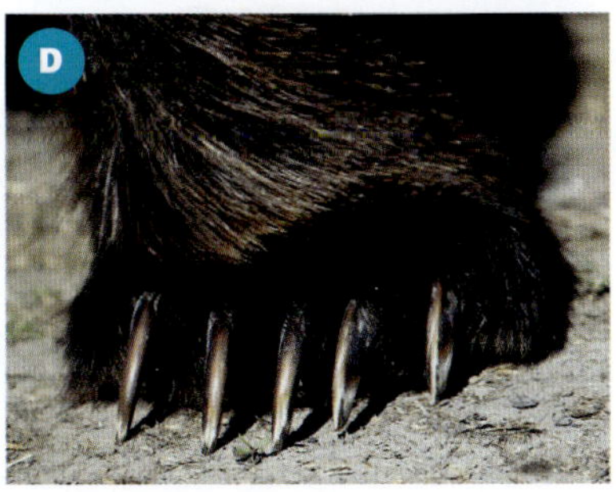

THINKSTOCK/GETTY IMAGES

THINKSTOCK/GETTY IMAGES

SUPERSTOCK RM/DIOMEDIA

Reflecting on the theme

As you have studied in this unit, it's essential that everyone becomes aware of animals' rights so they can be respected and treated humanely. What could you and your school do to ensure that everyone in your community is aware of the importance of animals' rights?

BEFORE WRITING

1. Read the animal fact file below and compare it to the one on page 110. Then choose the true sentences.

FACT FILE: Chimpanzee

Swahili Name: Sokwe Mtu

Size: 3 to 41/2 feet tall standing bipedal

Weight: 55 to 110 pounds

Habitat: Forest

Gestation: 8 months

Scientific Name: *Pan troglodytes*

Lifespan: 50 years

Diet: Omnivorous forager

Predators: Humans, leopards

THINKSTOCK/GETTY IMAGES

Noisy and curious, intelligent and social, the chimpanzee is the mammal most like a human. Chimpanzees fascinate humans and are favorites both in zoos and the wild.

Extracted from: <www.outtoafrica.nl/animals/engchimpanzee.html?zenden=2&subsoort_id=1&bestemming_id=1>. Accessed on: May 14, 2016.

- [ ] The texts in the animal fact files are usually short and objective.
- [ ] The information presented is untrue.
- [ ] An animal fact file can present information in topics or in short sentences.
- [ ] There are images in fact files.
- [ ] Animal fact files are always about mammals.

2. Complete this fact file with the information from the box.

Hippos spend most of their day in water.
Herbivorous.
The hippo's proportions reflect its sedentary, amphibious existence. Its plump and bulky body is set on short, stumpy legs, with each foot having four toes.
Rivers, swamps and protected areas.

THINKSTOCK/GETTY IMAGES

Description: ______________________________

____

____

Habitat: ______________________________

Diet: ______________________________

Fun fact: ______________________________

____

Adapted from: <www.outtoafrica.nl/animals/enghippo.html?zenden=2&subsoort_id=2&bestemming_id=1>. Accessed on: May 14, 2016.

WRITING

3. In pairs, create animal fact files. Follow the steps below.
    - Choose two animals you would like to write a fact file about. List some information you wish to include in your text.
    - Research the animals you chose. You might want to ask your Science teacher for some help, visit the library or research online.
    - Take notes of the information.
    - Find photos or make drawings to illustrate your fact files.
    - Write a draft of the fact files and ask a classmate to read it and evaluate if:
        - the fact files mention the animals' physical characteristics, where they live, what they eat and some curiosities;
        - the text is illustrated with a photo or drawing;
        - the text is organized in topics.
    - Adjust the text, if necessary.
    - Write the final version of the fact files on a separate sheet of paper.

AFTER WRITING

- Choose a place in your school to set up a bulletin board to post your fact files. Make sure you choose a place that most people at school can see.
- Post your fact files on the board.
- Ask staff and students to read your fact files. Take this opportunity to talk to people about the respect we must have for animals and why we must protect their rights.

SELF-EVALUATION

Check the true sentences about your learning in Unit 6.
In this unit you have learned to:

- [ ] read and write fact files about animals;
- [ ] name some animals;
- [ ] use adjectives in descriptions;
- [ ] describe animals.

Reflecting...

- **What did I learn about animal fact files?**
- **What did I learn about animals' rights?**
- **What would I like to know about endangered animals?**

Neutering and spaying

VVVITA/SHUTTERSTOCK

To neuter (castration) is to surgically remove the reproductive glands of a male animal.

To spay is to surgically remove the reproductive organs (ovaries, uterus, and fallopian tubes) of a female animal.

It is a good idea to spay or neuter puppies (baby dogs) and kittens (baby cats) of both sexes when they are six months old.

Cats and dogs can procreate until 10 years of age or older. In fact, female cats can start having babies when they are four months old. That's why more and more veterinarians (also called "vets") are spaying and neutering animals as young as eight weeks of age. This is to guarantee that the animals will never have an accidental pregnancy.

There are many advantages in neutering or spaying cats and dogs when they are young: they recuperate faster, have less discomfort, have a lower risk of cancer (an animal neutered before six months of age has almost a 0% chance of having prostate or ovarian cancer!), and become less aggressive.

Did you know?

- Dogs are ready to have babies for a period of about three weeks, once or twice a year.
- Cats are ready to have babies every 34 weeks from spring through fall.
- Pregnancy for both cats and dogs lasts 63 days.
- Cats can be pregnant again ten days after giving birth.

Adapted from: <www.friendsofanimals.org/programs/spaying-neutering/dont-delay-neuter-or-spay>. Accessed on: Dec. 6, 2015.

1. Research and find out: what is the name of the period in which cats and dogs can become pregnant?

____

2. Look at the poster. What is it about?

____

____

HTTP://WWW.ANIMALSHELTERING.ORG/

3. Now read the situation proposed, do the calculations and answer the question.

A cat named Kitty has six kittens. They are all female.

The kittens get pregnant after 4 months. After 63 days, they have six kittens each. They are all female.

These kittens get pregnant after 4 months too. After 63 days, they have six kittens each.

How many cats will there be in this family in about one year?

____

____

____

____

____

UNIT

7

A healthy life

ARCIMBOLDO, VERTUMNUS, C.1590

Giuseppe Arcimboldo was an Italian mannerist painter. In around 1590 he had the idea for *Vertumnus*, a painting in homage to the Roman mythological god. Vertumnus is the god of seasons, change and plants – that is, a god of nature and vegetation. The painting was commissioned by Rudolph II, emperor of the Holy Roman Germanic Empire. For that reason, the painter depicted Rudolf II as Vertumnus.

Your learning objectives for this unit are…

- to identify nutritional information in food labels;
- to read about cooking habits in other countries;
- to read and write a recipe.

ARCIMBOLDO, VERTUMNUS, C.1590

EXCHANGING IDEAS

1. Look at the image on the left. Describe the elements that compose the image.
2. The painting represents the god of seasons. What is the relation between the elements that compose the image and the seasons of the year?
3. In this unit, you will read texts about food and eating habits. What are healthy eating habits in your opinion?

- **www.giuseppe-arcimboldo.org/**

  Giuseppe Arcimboldo official website. His biography and all his works are available there.
- **www.youtube.com/watch?v=RwZY1jaw2EM&list=PLEB7B579138523955**

  Direction: James Colquhoun; Laurentine ten Bosch. *Food Matters* [*O alimento é importante*]. Australia, 2008. 80 min.

  Documentary that shows the importance of a healthy and conscious nourishment. It also presents the extensive agriculture vicious cycle that affects soil nutrients.

ARCIMBOLDO, Giuseppe. *Vertumnus*. 1590. Oil on wood, 70.5 cm × 57.5 cm. Bälsta, Skoklosters Slott, Sweden.

7 A healthy life

READING COMPREHENSION

TEXT 1

BEFORE READING

1. Anvisa (National Health Surveillance Agency) RDC 306 resolution of December 23, 2003 made mandatory the presence of nutritional information in the labels of all pre-packaged foods and beverages. Why is this Anvisa regulation important for the consumers?
2. Do you usually read the nutritional labels of foods and drinks? If so, which specific information do you look for? If not, why?
3. Read the label below quickly and answer: who would probably be interested in this product? Justify your answer.

READING

healthy: saudável
serving: porção

4. Read the text of the meal bar label and check the true sentences.

Nutrition Facts
Serving Size 1 bar (45g)
Servings Per Container 5

Amount Per Serving	
Calories 190	Calories from fat 80
	%Daily value*
Total Fat 9g	**14%**
Saturated Fat 3g	**14%**
Trans Fat 0g	
Cholesterol 0mg	**0%**
Sodium 180mg	**8%**
Total Carbohydrate 19g	**6%**
Dietary Fiber 9g	**35%**
Sugars 6g	
Protein 10g	**12%**

Vitamin A 20%	● Vitamin C 20%
Calcium 20%	● Iron 20%
Vitamin D 20%	● Vitamin E 20%
Thiamin 20%	● Robiflavin 20%
Niacin 20%	● Vitamin B6 20%
Folic Acid 20%	● Vitamin B12 20%
Phosphorus 15%	● Zinc 20%

*Percent daily values are based on a 2000 calorie diet. Your daily value may be higher or lower depending on your calorie needs

	Calories	2,000	2,500
Total fat	Less than	65g	80g
Sat Fat	Less than	20g	25g
Cholesterol	Less than	300mg	300mg
Sodium	Less than	2,400mg	2,400mg
Total Carbohydrate		300	375g
Dietary Fiber		25g	30g
Protein		50g	65g

Ingredients: Almonds, Chicory Root Extract, Soy Protein Isolate, Soy Protein, Soluble Corn Fiber, Vegetable Oil (Palm Kernel, Palm, Canola), **Sugar, Fructose, Chocolate Flavored Drops** (Sugar, Whey Protein Concentrate, Palm Kernel And Palm Oils, Cocoa Powder, Soy Lecithin), **Whole Grain Oats, Whey Protein Concentrate, Vegetable Glycerin, Soy Fiber, Cocoa Powder, Tapioca Starch, Tapioca Syrup, Dipotassium Phosphate. Contains 1% Or Less Of:** Rice Starch, Salt, Soy Lecithin, Water, Natural Flavor, Corn Syrup, Maltodextrin, Color Added, Baking Soda, Oil Of Rosemary Added To Retain Freshness. **Vitamins And Minerals: Calcium Carbonate, Vitamin C** (Sodium Ascorbate), **Zin And Iron** (Mineral Nutrients), **Vitamin E Actate, Vitamin A** (Palmitate), **A B Vitamins** (niacinamide), **Vitamin D3, Vitamin B6** (pyroxidine hidrochloride), **Vitamin B1** (thiamin mononitrate), **Vitamin B2** (riboflavin), **Vitamin B12, A B Vitamins** (folic acid).
CONTAINS ALMOND, SOY AND MILK INGREDIENTS.
DIST. BY GENERAL MILLS SALES, NC, MINNEAPOLIS, MN 55440 USA
3603825101 ©2013 General Mills

GENERAL MILLS

a. ☐ The daily energy intake needs may vary from person to person.

b. ☐ The packaging contains just one bar.

c. ☐ There are 6 grams of sugars per bar.

5. Read the information and answer the questions.

> The World Health Organization (WHO) recommends the maximum daily intake of less than 2 grams of sodium (less than 2,000 mg) for people aged 16 and older. Just 1 gram of refined salt that is used in cooking contains 400 mg of sodium and its excessive consumption may cause cardiovascular diseases, kidney failure, cerebrovascular accident (CVA), among other health problems.

a. How many of the bars on the previous page can someone consume without exceeding the recommended limit of sodium?

____

b. If someone consumes more bars than recommended, what precautions should he or she have while eating and drinking for the rest of the day?

____

____

6. Read this nutrition label and compare it to the one on page 128. Then check the product that presents more of the nutrients mentioned in the chart.

GTS/ SHUTTERSTOCK

	Meal bar	Cookies
total fat		
sodium		
cholesterol		
calories per serving		

> • **www.muitoalemdopeso.com.br.**
> Direction: Estela Renner. *Muito além do peso*. Brazil, Maria Farinha Filmes, 2012. 84 min.
> Documentary about Brazilian children nourishment and the impact that marketing has on them.

7. Use the words from the meal bar label on page 128 to complete the text below.

A good diet involves watching your c________________e count, including food rich in nutrients and vitamins, avoiding s________________d fats, as well as paying particular attention to all sources of f________________r [...]

Extracted from: <www.medicalnewstoday.com/articles/146935.php>. Accessed on: May 14, 2016.

AFTER READING

- As we have seen, the composition of the food and the amount ingested can directly affect our health. How do you evaluate your eating choices in terms of the benefits and damages to your health?
- Besides having eating habits that include fruits, vegetables and natural foods in general, what other practices are necessary to maintain a healthy lifestyle?

TEXT 2

BEFORE READING

1. In different parts of the world and the country, people have different eating habits. Give examples of foods that are typical of a country or a region.

____

2. Iran is a country located in the Middle East. Do you know what people eat there?

____

READING

3. Read the text about food habits in Iran. Then do the activities.

1 Iran was called Persia a long time ago. It's a land where we can see deserts and also mountains covered with snow, primitive villages and modern cities as well.

2 This country's hospitality is famous and every guest is considered 'God's gift.'

3 Yogurt is the food of rich and poor people. It's served with meals as a soup or as dessert, along with sugar, fruit, jam or honey. When the weather is hot, yogurt is mixed with water and salt to make a drink called *abdug*.

4 If you visit an Iranian home, your host is going to serve you tea, and a sugar cube to hold in your mouth. [...]

5 Today you can use a spoon and a fork to eat, but the old custom was to use only your fingers and a piece of bread.

Extracted from: MORAES, Liani. *The Table Is Set. Help Yourself!* São Paulo: Atual, 1996. p. 6 and 7.

Iran is an Islamic country located in the Middle East. Its capital is Tehran. The official language is Persian.

guest: hóspede
gift: presente
host: anfitrião

4. Write the number of the paragraphs where you can find the information below.

a. [ ] What is served to a guest in an Iranian home.

b. [ ] Geography of the country.

c. [ ] An ancient Iranian custom.

d. [ ] A popular method of serving food in Iran.

e. [ ] Iranian hospitality.

5. Answer the questions below. If necessary, read the text on page 130 again.

a. Which contrasts are there in Iran?

____

____

____

____

b. Why is yogurt a versatile food?

____

____

____

____

c. Are guests welcome in an Iranian home? How do you know that?

____

____

d. What is usually served to guests in an Iranian home?

____

____

____

e. Instead of their own fingers and bread, what do people use today when they eat?

____

____

AFTER READING

- Do some research about the eating habits of peoples from other regions of the world, such as Australia, England, South Africa. Find out about traditional foods and eating habits in these places.
- What are the differences between your eating habits and customs and the ones from the peoples you researched about?

FOCUS ON VOCABULARY

1. Unscramble the letters to form words that correspond to the definitions below. Then find the words in the word search.

a. (VGSERSIN) ________________ – the information measured in bars, cups, pieces and grams.

b. (MUSOID) ________________ – a mineral nutrient.

c. (NASTR AFT) ________________ – when liquid oil transforms into solid fat; for example, margarine.

d. (HOCSELOETRL) ________________ – a fat-like substance found in all cells of the human body.

e. (TAEDIYR ERFIB) ________________ – includes foods extracted from plants that are difficult to digest.

C	D	K	A	P	S	R	S	H	H	M	D	L	D	H	Y	T	S	Y	O
E	H	X	G	D	O	F	U	O	M	A	G	U	I	L	O	F	D	Y	I
Y	Q	W	N	M	D	Z	D	I	E	T	A	R	Y	F	I	B	E	R	T
O	B	A	M	E	I	R	P	X	H	L	Y	A	R	V	T	I	F	R	R
Z	G	P	V	T	U	X	J	G	G	I	L	M	T	C	G	R	B	T	A
D	A	E	T	G	M	V	A	C	W	L	A	A	A	H	M	Y	S	R	N
C	H	O	L	E	S	T	E	R	O	L	F	R	T	N	L	W	Q	A	S
V	W	B	M	V	Z	C	N	C	B	R	X	D	A	A	F	W	O	J	F
H	B	O	W	U	N	Q	H	P	Z	A	G	G	Q	B	D	Z	T	X	A
B	W	Z	X	S	E	R	V	I	N	G	S	Z	S	Q	E	E	M	P	T

2. These are some popular Iranian foods and drinks. Match the pictures to their names. Then listen and check your answers. 27

a. ☐ yogurt

b. ☐ soup

c. ☐ tea

d. ☐ jam

e. ☐ dessert

f. ☐ honey

1

AZITA

2

© FOOD COLLECTION

3

THINKSTOCK/GETTY IMAGES

4

THINKSTOCK/GETTY IMAGES

5

CHRISTIAN JUNG/SHUTTERSTOCK

6

THINKSTOCK/GETTY IMAGES

Colors / Fruits and vegetables

3. (28) Look at the food color wheel and read about some of the benefits fruits and vegetables give us. Use the names of the colors to complete the texts. Then listen and check your answers.

THINKSTOCK/GETTY IMAGES/ JULIAN ROVAGNATI/SHUTTERSTOCK/ PHOTOGRAPHEE EU/SHUTTERSTOCK/ VVOE/SHUTTERSTOCK

- **portalsaude.saude.gov.br/images/pdf/2014/novembro/05/Guia-Alimentar-para-a-pop-brasiliera-Miolo-PDF-Internet.pdf**
  Ministry of Health Guide for Brazilian people nourishment.

lung: pulmão
stroke: derrame
bones: ossos

a. ________________ fruits and vegetables help to prevent prostate, lung and stomach cancers. They're high in vitamin C. They are strawberries, apples and tomatoes.

b. ________________ and ________________ fruits and vegetables help to keep the skin and the eyes healthy. They're full of beta-carotene. They are peaches, corn, carrots and papayas.

c. ________________ fruits and vegetables are rich in dietary fiber. They help to prevent high cholesterol and reduce the risk of stroke. They are bananas, cauliflower, potatoes and onions.

d. ________________ fruits and vegetables help to prevent heart diseases. They maintain the bones and teeth strong. They are limes, broccoli, green grapes and avocados.

e. ________________ and ________________ fruits and vegetables are powerful antioxidants. They are eggplants, plums and blackberries.

Based on: <www.disabled-world.com/artman/publish/fruits-vegetables.shtml>. Accessed on: May 14, 2016.

IT'S YOUR TURN!

Walk around and ask three classmates about the colors of their favorite foods. Use the question: "What color is your favorite food?" Write their answers in your notebook and report the results to your classmates. You can say: "Jessica's favorite foods are red."

Imperative

1. Read the text and circle the words that refer to actions.

1 cup: 1 xícara (de medida)
1 tsp (a teaspoon): 1 colher de chá
blend: bater no liquidificador

THINKSTOCK/GETTY IMAGES

BANANA SMOOTHIE

1 medium banana
1 cup low-fat milk
1 tsp vanilla
1 tsp sugar
1 cup ice cubes (optional)

1. Peel banana and break into pieces.
2. Place all ingredients in a blender.
3. Blend until smooth, about 4 minutes.
4. Pour into a tall glass.

Makes 1 serving. Food Guide Pyramid servings: 1 fruit, 1.5 dairy.

Extracted from: <www.cdph.ca.gov/HealthInfo/healthyliving/childfamily/Documents/MO-NUPA-TeenCookbook.pdf>. Accessed on: May 14, 2016.

2. Check the correct alternatives and complete the sentences.

a. The words you circled in activity 1 are action verbs. They are in the imperative form. We use the imperative to ______________________.

☐ give instructions, orders and advice ☐ make questions and give answers

b. The imperatives in activity 1 are in the ______________ form.

☐ negative ☐ affirmative

c. We use ______________ (do + not) before the main verb to form the negative imperative form.

☐ don't ☐ not

3. Use the words from the box to complete the sentences. Then match the sentences to their corresponding signs.

Be	Do not (2x)	Turn

[ ] ______________________ litter.

[ ] ______________________ quiet!

[ ] ______________________ enter.

[ ] ______________________ right.

To make a polite request, use **please** with the imperative.

Please, don't speak so loud.

Follow my instructions, **please**.

A

ALAMY

B

THINKSTOCK/GETTY IMAGES

C

THINKSTOCK/GETTY IMAGES

D

THINKSTOCK/GETTY IMAGES

Some / Any

4. Read the text and check the sentences that are correct.

Community garden

– Is there **any** restriction to the hours that the garden is open? [...]

WATER: Easy access to water is vital to garden success. If there isn't **any** running water on the site, investigate the cost of providing it. [...] The committee should purchase **some** rain barrels (there are several good ones on the market these days) and the gardeners encouraged to practice water conservation techniques, such as mulching and bottle drip irrigation. [...]

GETTING TO KNOW YOU A community garden can provide opportunity for people to be creative in ways that they haven't explored since childhood. **Some** of the most successful community gardens offer many ways in which to grow. [...]

– Do you need **any** of the following: rain barrels, hoses, buckets, watering cans, tools? [...]

CELEBRATE! Your ideas and hard work have finally become a community garden. What's next? Celebrate!! Have a grand opening, barbecue, or **some** other fun event to give everyone who helped to make this happen a special thank-you. [...]

Adapted from: <foodshare.net/custom/uploads/2015/11/Community_Gardening_101.pdf>. Accessed on: May 14, 2016.

a. [ ] **Some** and **any** are expressions of time.

b. [ ] **Any** is used in negative and interrogative sentences.

c. [ ] **Some** is used in affirmative sentences.

- **www.youtube.com/watch?v=1sHrxvC73GE**

Direction: Thereza Jessouroun. *Por uma vida melhor*. Brazil: CECIP; CESE; IBASE, 2012. 30 min.

Documentary about nourishing and nutritional security in Brazil, access to water and appropriate nourishment.

- ***As viagens dos alimentos*: as trocas entre os continentes**

Janaina Amado; Luiz Carlos Figueiredo. São Paulo: Saraiva, 2014.

This book presents interesting facts about the importance of Portugal maritime shipments to the Brazilian nourishment.

5. Look at the two dishes below. Write sentences using **some** or **any** to describe each dish.

THINKSTOCK/GETTY IMAGES

FERNANDO FAVORETTO/CRIAR IMAGEM

______________________________ ______________________________

______________________________ ______________________________

______________________________ ______________________________

______________________________ ______________________________

To like, to love and to prefer

6. Read the sentences about eating habits. Write **P** for preference, **D** for dislike or **L** for like.

a. ☐ He **doesn't like** chicken or green vegetables but will eat some fruit.

b. ☐ He **prefers** processed, pre-packaged meals.

c. ☐ I cannot eat cooked vegetables. I can eat most vegetables uncooked, even if I **don't like** them much.

d. ☐ I don't eat cooked carrots or cooked broccoli – which is strange, because I **love** them raw.

Adapted from: <www.bbc.co.uk/news/world-us-canada-10959879>. Accessed on: May 14, 2016.

7. Complete the sentences with information about you. Use a dictionary if necessary.

a. I like ______________________________.

b. I don't like ______________________________.

c. I prefer ______________________________.

d. I love ______________________________.

HANDS ON!

Imagine a classmate is changing his/her eating habits. Make up a list of instructions you think are good for him/her to plan a healthy diet. You can use a dictionary to help you. Then report your ideas to your teacher and classmates.

Imperative

Use the imperative to give orders or instructions.

Affirmative	Negative
Infinitive without **to**	Don't + infinitive without **to**
Do your homework.	**Don't be** late for class.
Read this book for next week.	**Don't call** before 8:00 am.
Make the cake for the party.	**Don't speak** Portuguese in the English class.

For more formal situations, or to describe signs, use **do not** in the negative form.

MOODBOARD/THINKSTOCK/GETTY IMAGES

Some / Any

Some and **any** are used to describe non-specific quantity or amount.

Affirmative sentence	 THINKSTOCK/GETTY IMAGES	There are **some** apples in the basket.
Negative sentence	 THINKSTOCK/GETTY IMAGES	There aren't **any** apples in the basket.
Interrogative sentence	 SHUTTERSTOCK	**A:** Are there **any** bananas in the basket? **B:** No, there aren't.

To like, to love and to prefer

I **love** Italian food, but I **don't like** pizza.

Eduardo **likes** yogurt and Paula **prefers** orange juice for breakfast.

My dog **loves** cold water, but he **doesn't like** cold food.

We **prefer** vegetarian food.

They **love** my friends.

1. Complete the instructions to make a cereal bar with the affirmative or negative imperative of the verbs in the box.

add cook cut eat mix pour use

EKATERINA KHOROSHILOVA/SHUTTERSTOCK

1. Melt 100 g butter (_______________ margarine!) and _______________ ½ cup of honey and ¼ cup of sugar.

2. Cook for about 5-6 minutes. _______________ for more than 7 minutes.

3. _______________ 3 cups of cereals, 1 and ½ cup of dried fruit and some coconut in a large bowl.

4. _______________ the sugar mixture to the bowl and mix everything.

5. Press the mixture in a tray and bake it for 15-20 minutes.

6. _______________ it hot! Refrigerate for about 2 hours and then _______________ into slices (about 2 cm x 6 cm).

2. Look at the refrigerator below and complete the telephone conversation using **some** and **any**.

A: I'm at the supermarket, do we need anything?

B: Let me open the refrigerator... I think we need _______________ yogurt.

ANNA OMELCHENKO/THINKSTOCK/GETTY IMAGES

A: OK. Are there _______________ apples in the refrigerator?

B: Yes, there is one apple. But there aren't _______________ grapes. I know you love grapes...

A: Yes! Grapes. What else?

B: There isn't _______________ butter.

A: Got it. Are there _______________ eggs? Potatoes?

B: Yes, there are _______________ eggs and _______________ potatoes. Oh, there isn't _______________ cheese.

A: OK. So, just checking: we need _______________ yogurt, grapes, butter and cheese.

B: Yes, that's it.

3. Circle the correct option to complete the sentences.

a. My best friend **doesn't like/loves** Japanese food. I **like/don't like** Japanese food too, but I **prefer/don't like** Brazilian food, specially food from Bahia!

b. My grandfather **doesn't like/loves** mango juice, he **prefer/prefers** orange or lemon juice.

c. I **don't like/like** beef, I'm a vegetarian.

LISTENING COMPREHENSION

BEFORE LISTENING

1. Check what you can use to make lemonade.

A

THINKSTOCK/GETTY IMAGES
☐

B

VIKTORIA GAVRILINA/SHUTTERSTOCK
☐

C

GYVAFOTO/SHUTTERSTOCK
☐

D

THINKSTOCK/GETTY IMAGES
☐

E

THINKSTOCK/GETTY IMAGES
☐

F
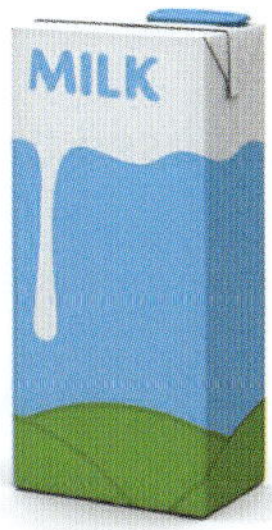

THINKSTOCK/GETTY IMAGES
☐

2. Which sentences can you probably find in a lemonade recipe? Check.

A

SUE WILSON/ALAMY/LATINSTOCK

☐ Slice the lemons.

B

THINKSTOCK/GETTY IMAGES

☐ Squeeze the lemons.

C

DORLING KINDERSLEY/GETTY IMAGES

☐ Peel the lemons.

D

ALEXEYSUN/SHUTTERSTOCK

☐ Dilute the lemon juice with water.

E

THINKSTOCK/GETTY IMAGES

☐ Add some sugar.

LISTENING

3. Listen to a recipe of homemade lemonade and number the steps.

29

____

____

____

4. Listen again and answer the questions.

30

a. How many lemons are necessary to make this lemonade?

____

b. What ingredients are included?

____

c. What is used to garnish the glass of lemonade: a slice of lemon or ice cubes?

garnish: decorar

____

AFTER LISTENING

- Read the three steps of the lemonade recipe. In pairs, change or add one more step.

  Step 1: Squeeze the lemons. Use a juicer to squeeze 10 lemons. Pour the juice into a large pitcher.

  Step 2: Add sugar. Measure one cup of sugar and pour into the pitcher. Stir until the sugar dissolves.

  Step 3: Dilute with water. Fill the pitcher 3/4 full with cold water.

____

____

- What is your favorite juice?

____

- Do you know how to prepare it? If you do, are the steps for this juice similar to the ones suggested for the lemonade? List them below.

SPEAKING

1. Think of a recipe that includes some of the ingredients and verbs below. Mime the recipe to a classmate. He/she has to say the ingredients and the steps to prepare this recipe.

Ingredients

GTRANQUILLITY/SHUTTERSTOCK

ice cream

DIOMEDIA / DENKOU IMAGES

milk

FOODCOLLECTION/GETTY IMAGES

bread

DEBORAH PENDELL/GETTY IMAGES

strawberries

SCOTT PHILLIPS/CORBIS/LATINSTOCK

tomato

STEPAN POPOV/ALAMY/LATINSTOCK

cheese

THINKSTOCK/GETTY IMAGES

condensed milk

DIOMEDIA / INGRAM PUBLISHING

bacon

Verbs of instructions

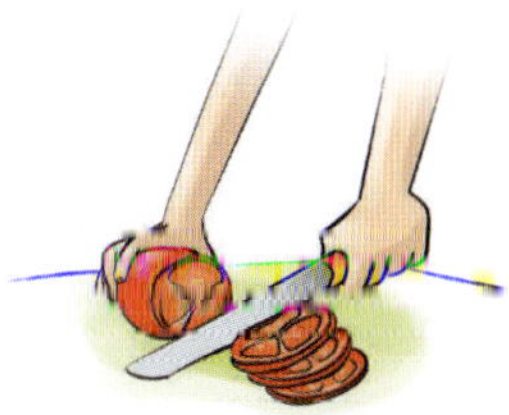
slice

mix

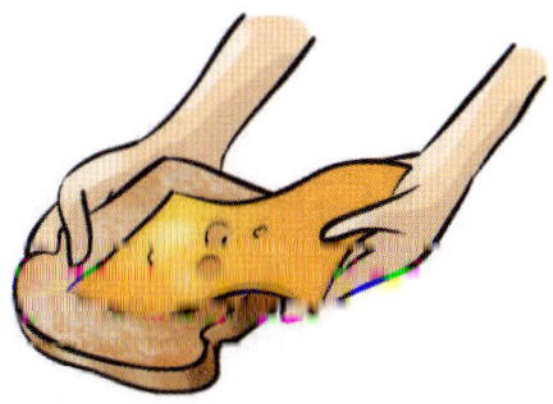
put

ILUSTRAÇÕES: VICENTE MENDONÇA

pour

add

Reflecting on the theme

What should people consider while choosing ingredients to cook a healthy meal?

Choose a healthy recipe and present it to the group. Explain why you chose it.

WRITING

BEFORE WRITING

1. Compare the recipe below to the one on page 134. Read the sentences and write 1 for the banana smoothie recipe and/or 2 for the chocolate-banana sundae.

1 pint: 473 ml (US), 568 ml (UK)
shredded coconut: coco ralado

DIOMEDIA/SOZAIJITEN/DATACRAF CO., LTD

Chocolate-Banana Sundae

Preparation: 10 minutes
Cooking time: 10 minutes
Serves 4

- **INGREDIENTS**

4 small bananas
1 pint vanilla ice cream
¼ cup chocolate sauce
¼ cup sweetened shredded coconut

- **DIRECTIONS**

1. Peel and slice the bananas.
2. Scoop the ice cream into 4 bowls.
3. Top with the bananas, chocolate sauce, and coconut.

Adapted from: <www.realsimple.com/food-recipes/recipe-collections-favorites/kid-friendly-recipes>. Accessed on: May 14, 2016.

a. ☐ There is a list of ingredients and instructions on how to prepare it.

b. ☐ There is more than one step to make it.

c. ☐ Each part of the recipe has a label.

d. ☐ There is information about servings.

e. ☐ Preparation time is informed.

f. ☐ The verbs express instructions.

g. ☐ Cooking time is mentioned.

2. Read the recipe again and answer the questions.

a. How many bananas would you need in this recipe to serve six people?

____

b. Would there be any changes in relation to the number of cooking tools used? Which ones?

____

WRITING

3. Follow the steps below and write a special recipe.
   - Talk to a classmate about what you love to eat.
   - Choose your favorite ingredients and write a recipe to use them all.
   - If desired, adapt a recipe you are already familiar with.
   - Write a draft for the recipe. Use command verbs.
   - Organize your text so that the steps are clear.
   - Draw something to illustrate your recipe and name it.
   - Exchange recipes with a classmate and check if:
     - the recipe is divided in two parts: ingredients and instructions;
     - there are command verbs;
     - the amount for each ingredient is indicated.
   - Then, make the necessary adjustments in your recipe and ask the teacher to review the final text.

AFTER WRITING

- Write your recipe on a separate piece of paper.
- With the whole class, collect and organize the recipes to create a recipe book.
- Choose a title for the book and create a cover page.
- Sort out the recipes by groups: salads, meats, pastas, desserts, etc.
- Compile the book and ask the teacher to, if possible, make enough copies or make a digital version available to every student.

SELF-EVALUATION

Check the true sentences about your learning in Unit 7.
In this unit you have learned to:

- [ ] identify nutritional information in food labels;
- [ ] read about cooking habits in other countries;
- [ ] read and write a recipe.

Reflecting...

- **What did I learn about reading and writing recipes?**
- **What did I learn about eating habits and customs in other countries?**
- **What would I like to learn about the eating habits in other countries?**

UNIT

8

Can you play soccer?

Francisco Rebolo is considered one of the most important landscape painters in Brazilian art. [...] Francisco Rebolo Gonsales was born in São Paulo, in 1902, the fifth son of a Spanish immigrant family. [...] Rebolo's career in painting starts in the early 1930s, after quitting his soccer career. [...]

Translated from: <www.mercadoarte.com.br/blog/francisco-rebolo/>. Accessed on: Mar. 12, 2015.

Your learning objectives for this unit are...

- to read and write news;
- to identify sports and safety equipment used by athletes and sportspeople;
- to use verbs that express the idea of ability and permission.

FUTEBOL, REBOLO, 1936

EXCHANGING IDEAS

1. How is Rebolo's life story related to the theme of this painting?
2. This piece is from 1936, when soccer was an elite sport that did not accept black players. Based on this information, what must have been the impact and relevance of this painting at that time?
3. Do you practice any sport? Which one? If you are not practicing any sport at the moment, which one would you like to?
4. Which sports competitions do you follow and like to watch live or on TV?

- ***Pelé***

  Rod Smith. Penguin Graded Readers, Level 1. 2. ed. São Paulo: Pearson Education do Brasil, 2010.

  Biography about Pelé, considered by many people as the best football player of the world.

REBOLO, Francisco. *Futebol*. 1936. Oil on canvas, 86 cm × 36 cm. Private collection.

8 Can you play soccer?

READING COMPREHENSION

TEXT 1

BEFORE READING

1. Practicing sports is important to improve people's quality of life. How do young people benefit from it?
2. Female soccer players have been on the spotlight lately. Do you know any soccer player who has been with the Brazilian national team? Which one?
3. Read the news below quickly. What is it about?

READING

4. Read the news and answer the questions.

ftw.usatoday.com/2014/12/u-s-womens-soccer-loses-no-1-ranking-for-the-first-time-in-7-years

U.S. Women's Soccer loses No. 1 ranking for the first time in 7 years

By: LAKEN LITMAN December 19, 2014 11:14 am ET

For the first time in seven years, the U.S. is not the world's No. 1 team in women's soccer.

FIFA announced this year's final Women's World Rankings on Friday, and it was Germany that came out on top. The Germans earned this spot after recent victories over Sweden and England, while the Americans lost to Brazil and tied China during the current 2014 International Tournament of Brasilia. They beat Argentina 7-0 on Thursday, and will face Brazil again in the final on Sunday.

[...]

EVARISTO SA/AFP

Carli Lloyd goes up against Brazil star Marta in the International Tournament of Brasilia.

Extracted from: <ftw.usatoday.com/2014/12/u-s-womens-soccer-loses-no-1-ranking-for-the-first-time-in-7-years>. Accessed on: May 14, 2016.

FIFA (Fédération Internationale de Football Association) supervises soccer confederations and international competitions worldwide. It was created in Paris (1904) and its headquarter is located in Zurich, Switzerland.

a. Who are the players in the picture?

____

____

b. What are their nationalities?

____

____

c. What was the world's No. 1 team in 2014?

____

____

5. What is the headline of the news on page 146?

____

6. Read the caption of the photograph. Check its function.

a. ☐ It describes the action in the photograph.

b. ☐ It reveals the main idea of the news.

7. Read the news again and match the questions to their answers.

a. Who announced the fact? ☐ The 2014 Women's World Rankings.

b. What was announced? ☐ December, 2014.

c. When was it announced? ☐ FIFA.

8. Read the article again and complete the chart with the words from the box.

Argentina Brazil China England Sweden

Team	Won against	Tied with	Lost to
Germany			
The U.S.			

AFTER READING

U.S.: the U.S.A. (The United States of America)

- Research about other prominent female athletes. There are renowned pole vault athletes, judo fighters, Olympic gymnasts and others in Brazil. Share the information you find with your classmates.
- Do female athletes have the same media coverage as men?

TEXT 2

BEFORE READING

1. Read the magazine article below. What does it have in common with the news on page 146?
2. Which sport is covered in the article? What do you know about this sport and this athlete?

- **vimeo.com/113869939**

Direction: Jason Horton; See Food. *Shaping Medina*. United States, 2014. 11 min.

This short film begins with the Brazilian surfer Gabriel Medina's first victory in 2011. After that, it presents Medina's most important accomplishments until the 2014 season, when he became the world champion.

READING

3. Read the magazine article. Then do the activities.

www.surfermag.com/features/gabriel-medina-first-brazilian-champ

Gabriel Medina: Brazil's First Champ

Junior Faria, Brazilian surf journalist, on Medina's impact

By Surfer

POSTED ON DECEMBER 19, 2014

It's official – Gabriel Medina is the new World Champion. For the first time in history a South American holds the WCT World Title. The 20-year-old phenom from the beachbreaks of São Paulo, Medina now joins Kelly Slater as one of the two youngest World Champions ever. He takes home a trophy that thousands of passionate Brazilian surf fans dreamed about since Victor Ribas finished in 3rd place in 1999. A lot of celebration is expected in Brazil.

KENT NISHIMURA/AFP

Gabriel Medina, the new No. 1 in the world. [...]

[...] Medina represents the ultimate surfing competitor: talented, passionate, and hungry for victory.

Medina is a surfer that is not afraid to admit that winning is his main goal. [...] Medina's popularity has pushed surfing's notoriety in Brazil to new levels. His career path has a lot of similarities to big names in soccer, like Neymar Jr. But now Medina has a title that slipped through Neymar's hands in the last World Cup. And that is one of the reasons why Medina is becoming bigger than surfing in Brazil.

Medina comes from a humble family. He is a local hero at one of the country's most famous surfing spots and has earned worldwide recognition through sheer talent. A life story that has many similarities with Brazilian soccer superstars. [...]

Raise the green, yellow, and blue flag up high, Gabriel – with rage, passion, and a big smile on your face.

Extracted from: <www.surfermag.com/features/gabriel-medina-first-brazilian-champ>. Accessed on: May 14, 2016.

4. Read the text and look at the picture on page 148. Write **T** (true), **F** (false) or **NM** (not mentioned).

a. ☐ It is the first time a surfer from South America holds the WCT World Title.

b. ☐ Medina is a 20-year-old surfer from São Paulo.

c. ☐ Slater isn't a world champion in surf.

d. ☐ Medina's family isn't rich.

e. ☐ Medina gets a lot of money as a surfer.

5. Answer the questions below.

a. What do Gabriel Medina and Kelly Slater have in common?

b. Did Medina's talent receive due recognition? Write the sentence in the article that supports your answer.

c. What is Medina's main objective in surf competitions?

d. Why is Medina compared to a soccer player?

KENT NISHIMURA/AFP

6. Look back to the article and find...

a. ... two adjectives that describe Medina: ____________________

b. ... Medina's age: ____________________

c. ... Medina's title: ____________________

AFTER READING

- Gabriel Medina's WCT World Title brought more interest to surf. Why is this title important for future generations of surfers?

FOCUS ON VOCABULARY

1. Go back to text 1 on page 146 and find the words "beat", "victory", "lost" and "tie". Read the sentences they are in and guess what they mean. Then complete the texts.

www.9and10news.com/category/217908/sports

a. NASHVILLE, Tenn. (AP) – Tomas Tatar broke a ______________ on a power play at 9:06 of the third period in the Detroit Red Wings' 4-3 victory over the Nashville Predators on Saturday.

NATIONAL HOCKEY LEAGUE

b. COLLEGE PARK, Md. (AP) – Melo Trimble scored 19 points, and No. 14 Maryland ______________ Michigan 66-56 Saturday to complete an undefeated season at home in the Big Ten.

REPRODUÇÃO

c. LAKELAND Fla. (AP) – Julio Teheran allowed one run in a two-inning spring debut, leading the Atlanta Braves to a 6-4 ______________ over the Detroit Tigers on Thursday.

REPRODUÇÃO

d. SARASOTA, Fla. (AP) – [...] Baltimore Orioles ______________ to the Detroit Tigers 5-4 Wednesday.

Extracted from: <www.9and10news.com/story/28228857/tomas-tatar-lifts-red-wings-past-predators-4-3>; <www.9and10news.com/story/28228074/no-14-maryland-beats-michigan-66-56-for-5th-straight-win>; <www.9and10news.com/story/28275092/teheran-simon-make-spring-debuts-tigers-beat-braves-6-4>; <www.9and10news.com/story/28263469/machado-wieters-return-for-orioles-in-loss-to-tigers>. Accessed on: May 9, 2016.

2. Read the text on page 148 again and find the words that correspond to the definitions below.

a. ______________: a person that is extremely good at doing something.

b. ______________: a person with modest behavior and attitudes.

3. Check the flag mentioned in the text on page 148.

A

PRESIDÊNCIA DA REPÚBLICA

☐

B

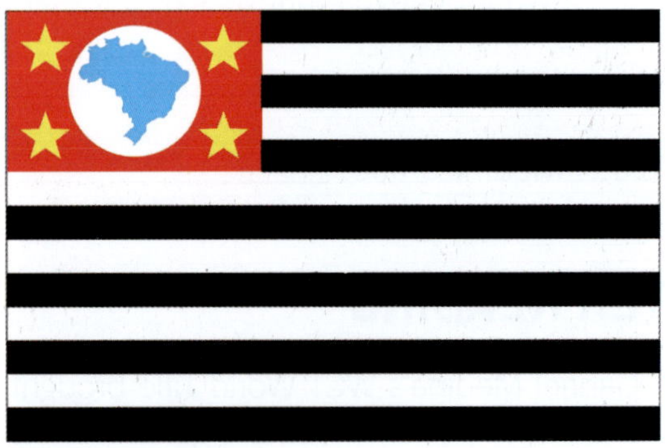
GOVERNO DO ESTADO DE SÃO PAULO

☐

Sports and safety equipment

4. Label the pictures using the words from the box. Listen and check your answers. Underline the sports you would like to practice.

31

basketball	cycling	judo	soccer	swimming	tennis

A

TIM DE WAELE/CORBIS/LATINSTOCK

____

B

JASON MILLER/GETTY IMAGES

____

C

CLIVE ROSE/AFP

____

D

EDUARDO KNAPP/FOLHAPRESS

____

E

JOSÉ MANUEL RIBEIRO/AFP

____

F

FREDERIC J. BROWN/AFP

____

5. These are some sports uniforms and equipment that athletes wear. Match them to the sports mentioned in activity 4. Use a dictionary to help you.

- [ ] soccer cleats and shin guards
- [ ] martial arts uniform and black belt
- [ ] goggles and swim cap
- [ ] wristband
- [ ] knee pad
- [ ] bike helmet and gloves

- **www.youtube.com/watch?v=dSHbXdkUlsA**
  High School Musical 3 (Senior Year Cast scene). *Now or Never*. Lyrics by Matthew Gerrad & Robbie Nevil. 2008.
  Song about team work in a basketball team.

IT'S YOUR TURN!

In pairs, choose a sport from activity 4 and mime the corresponding action to a classmate. He/She has to guess the name of the sport. Student A asks: *Is it cycling?* Student B answers: *Yes, it is. / No, it isn't. It's...*

LANGUAGE IN USE

Can

1. Read the comic strips and answer the questions.

Comic strip 1

Calvin and Hobbes are characters created by American cartoonist Bill Watterson in 1985. Calvin is a 6-year-old boy and his best friend, Hobbes, is a stuffed tiger. Hobbes is as real to Calvin as the other characters in this cartoon series. The last Calvin and Hobbes strip was published on December 31, 1995.

a. Calvin complains that sometimes his words do not follow his thoughts. Why?

____

____

b. In "[...] we think faster than we can speak.", the verb **can** expresses an ability or a permission?

____

Comic strip 2

c. In "Can Hobbes come?", the verb **can** expresses an ability or a permission?

____

d. Does Calvin's mother grant permission at first?

____

e. On the last panel, Calvin gives a bad advice to those who don't get what they want. What is it? What do you think about it?

____

____

____

2. Read the comic strips in activity 1 again. Then choose the correct options to complete the sentences.

a. The ________ form **can** and the ________ form **can't** are used for all subjects.

☐ affirmative / negative ☐ negative / affirmative

b. To form the interrogative sentence, we use **can** ________ the subject.

☐ after ☐ before

c. The main verb used with **can** or **can't** is in the ________.

☐ infinitive form without **to** ☐ present tense

3. Use **can** and the clues given to write questions. Then complete the answers.

a. I / take my racket and tennis ball / to the classroom

Student: ____

Teacher: No, ____.

b. Dad, / we / play volleyball / after school

Son: ____

Dad: Sure _______________________________.

c. you / the ball / pass me

Rita: It's my turn. ____, please?

Vincent: Of course _______________________________.

d. Adam / play basketball

Miles: ____

Kellen: No, _______________________________. But he can play soccer well.

e. a goalkeeper / use her hands / in soccer

Mirna: ____

Coach: _______________________________ She can use her hands to touch the ball in the penalty area.

To play (simple present – affirmative form)

4. Read these photo captions. Then underline the correct alternatives in the sentences that follow.

MARK HAMILTON/BBC SCOTLAND

I **play** solo concerts from time to time.

HANNAH PETERS/AFP

Maria Sharapova **plays** a backhand in her match against Zarina Diyas.

BRUNO GALLARDO

We **play** beach soccer with amputees on a Sierra Leone beach.

a. The verbs in the sentences above are in the simple present and express **repeated actions, a permanent situation or a habit** / **instructions**.

b. In **negative** / **affirmative** sentences, we use the verb in the infinitive form without **to** for **I** and **we**. For **she** we add **-s** to the end of the verb.

5. Complete the conversation between classmates Hayden and Carter. Use the words/expressions from the box.

can teach	can't play	play	plays

Carter: Hey, Hayden! There is a soccer game at the club today. Would you like to play with us?

Hayden: Ah, I'm sorry, Carter. I ______________________ soccer.

Carter: What? I can't believe it! Come on! We ______________________ you.

Hayden: I don't know... Timothy ______________________ very well, and Tyler and Blake ______________________ for the school team. They are all very good players. I'm not.

Carter: That's not true. Come on, man.

Hayden: All right, let's go!

HANDS ON!

Let's take a classroom survey. Ask six classmates about their abilities in sports. You can ask: "Can you play...?" or "Can you swim / dance / ride a bike?" Then report the results of the survey to your classmates. Tell them, for example: "Three of my classmates play tennis." "They are Paul, Jessica and Jack."

Can

We use **can** to express ability and permission.

Affirmative
Subject + can + verb + complement
I **can** play soccer. He **can** play tennis.

Interrogative
Can + subject + verb + complement
Can I play soccer with you? **Can** she play soccer well?

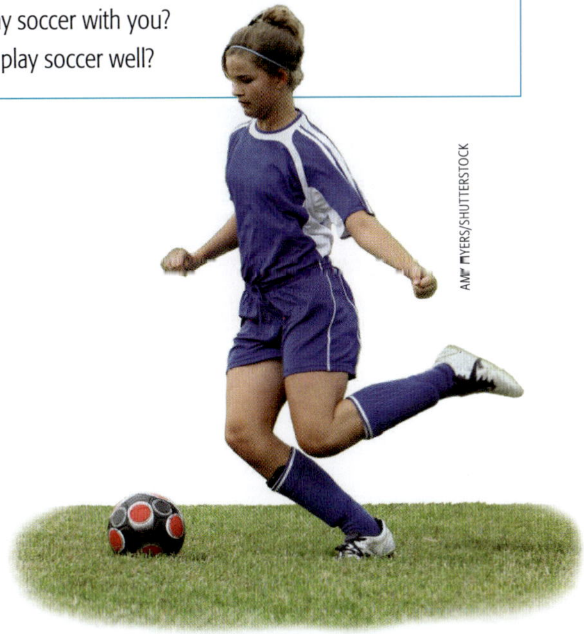

AMY MYERS/SHUTTERSTOCK

Negative
Subject + can't + verb + complement
I **can't** play soccer. He **can't** play tennis.

To play (simple present)

THINKSTOCK/GETTY IMAGES

Affirmative form (I, you, we, they)
Subject + verb + complement
I **play** soccer. You **play** soccer. We **play** soccer. They **play** soccer.

Affirmative form (he, she, it)
Subject + verb + -s + complement
He **plays** tennis and she **plays** soccer.

THINKSTOCK/GETTY IMAGES

1. Complete the sentences about the people in the photos.

SHUTTERSTOCK

________ surf very well.

SHUTTERSTOCK

________ play basketball well.

NICK STUBBS/SHUTTERSTOCK

________ tennis?

DELFIM MARTINS/PULSAR IMAGENS

They ________ soccer on this street.

2. Complete the conversation below. Use the words/expressions from the box.

can	can practice	can teach
can't	play	plays

IMAGE SOURCE/GETTY IMAGES

Steven: Hi, Mary! We have a new video game at home: *Fifa 16*! Would you like to come and play?

Mary: Sure! But I ________ play it very well.

Steven: No problem. My brother ________ you. He is good.

Mary: And you? ________ you play it well?

Steven: Well... I ________ OK, but my brother ________ it better.

Mary: We ________ together then.

3. Complete these sentences with information about yourself. Use the verbs in parentheses.

a. (play) I ________ very well. My best friend ________ very well.

b. (love) My mother ________. I ________.

c. (like) I ________. My brother/sister ________.

LISTENING COMPREHENSION

BEFORE LISTENING

1. Look at the Paralympic athletes in the pictures. Match them to the sports they practice.

CHRISTOPHER LEE/GETTY IMAGES

PHIL COLE/GETTY IMAGES

BUDA MENDES/GETTY IMAGES

CHIEN-MIN CHUNG/GETTY IMAGES

☐ Terezinha Guilhermina is a Brazilian runner.

☐ Daniel Dias is a Brazilian swimmer.

☐ Tim Angle is an American sailor.

☐ Daniela Di Toro is an Australian tennis player.

- **www.paralympic.org**
  Paralympic Games official website.

The Paralympic Games is an event with sports adapted to athletes with a range of motor and sensory disabilities. The Paralympic Games are held in the same city as the Olympic Games.

2. Order the sentences below to form a meaningful interview.

☐ Edward: Yes, I'm very happy. I'm already training for the 2020 Olympics in Tokyo.

☐ Reporter: Wow! How many times a day do you train?

1 Reporter: Good morning, everyone. Today we'll interview our local athlete Edward Craig. Thank you, Edward, for talking to us at World News. Can you tell us about your training routine?

☐ Reporter: Oh, I see. But are you happy with your performance results?

☐ Edward: In fact, I train twice a day. In the afternoon I go for a run; then I have a body and muscle massage. I go to bed early. It is very… huh… very tiring.

☐ Edward: Good morning, everyone, and thanks for inviting me to the program. Uh, well, my life is not easy. I wake up before 6 am every morning and I run for an hour and a half. Then, I have a shower and go to the gym.

☐ Reporter: Really? That's good news. We wish you success! And once again, thanks for coming.

LISTENING

3. Listen to an interview with Tommy Des Brisay, a Canadian Paralympic athlete with autism. Use the words from the box to complete the text. Then, listen to the interview again and check.

32

become	compete	has	run	seven

[...]

Reporter: Tommy Des Brisay loves to __________ and he runs a lot. Just about every day he is at the track, on a treadmill or outdoors trying to __________ even faster.

Des Brisay: I have been running for so long. Five years ago, on August 2nd, 2006.

Reporter: Des Brisay __________ autism. He suffers from a developmental disorder of the brain which impacts social and communication skills. He was __________ years old when he uttered his first word.

Do you get nervous when you run, when you __________?

Des Brisay: Not really. I'm not nervous. I'm... I'm too excited.

[...]

2014 AUTISMMEANSFRIENDSHIP

uttered: pronunciou, proferiu

4. Listen to the interview once again and check the correct answers.

33

a. What does he do to become even faster?

- [ ] He's at the track, on a treadmill or outdoors almost every day.
- [ ] He goes to the gym every day.

b. How does Tommy feel when he runs?

- [ ] nervous
- [ ] excited

AFTER LISTENING

- In pairs, imagine you can ask Tommy Des Brisay a question. What would you like to ask him? Tell your teacher and classmates. Justify your answer.

SPEAKING

1. Are you a sports fan? In pairs, ask and answer the quiz. Then share the results.

Are you into sports?

1 Do you play any sports?
- ◯ Yes, I do. ◯ No, I don't.

2 Can you swim?
- ◯ Yes, I can. ◯ No, I can't.

3 Do you like to run?
- ◯ Yes, I do. ◯ No, I don't.

4 Do you go to the gym?
- ◯ Yes, I do. ◯ No, I don't.

5 Can you play tennis?
- ◯ Yes, I can. ◯ No, I can't.

6 Do you watch sports on TV?
- ◯ Yes, I do. ◯ No, I don't.

7 Do you think it's important to practice sports?
- ◯ Yes, I do. ◯ No, I don't.

8 Do your parents exercise regularly?
- ◯ Yes, they do. ◯ No, they don't.

Answers:

Positive answers = 3 points

Negative answers = 1 point

Score:

17-24 points – You are definitely a sports fan. Keep it up!

9-16 points – You are not a sports fan, but you like sports to a certain degree.

8 points – Reconsider your attitude towards sports. Try to find an activity you enjoy.

Reflecting on the theme

You read about many champions in this unit. What qualities does it take to be successful in a sport?

WRITING

BEFORE WRITING

1. Read the piece of news and do the activity.

www.gazetteseries.co.uk/news/12897073.Young_athlete_from_Kingswood_wins_young_citizen_award_in_Belfast_ceremony/

Young athlete from Kingswood wins young citizen award in Belfast ceremony

Chloe Ball-Hopkins, 18, received Rotary Great Britain and Ireland's Young Citizen Award at a ceremony on Saturday, April 11.

Chloe was selected as the first recipient of a new award, the Rotary Young Citizen Para-Athlete Award, after being nominated by the Rotary Club of Cotswold Tyndale.

[...]

"I'm so pleased and privileged to be the first person to win the award, especially as it's a brand new category."

[...]

Tipped for the GB Paralympic Squad in Archery for 2016, Chloe suffers from muscular dystrophy.

From an early age she has been a fundraiser and has helped to increase awareness of the muscle-wasting, life-limiting condition.

[...]

Extracted from: <www.gazetteseries.co.uk/news/12897073.Young_athlete_from_Kingswood_wins_young_citizen_award_in_Belfast_ceremony/>. Accessed on: May 14, 2016.

Read the headline of the news article above and answer the questions.

Who? ___

What? ___

Where? ___

2. Read the news article headlines on pages 146 and 148 again and answer: what do they have in common?

___

___

WRITING

3. What kind of news would you like to read and write? Follow the steps to create your own news.
   - Choose a newspaper, magazine or website news that you would like to read. Here are some possibilities:
     - your school was awarded for the excellent performance of the students;
     - your team won an important title;
     - a cure for a terminal disease has been discovered;
     - you were voted the most creative student in school.
   - Think of a headline that summarizes what the news is about.
   - Read the headline again and check if:
     - it highlights the main information (who, what, where);
     - it captures the reader's attention.
   - Show your draft to the teacher.
   - Make any necessary adjustments according to the teacher's suggestions.

AFTER WRITING

- Write the news on a piece of paper and include an image for illustration with a proper caption.
- Exchange your news with other students until everybody has read them all.
- As a whole group, organize a school board news in an area of high circulation of people.
- Invite students from other classes and teachers to read them.

SELF-EVALUATION

Check the true sentences about your learning in Unit 8.
In this unit you have learned to:

- [ ] read and write news;
- [ ] identify sports and safety equipment used by athletes and sportspeople;
- [ ] use verbs that express the idea of ability and permission.

Reflecting...

- What did I learn about writing headlines?
- What did I learn about verbs that express an ability and a permission?
- What questions do I have about the use of the verb can?

Moving the body

"The ideal fitness is the attainment and maintenance of a uniformly developed body with a sound mind fully capable of naturally, easily, and satisfactorily performing our many and varied daily tasks with spontaneous zest and pleasure."

Joseph Pilates

zest: entusiasmo

Joseph Pilates was the founder of the Pilates method. He was born in Germany in 1880. He was a fragile child with rickets, asthma, and rheumatic fever. But he was determined to become stronger. He worked his body and his mind through practices such as yoga and ancient Roman and Greek exercises. His practice worked and he became an accomplished gymnast, skier, boxer, and diver.

I.C. RAPOPORT/GETTY IMAGES

During World War I, Pilates was in prison camp because he was a German citizen working in England. Pilates became a nurse. During this time, he created a unique system using a hospital bed in order to help patients recover strength and movement. He learned the importance of training the core abdominal and back muscles. This was the foundation for exercises and the equipment associated with the Pilates method.

The German government invited Pilates to use his methods to train the army in 1926. He emigrated to the United States and opened the first Pilates studio in New York City. Many dancers, actors, and athletes went to his studio to practice with him.

Joseph Pilates died at age 87.

Based on: <www.encyclopedia.com/topic/Pilates/aspx>. Accessed on: Dec. 7, 2015.

HOW TO DO THE SPINE TWIST

Pilates on the mat for waist

Step 1

Inhale

ILUSTRAÇÕES: ZUBARTEZ

- Sit back straight on the floor.
- Open legs wide pointing toes up.
- Elevate arms while bringing hands together.

Step 2

Exhale

- Twist body at waist to your right.
- Make sure weight is evenly distributed.

Step 3

Inhale

- Restore torso back to center.

Step 4

Exhale

- Turn body to the left.

Step 5

Inhale

- Restore torso back to center.
(Repeat 1~5) x 3

Extracted from: <http://slism.com/diet/mat-pilates-exercises-at-home.html>. Accessed on: May 16, 2016.

1. Research online and find out what kinds of activities people used to do to keep fit when Joseph Pilates founded the Pilates method.

____

____

2. Ask for your Physical Education teacher's help and perform the pilates exercise above.

FURTHER PRACTICE 1

1. Read the comic strip and answer the questions.

a. Which word refers to the identification card?

____

b. Which word refers to a part of the dog's body?

____

c. Why does the security officer check the document carefully in the second panel?

____

____

d. Which feelings does the dog express in each panel?

1: ______________________________________

____

2: ______________________________________

____

3: ______________________________________

____

e. What did the dog expect when he handed the document to the officer?

____

2. Read the comic strip and check the correct answers.

2015 KING FEATURES SYNDICATE/IPRESS

a. The dog wants to pay for the ice cream by

☐ credit card. ☐ check.

b. In "This isn't your MasterCard", the word **your** refers to

☐ Mother Goose's MasterCard. ☐ the dog's MasterCard.

c. In "I know. She's my master", the word **She** refers to

☐ Mother Goose. ☐ the dog's mother.

3. Which word used in the comic strip is more common in oral texts? Why does the salesperson say this word?

____

4. Use the information in this extract of a biography to complete the chart.

Will Smith Biography

Birthdate: September 25, 1968

Birthplace: Philadelphia, PA

Will Smith went from rapper, to actor, to the world's biggest box office star. Kidzworld checks out the Prince of Hollywood. [...]

Extracted from: <www.kidzworld.com/article/13748-will-smith-biography>. Accessed on: May 16, 2016.

RUSS ELLIOT/ADMEDIA/CCRUS/...STOCK

First name	
Last name	
Date of birth	
City of birth	
Two occupations	

5. What is Will Smith's nationality? ______________________________

6. Listen to the first part of the interview with Paul and Cristina and answer the questions.

34 **a.** Cristina's surname is

☐ Romera. ☐ Romira.

b. Paul's surname is

☐ Achatz. ☐ Acaetz.

7. Listen to the second part of the interview and complete each gap with one word.

35 **Interviewer:** Paul, where do you ________________ from?

Paul: From ________________.

Interviewer: Do you study ________________ at school?

Paul: Yes.

Interviewer: Do you ________________ it?

Paul: ________________, it's very funny and... yeah.

Interviewer: Thank you. Cristina, ________________ do you come from?

Cristina: I come from ________________.

8. Listen to Paul talking about his free time. What does he enjoy doing? Check the true sentences.

36

☐ He plays football.

☐ He talks to his friends and neighbors.

☐ He never watches TV.

☐ He plays computer games.

☐ He stays outside.

9. Listen to Cristina talking about her family. Complete the sentence with words from the box.

37

aunt	uncles	brother	
cousins	parents	granddad	granny

Cristina lives with her ________________ and her little ________________.

10. Listen to these movie extracts and underline the correct option according to what you hear.

38 **a.** **Where's / Where is** Selvam?
(*Life of Pi*)

b. **I am / I'm** from the ocean.
(*Finding Nemo*)

c. **We're / We are** not chickens, **we're / we are** geese!
(*The Aristocats*)

d. **They're / They are** savages!
(*Madagascar*)

11. Read the news article about foreigners in London and decide if the sentences are **T** (true) or **F** (false).

www.standard.co.uk/news/270-nationalities-and-300-different-languages-how-a-united-nations-of-workers-is-driving-london-forward-6572417.html

In the past six or seven years, London has become the Babel of the modern world. More than a third of Londoners are now foreign born – that's around 2.5 million people. Our city encompasses more than 270 nationalities and 300 languages.

[...]

Before the growth in immigration from around 1998, London was already by far the most important destination for migrants to the UK. But in 1986, half the city's immigrants were made up of those from just five countries with Commonwealth ties – India, Kenya, Jamaica, Cyprus and Bangladesh – as well as Ireland. Since 1990, those have been joined by significant numbers from nations both from outside the EU – Nigeria, Turkey, Somalia and others – as well as from Europe. And since 2004 especially, when 10 new states joined the EU, large numbers of Eastern Europeans, especially Poles, have arrived. In fact, almost 40 per cent of all the UK's migrants now live here.

So it is that London has achieved what one recent report calls "superdiversity", a melting pot of nationalities, ethnicities and languages unequalled in Europe. It's a fantastically complicated picture – and one that's full of surprises. Who knew that Americans, for example, are one of the biggest groups from outside the EU? Many foreign-born Londoners – 43 per cent – are now British citizens, and that rises to more than four out of five of the city's foreign-born Afro-Caribbeans.

[...]

REBECCA REID/EYEVINE

Cultural flavours: staff at the restaurant Sketch come from a smorgasbord of countries. From left to right, back row: Masanori Ito (Japan), Magalie Boullery (Reunion), Victoria Brooks (UK), Daniel Fisher (Australia), Joseph Arowolo (Nigeria), Jorge Quintero (Colombia), Orlentha Russell (Jamaica), Harpreet Pal (India) and Daiva Belkiene (Lithuania). From left to right, front row: Rian Steel (USA) and Gadis Sadiqah (Indonesia).

EU: União Europeia

Extracted from: <www.standard.co.uk/news/270-nationalities-and-300-different-languages-how-a-united-nations-of-workers-is-driving-london-forward-6572417.html>. Accessed on: May 16, 2016.

a. ☐ "Londoners" are people that live in London.

b. ☐ There are over 270 nationalities and 300 languages in the world.

c. ☐ Indians, Kenyans, Jamaicans, Cypriots, the Bangladeshi, and the Irish were half of the immigrants in 1986.

d. ☐ The Polish, mentioned in the text as "Poles", are from the Eastern European country of Poland.

e. ☐ There is a small percentage of people from the United States among the immigrants in London.

1. Read the infographic published by United Nations Educational, Scientific and Cultural Organization (UNESCO) in 2013 about the global progress and gaps in education. Then write **T** (true) or **F** (false).

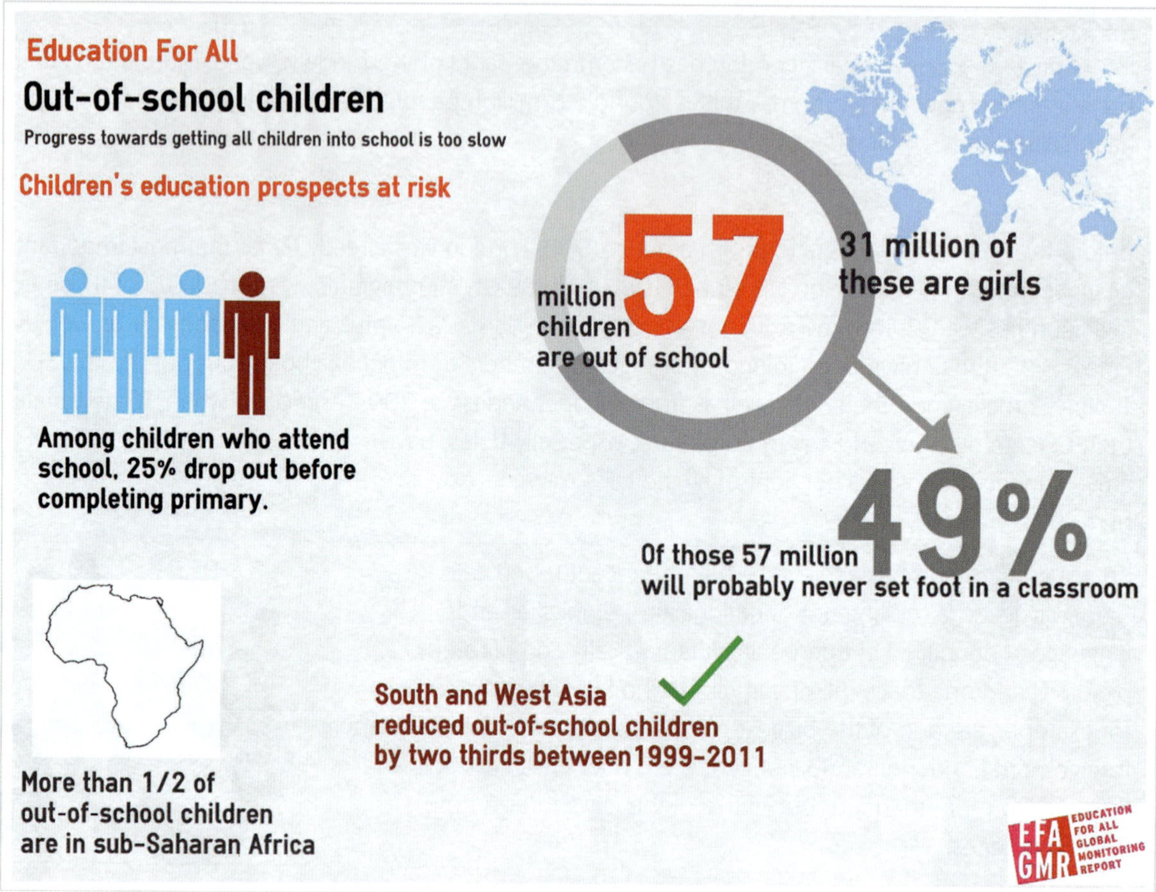

UNESCO

a. ☐ There are more than 50 million children out of school.

b. ☐ There are more boys than girls out of school.

c. ☐ 75% of children who attend school complete primary school.

d. ☐ Many out-of-school children live in sub-Saharan Africa.

e. ☐ 50% of out-of-school children are in West Asia.

2. Check the appropriate alternative to complete the statement.

According to the infographic, we can infer that there are many children out of school and

a. ☐ the progress being made to solve this problem isn't adequate.

b. ☐ there isn't a solution to this problem.

- **www.uis.unesco.org/Education/Pages/reaching-oosc.aspx**
  A video with statistical data about education and children throughout the world.

3. Read the cartoon and answer the questions.

a. Who are the members of the family in the cartoon?

☐ They're the lady and her dogs.

☐ They're the lady and her cats.

b. Why does the lady look happy?

☐ Because she loves her pets.

☐ Because she has a traditional family.

4. Read the comic strip and answer the questions.

a. Which word in "On your chair" caused the misunderstanding?

____

b. What does the girl say to clarify the misunderstanding?

____

5. Read the text and complete it using the words from the box. Then listen and check your answers. 39

aunts	grandnieces	grandparents	niblings	
siblings' children	their (2x)	these	uncles	your

You have parents, and your parents have parents. ______________ are your ______________, who also have parents – ______________ great-grandparents. Keep adding parents, keep adding "greats". [...] You have siblings, and so do your parents. These are your ______________ and ______________. [...] Now down the tree, your ______________ are your nieces and nephews, collectively, ______________, and you are ______________ aunt or uncle. Their children are your ______________ and nephews, and you are ______________ grandaunt or uncle. [...]

siblings: irmãos e irmãs

6. Draw a tree with the family members mentioned in the text above.

7. Listen to Lauren Chu talking about Chinese families and do the activities below.

40

a. Check the family members that typically make up the traditional Chinese family.

- [ ] pets
- [ ] parents
- [ ] uncles
- [ ] one to two kids
- [ ] one to three kids
- [ ] aunts

b. Underline the correct alternatives to complete the sentences.

I. In China, **one of the parents normally works / both parents normally work**.

II. Some parents bring their **retired** **parents / brothers and sisters** to live with them, so that they can take care of their little children while they are at work.

retired: aposentados

8. Now listen to Lauren talking about homes in China again. What is there in most homes? Circle the items that she mentions.

41

In most Chinese homes there is... / there are...

a couple of bathrooms	garden
a few bedrooms	kitchen
balcony	living room
dining room	storeroom
garage	

9. Write true sentences about the typical Chinese home using the words from activity 8.

In most Chinese homes there is a living room.

____

____

____

____

____

____

____

10. Are Chinese families and homes similar to the ones in Brazil? Why?

____

____

____

____

1. Read the flyer and check the true sentences.

a. ☐ This is a six-day event.

b. ☐ The event promotes parks in Philadelphia.

c. ☐ Different institutions support the event.

2. Read the flyer again and answer the questions.

a. Where can you find more information about volunteering for **Love Your Park Week**?

____

b. When is **Love Your Park Week**?

____

3. Look at the map of the French Quarter, the historic neighborhood in New Orleans, the USA, and choose the appropriate answers to the following questions.

CREDITS/SOURCE

a. Is there a cathedral in the French Quarter?

☐ Yes, there is a cathedral on Chartres Street.

☐ Yes, there is a cathedral next to a theater.

b. Where is the French Market?

☐ It's on Decatur Street.

☐ It's on Canal Street.

c. Where is Louis Armstrong Park?

☐ It's in front of the cathedral.

☐ It's near St. Louis Cemetery #1.

d. Is there a theater on the corner of Canal St. and Rampart St.?

☐ Yes, there is.

☐ No, there isn't.

4. Look at the picture and underline the correct options.

a. The piglet is resting **on** / **under** its mother's mouth.

b. A piglet is a **baby** / **mother** pig.

c. The mother pig is **big and furry** / **small and fast**.

5. Listen to some interesting fun facts and match the name of the animal to the corresponding information. (42)

a. camel

b. elephant

c. giraffe

d. polar bear

e. koala

☐ Its trunk is made up of more than 100,000 muscles and no bones.

☐ Its fingerprints are similar to human fingerprints.

☐ This animal can drink up to 100 liters of water in 10 minutes.

☐ This animal only sleeps for about two hours a day.

☐ This animal has a well-developed sense of smell.

6. Complete the conversation using the articles **a**, **an**, or **the**. Then complet the chart by writing the name of the animals in the singular or plural column.

A: This farm is amazing! ______________ animals look so happy here!

B: It's really fantastic. Look! There is ______________ ostrich near those sheep and horses.

A: Wow! There is ______________ cow near ______________ puppies over there. Let's get a little closer.

Singular	Plural
	cows
horse	
puppy	
sheep	
	ostriches

7. Read the text on the T-shirt and answer the question.

THINKSTOCK/GETTY IMAGES

What can we infer about the author's opinion of human and animal rights?

____

____

____

____

____

____

1. Read the article below and underline the correct options.

o.canada.com/sports/soccer/world-cup/carrie-serwetnyk-blind-football-in-brazil

Carrie Serwetnyk: Blind Football in Brazil

HAROLDO ABRANTES/AG. A TARDE/AGÊNCIA O GLOBO

Athlete Jeferson da Conceição Gonçalves, known as Jefinho, who is considered the best visually impaired football player in the world.

Carrie Serwetnyk

Published: July 2, 2014, 11:47 am

[...]

RIO DE JANEIRO – It can be difficult enough to get to the bathroom in the darkness of the middle of the night let alone play a game like soccer without sight. But that's the case for athletes like Jeferson da Conceição Gonçalves, known as Jefinho, who is considered the best visually impaired football player in the world.

Yes, there is such a sport and of course, Brazil is number one.

[...]

The sport was introduced during the Paralympic Games in 2004 in Athens and les canarinhos have won all of the championships.

Teams play five a side with a ball that rattles. Goalies are the only players who have sight and there is a "technical committee guide" who provides direction during the play.

All the games must be silent and fans can only cheer after goals!

Extracted from: <o.canada.com/sports/soccer/world-cup/carrie-serwetnyk-blind-football-in-brazil>. Accessed on: May 16, 2016.

a. Jeferson da Conceição Gonçalves is an athlete. He can't **speak** / **smell** / **see**.

b. Jefinho is Jeferson's **surname** / **nickname** / **name**.

c. Football fans can't **speak** / **play** / **eat** during the game.

d. There are five **players** / **goalkeepers** / **teams** on each side.

let alone: quanto mais
visually impaired: deficiente visual
rattle: chacoalha
cheer: animar-se, festejar

2. Go back to the text on page 176 and find words to complete the sentences below.

a. Brazil is number one in blind ____________________.

b. Fans must be ____________________ during the games.

c. Fans can cheer after ____________________ are scored.

3. Look at the picture and read the text. Then match both parts of the sentences.

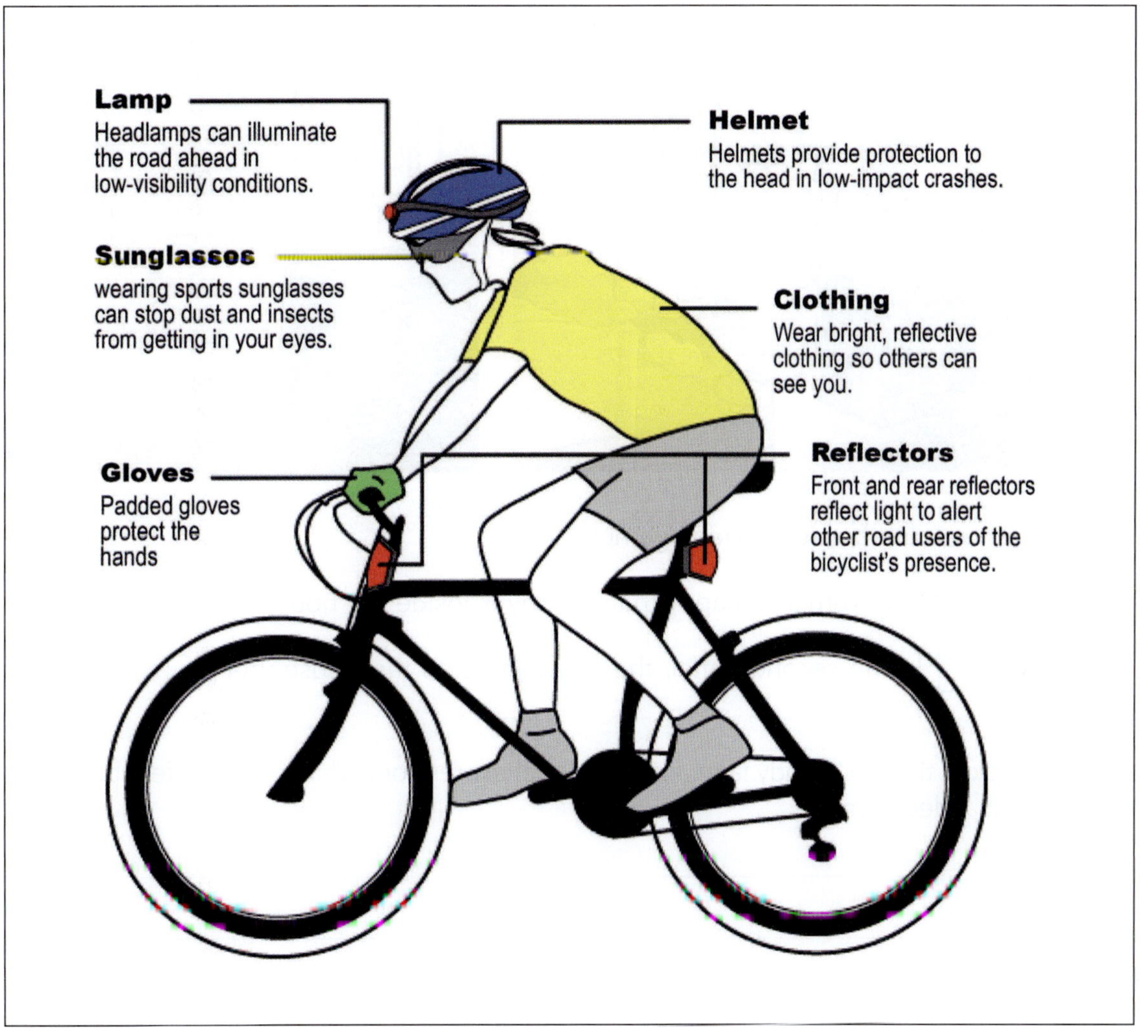

MISSOURI BICYCLE AND PEDESTRIAN FEDERATION, AMERICAN ACADEMY OF FAMILY PHYSICIANS

a. Sunglasses

b. A helmet

c. The light of the reflectors can alert

☐ other people that there is a cyclist on the road.

☐ can protect the cyclist's eyes.

☐ can protect the cyclist's head in case of an accident.

4. Read the cartoon and check the true statements.

a. ☐ The boy loves video games.

b. ☐ The woman is happy that the boy is inside the house.

c. ☐ In the second panel, the boy is outside the house, but he is still playing video game.

5. Look at the boy's body language and facial expression. What can we infer about his relation with video games?

____

____

____

____

6. Listen to a girl talking about her favorite athlete. Underline the correct words in the sentences below according to what you hear. (43)

a. Freya plays **football** / **volleyball**.

b. Freya is the narrator's **mother** / **sister**.

c. She is **seven** / **eleven** years old now.

d. She practices **fifteen** / **five** times a week.

e. Freya wants to be a professional football player for Iceland's **national** / **international** team.

7. Use **some** or **any** to complete the questions and answers about Freya.

a. **A**: Does Freya get ____________________ help when she practices sport?

B: Yes, she gets ____________________ help from her dad and her friends from school.

b. **A**: Does she want to play for ____________________ professional team?

B: Yes, she wants to become a professional player for Iceland's national team.

8. Jamie Oliver, the English celebrity chef, is famous for his campaign for better food education and his cooking shows. Read what he says about school meals and answer the questions.

> [...]
>
> Why is it so important to give kids a hot meal? Because we need to react to the sad state of health of the nation's kids, who are suffering from a man-made health problem. We need to get kids off the junk. This could be the chips they buy from local shops, the fizzy drinks, sweets and crisps they eat every day instead of proper food. These foods are full of salt, fat and sugar and eating them on a daily basis will reduce the brainpower and life expectancy of the kids in your care. Think about it!
>
> [...]

Extracted from: <www.jamieoliver.com/media/jo_sd_school_pack.pdf>. Accessed on: Mar 14, 2015.

a. Find the words in the text that correspond to the ones in Portuguese below.

refrigerante: ____________________

batata chips: ____________________

batata frita: ____________________

doces: ____________________

sal: ____________________

gordura: ____________________

açúcar: ____________________

b. According to the text, are the sentences true (**T**) or false (**F**)?

☐ Kids in Britain eat healthy food at school.

☐ Crisps, chips, and fizzy drinks are examples of unhealthy food.

☐ It is healthy to eat a lot of sugar, fat, and salt.

PROJECT 1

Be a water-conscious citizen

In this project you will:

- understand the importance of using water as a sustainable resource;
- take actions to encourage water conservation;
- make a poster to raise people's awareness about water conservation.

1. Read the text and answer the following questions with a classmate.

How Much Water is On Earth?

by Brett Israel | September 09, 2010 01:52pm ET

If the Earth was the size of a basketball, all of its water would fit into a ping pong ball. How much water is that? It's roughly 326 million cubic miles (1.332 billion cubic kilometers), according to a recent study from the U.S. Geological Survey. Some 72 percent of Earth is covered in water, but 97 percent of that is salty ocean water and not suitable for drinking.

"There's not a lot of water on Earth at all," said David Gallo, an oceanographer at the Woods Hole Oceanographic Institution (WHOI) in Massachusetts.

Oceans create a water layer spanning 15,000 miles (24,000 kilometers) across the planet at an average depth of more than 2 miles (3.2 km). If you poured all of the world's water on the United States and could contain it, you'd create a lake 90 miles (145 km) deep.

This seems, and looks, like a lot of water, Gallo told Life's Little Mysteries, but looks can be deceiving.

If the Earth was an apple, Gallo said, the water layer would be thinner than the fruit's skin. The Earth's freshwater is even rarer.

"For humanity to thrive, or even exist, we need to sprinkle that teeny bit of fresh water in the right places, at the right times and in just the right amounts," Gallo said. [...]

Extracted from: <www.livescience.com/29673-how-much-water-on-earth.html>. Accessed on: May 16, 2016.

DAVE GALLO/WOODS HOLE

suitable: própria, adequada
spanning: abrangendo
deceiving: enganoso
thrive: desenvolver-se
sprinkle: borrifar
stripped: despida

The Earth stripped of its water (left). All of the Earth's ocean water (middle) and freshwater (right).

a. The surface of the planet consists of freshwater and salty water. How much salty water is there?

____

b. If we consider a basketball to represent the size of the Earth, the amount of freshwater is equivalent to:

- [ ] a ping pong ball.
- [ ] a ball much smaller than a ping pong ball.
- [ ] an apple.
- [ ] a football.

c. By reading the text, can we conclude that there is very little drinking water on the planet?

____

Group discussion

- If we keep on using water thoughtlessly or managing this resource poorly, the planet will soon face a worldwide water shortage. How different would your life be if water supply were severely reduced and controlled? What do you think we can do now to avoid a catastrophic scenario in the future?

2. Check the pictures below that show correct actions about the use of water.

MARTA NARDINI/GETTY IMAGES

THINKSTOCK/GETTY IMAGES

THINKSTOCK/GETTY IMAGES

THINKSTOCK/GETTY IMAGES

Project

- In pairs, talk to your Science and Geography teachers about the sustainable use of water and the access to fresh water in different areas of the world.
- Research about water conservation and make notes. If possible, use English sources (books or websites). See some research suggestions below.
- Organize the notes in topics in your notebook.
- Make sure all your notes are in English. If necessary, ask your teacher for help.
- Ask your teacher to check your text and then correct it accordingly.
- Make a poster using your notes. Illustrate it using photos or drawings that express the idea of water conservation. Make sure your poster has visual impact.
- Put together a bulletin board at school to hang all the posters produced by the class.
- Invite the school staff and other students to check out the class projects. Encourage them to take actions to use water sustainably.

Research suggestions

- ypte.org.uk/factsheets/environment/water#section
- wateruseitwisely.com/tips/category/kids/
- www.thewaterpage.com/water-conservation-kids.htm
- www.scottishwater.co.uk/clearer-fresher-learning/all-about-water/all-about-water

PROJECT 2

Healthy mind, healthy body

In this project you will:

- understand the importance of having a healthy mind and a healthy body;
- create a quiz about mind-body health;
- analyze the results of the quiz.

1. Read the text and do the activities.

pbskids.org/itsmylife/school/teststress/article7.html

Test Stress: Keeping a Healthy Body and Mind

In the middle of studying and stressing, it's easy to forget to take care of the most important thing: ourselves! Staying healthy – both physically and mentally – is a very big part of dealing with all kinds of stress, including test stress. Here are some important tips:

- **Get** enough **sleep.** Being tired can make your stress levels go up, and a good night's sleep is one of nature's most awesome stress-beaters. Make sure you go to bed on time and try to get at least eight hours (or more) of sleep at night. [...]
- **Eat right.** Keep a balanced, nutritious diet. Your brain does its best work when it gets turbo fuel from good food. Eat plenty of protein, fruits, vegetables, and whole grains. [...] Avoid junk foods made with chemicals and who-knows-what. [...]
- **Get plenty of exercise.** [...] Do some jumping jacks. Go for a walk. Hop on your bike. Or just turn up the music in your room and DANCE. [...]
- **Have some fun.** [...] Although school and studying are important, we can't survive without some good old fashioned F-U-N. [...] If you're happy and relaxed, your mind will be ready to hit the books and prepare for the test. [...]
- Be aware **of your emotions.** If other things are bothering you, like difficulties at home or troubles with your friends, a big test might seem much worse than it really is. [...] This is why it's very important to be aware of your feelings, and to get some help when you need it. [...]

Extracted from: <pbskids.org/itsmylife/school/teststress/article7.html>. Accessed on: May 16, 2016.

dealing: lidar
enough: suficiente
brain: cérebro
fuel: combustível

junk foods: alimentos de baixo valor nutricional e alto teor calórico
be aware: tenha consciência
bothering: incomodando

a. Which of the tips do you frequently follow?

b. Add a different tip to the list.

Group discussion

- Being healthy is not synonymous with not being sick. Our health is closely related to our well-being. What we eat, the physical activities we do and our daily routines affect our mind-body health.
- Do you have healthy habits? What would you like to change about your habits?

Project

- Form four groups.
- Each group will be responsible for one of the following topics related to health: food, physical activity, sleep and fun. The groups will prepare a quiz to interview people about their habits concerning each topic.
- Talk to your Physical Education and Science teachers and ask them to suggest interesting questions to include in your quiz.
- Research about your topic and make notes. If possible, use English sources (books or websites). See some research suggestions below.
- Based on your research, create two questions in English. Example: "How often do you do physical exercise?" (a. Once a week / b. Twice a week / c. Three times a week or more).
- Ask your teacher to check your text and then correct it accordingly.
- Collect the questions created by the four groups (you should have eight questions) and rewrite them in a single sheet of paper.
- Make copies of the quiz. Each group should interview five people at school, making up a total of 20 people interviewed by the class.
- Talk to your classmates about the answers and analyze the results.

Research suggestions

- www.eufic.org/article/en/expid/10-healthy-eating-tips-kids/
- www.health.govt.nz/your-health/healthy-living/food-and-physical-activity/physical-activity/activities-children-and-young-people
- www.nhs.uk/Livewell/Goodfood/Pages/healthy-eating-teens.aspx
- www.caringforkids.cps.ca/handouts/teens_and_sleep
- gb.cmha.ca/programs_services/mental-health-tips-for-youth/#.VPjMTfnF-Ck

Subject pronouns / Verb to be (present)

Os *subject pronouns* correspondem aos pronomes pessoais do caso reto da língua portuguesa. São usados para evitar a repetição dos nomes em posição de sujeito nas orações. *You* apresenta a mesma forma para a segunda pessoa do singular e do plural; é o contexto que determina a qual das duas pessoas ele se refere.

O verbo *to be* corresponde, em português, aos verbos **ser** ou **estar**.

Observe os quadros abaixo. No primeiro você encontrará os pronomes pessoais e as formas – não contraídas e contraídas – do verbo *to be* correspondentes a cada pronome. Nos quadros seguintes, você vai encontrar exemplos de frases afirmativas, negativas e interrogativas.

	Subject pronouns	Verb to be	Full forms	Contracted forms
Singular	I	am	I am	I'm
	You	are	You are	You're
	He	is	He is	He's
	She	is	She is	She's
	It	is	It is	It's
Plural	We	are	We are	We're
	You	are	You are	You're
	They	are	They are	They're

Affirmative sentences

I am / I'm	Grace.
You are / You're	a new student.
He is / He's	my friend.
She is / She's	at school now.
It is / It's	a new restaurant.
We are / We're	Brazilian.
You are / You're	teachers.
They are / They're	in Porto Alegre today.

Com exceção da primeira pessoa do singular, há três maneiras diferentes de formar as frases negativas. Atente-se aos exemplos no quadro ao lado.

Negative sentences

I am not / I'm not	Grace.
You are not / You're not / You aren't	a new student.
He is not / He's not / He isn't	my friend.
She is not / She's not / She isn't	at school now.
It is not / It's not / It isn't	a new restaurant.
We are not / We're not / We aren't	Brazilian.
You are not / You're not / You aren't	teachers.
They are not / They're not / They aren't	in Porto Alegre today.

Interrogative sentences

Am I	in the right class?
Are you	a new student?
Is he	your friend?
Is she	at school now?
Is it	a new restaurant?
Are we	late?
Are you	teachers?
Are they	in Porto Alegre today?

Short answers – Affirmative and negative

Yes, I am.	No, I'm not.
Yes, you are.	No, you aren't. / No, you're not.
Yes, he is.	No, he isn't. / No, he's not.
Yes, she is.	No, she isn't. / No, she's not.
Yes, it is.	No, it isn't. / No, it's not.
Yes, we are.	No, we aren't. / No, we're not.
Yes, you are.	No, you aren't. / No, you're not.
Yes, they are.	No, they aren't. / No, they're not.

Possessive adjectives

Os *possessive adjectives* são pronomes usados antes de substantivos para indicar posse. Observe os exemplos no quadro abaixo.

This is **my** cat, Garfield.	**Its** tail is long and furry.
Is she **your** friend?	**Our** birthdays are in December.
His name is Jon.	Are they **your** new teachers?
Her full name is Malala Yousafzai.	These are **their** books.

Question words (wh-questions): who, what, where

As *question words* são palavras interrogativas usadas para obter informações específicas sobre alguém, alguma coisa, algum lugar etc. Observe alguns exemplos das *question words* estudadas neste volume.

Who

A: **Who** is this boy?
B: He's my brother. His name's Louis.

Where

A: **Where** are you from?
B: I'm from Brazil.

What

A: **What** is this?
B: It's my new mechanical pencil.

A: **What**'s his name?
B: His name's Gian.

Demonstrative pronouns

Os *demonstrative pronouns* são usados para demonstrar a posição de alguém ou de alguma coisa em relação a quem fala. No singular, usamos *this* quando queremos demonstrar que alguém ou alguma coisa está próxima de quem fala e *that* quando queremos demonstrar que alguém ou alguma coisa está distante de quem fala.

A: Mark, who is **this** girl here?
B: She's my Chinese friend. Her name's Quon.

A: Who is **that** man over there, Emma?
B: That's my History teacher. His name's Joseph.

LANGUAGE REFERENCE

Genitive case

Usamos o *genitive case* para indicar posse, para declarar que alguém possui alguma coisa. Em geral, formamos o *genitive case* acrescentando o apóstrofo + s ('s) ao substantivo. Observe os exemplos abaixo:

This is Jacob**'s** family.
Are you Mr. Hunt**'s** son?
This isn't the teacher**'s** bag.

There to be (present)

There to be é usado para indicar a existência de alguma coisa ou alguém. Usamos *there is* para complementos no singular e *there are* para complementos no plural. Observe os exemplos abaixo:

Affirmative sentences

There is a black pencil on the desk.
There are two nice pictures on the wall.

Negative sentences

There isn't an air conditioner in the classroom.
There aren't any schoolbags on the floor.

> **Contracted forms**
> There is: There's
> There is not: There isn't/There's not
> There are not: There aren't

Interrogative sentences

Is there a book on the teacher's desk?
Are there any students in the classroom?

Short answers

Yes, **there is**./No, **there isn't**.
Yes, **there are**./No, **there aren't**.

Indefinite articles

Os *indefinite articles* – *a*, *an* – correspondem aos artigos indefinidos em português, portanto, são usados antes de substantivos contáveis no singular.

A é utilizado antes de substantivos que iniciem com som de consoante, com y ou com o *h* sonoro.

Alguns exemplos são: **a** boy / **a** uniform / **a** year / **a** house.

An é utilizado antes de substantivos que iniciem com som de vogal ou com *h* mudo.

Alguns exemplos são: **an** eraser / **an** umbrella / **an** hour.

Prepositions of place

Para falar sobre a localização de alguém ou de alguma coisa, podemos usar as preposições de lugar a seguir mencionadas. Observe:

ILUSTRAÇÕES: QBS LEARNING

There are some black pencils **in** his pencil case.

The new pharmacy is **next to** the park.

Her schoolbag is **behind** the desk.

There are stores **near** our building.

His dog is **on** the sofa.

Katryn is **between** Douglas and Lucas.

The car is **in front of** my house.

Look at that! Your cat is **under** your bed!

Definite article

O *definite article* – *the* – corresponde aos artigos definidos em português. Ao contrário do que acontece em língua portuguesa, o *definite article* é invariável quanto ao gênero. Ele é usado antes de um substantivo já conhecido pelo leitor. Atente-se aos exemplos abaixo:

There is a new pet shop on the corner. **The** pet shop is open every day.
I know **the** cats there are for adoption. Are **the** dogs for adoption too?

Simple present (to have)

O verbo *have* corresponde ao verbo ter em português e expressa posse.

I **have** a puppy. Its name is Gogo.

You **have** a beautiful name, Milley.

We **have** seven cousins.

They **have** no children.

Plural nouns

Em geral, para formar o plural dos substantivos em inglês, assim como em português, acrescentamos s aos substantivos. Seguem alguns exemplos:

book – books　　day – days　　house – houses

Existem, contudo, algumas exceções. Veja:

- Acrescentamos *es* para formar o plural dos substantivos terminados em *ch*, *sh*, *s*, *ss*, *x* e a maior parte dos substantivos terminados em *o*:

peach – peach**es** | bus – bus**es** | box – box**es**
tomato – tomato**es** | brush – brush**es**

Nota: Os substantivos *piano*, *photo*, *radio* e *video* são algumas exceções a essa regra e formam o plural com o acréscimo apenas de *s*: *pianos*, *photos*, *radios* e *videos*.

- Nos substantivos terminados em consoante + *y*, substituímos o *y* por *i* e, em seguida, acrescentamos *es*:

strawberry – strawber**ries** | baby – bab**ies** | family – famil**ies**

- Nos substantivos terminados em *f* ou *fe*, substituímos essas letras por *ves*:

wife – wi**ves** | life – li**ves** | half – hal**ves**

Nota: Os substantivos *dwarf*, *scarf* e *staff* são algumas exceções a essa regra, tendo seu plural formado das duas maneiras: *dwarfs* ou *dwarves*, *scarfs* ou *scarves*, *staffs* ou *staves*.

- No caso de alguns substantivos, o plural é formado de maneira irregular:

mouse – **mice** | tooth – **teeth** | woman – **women**
foot – **feet** | man – **men** | person – **people**

- Alguns substantivos possuem a mesma forma tanto para o singular quanto para o plural.

sheep – **sheep** | money – **money** | jeans – **jeans** | shorts – **shorts**

Imperative

Usamos verbos no modo imperativo para dar instruções e/ou ordens. Na forma afirmativa, o imperativo é formado pelo verbo no infinitivo sem o *to*. Na forma negativa, acrescentamos *don't* ou *do not* antes do verbo.

Close your books.
Open your eyes.
Do not feed the animals.
Don't use your cell phones here!

Some / Any

Some é um pronome indefinido que corresponde a **algum**, **alguns**, **alguma**, **algumas** em português e é geralmente usado em frases afirmativas. Pode ser usado também em frases interrogativas quando oferecemos alguma coisa a alguém.

Some é acompanhado de substantivos contáveis ou incontáveis, no singular ou no plural.

There is **some** food in the fridge.
Do you want **some** cookies?
There are **some** oranges in the bowl.

Any é também um pronome indefinido que corresponde a **algum**, **alguns**, **alguma**, **algumas**, **nenhum**, **nenhuma** em português. Pode ser usado em frases negativas e interrogativas. Assim como *some*, *any* é acompanhado de substantivos contáveis ou incontáveis, no singular ou no plural.

There aren't **any** girls in my class.
Are there **any** snack bars in your neighborhood?
Is there **any** more milk?

Expressing likes and preferences

Usamos *like* para expressar que gostamos de algo, *love* quando adoramos algo e *prefer* para indicar uma preferência. Para dizer que não gostamos de algo, usamos a negativa de *like*.

I **like** animals!
You **like** me, right?
He **likes** strawberries.
She **likes** reading.
It **likes** milk.
We **like** purple.
They **like** English and Geography.

I **love** Italian food.
You **love** Andrew.
He **loves** Math.
She **loves** her work.
It **loves** water.
We **love** our planet!
They **love** their family.

I **don't like** chocolate cake.
You **don't like** TV series.
He **doesn't like** summer.
She **doesn't like** grapes.
It **doesn't like** to take bath.
We **don't like** History.
They **don't like** museums.

I don't like dogs. I **prefer** cats and you **prefer** cats, too, right?
My parents like sweets, but my brothers and I **prefer** healthy food.
She doesn't like Math. She **prefers** Science.
Paul doesn't like honey. He **prefers** sugar.
My friends and I don't like horror movies. We **prefer** drama.
They don't like e-books. They **prefer** paper books.

Can

Usamos *can* para expressar habilidade, pedir permissão ou fazer pedidos. Observe o uso de *can* nas frases afirmativas, negativas e interrogativas abaixo.

I **can speak** Spanish.
They **can watch** TV in the afternoon.
He **can't find** his car keys.
We **can't surf**.
Can she **play** golf?
Yes, she **can**./No, she **can't**.
Can you **come** here?
Yes, I **can**./No, I **can't**.

Simple present (play)

I play the guitar and **my friend Doug plays** the drums for the school band.
You play soccer but **your sister plays** volleyball and handball.
His dog is really cute. **It plays** with its ball all the time.
They play rugby very well, but **we play** rugby very well, too.

AUDIO SCRIPTS

UNIT 1

TRACK 2

Page 17. Activity 6

Listen and check.

A – B – C – D – E – F – G – H – I – J – K – L – M – N – O – P – Q – R – S – T – U – V – W – X – Y – Z

TRACK 3

Page 17. Activity 8

Listen to the conversations. Circle the names people spell.

a. Man: Veruca? Can you spell that for us, please?
Girl: V-E-R-U-C-A. Veruca Salt.

b. Man: Streatfield. How do you spell that?
Woman: S – T – R – E – A – T – F – E – I – L – D

c. Interviewer: How do you spell Gyllenhaal?
Interviewee: G – Y – L – L – E – N – H – A – A – L

Extracted from: *A Fantástica Fábrica de Chocolate* (00:17:56-00:18:03); *Mensagem para Você* (01:24:32-01:24:42); *Entrevista com Jake Gyllenhaal* <www.youtube.com/watch?v=j3GN_YOKR1k> (0:21-0:23; 0:33-0:42). Accessed on: May 12, 2016.

TRACK 4

Page 19. Pronunciation practice

Underline the words you hear.

a. I am an assistant to the mayor of the city. Hello!
b. Yes, he's one of my minions.
c. What's your name?
d. She's from Italy. Florence, I think.

Extracted from: *Escola de Rock* (00:04:17-00:04:20); *Meu Malvado Favorito 2* (00:26:43-00:26:44); *Monstros S.A.* (00:04:50-00:04:51); *Os Feiticeiros de Waverly Place* (00:09:59-00:10:01).

TRACK 5

Page 24. Activity 5

Listen to conversation 1 and check your answer to activity 4.

Conversation one

Keith: What's your name?
Jaq: I'm Jaq Mackenzie.
Keith: Jaq?
Jaq: Yeah.
Keith: J-A-Q?
Jaq: Yeah.
Keith: I like that.
Jaq: Thank you.
Keith: Where're you from, Jaq?
Jaq: I'm from Santa Monica, California.
Keith: And what do you do there?
Jaq: Ah, I go to school at Los Angeles County High School for the Arts.
Keith: Yeah?
Jaq: Yeah.

Extracted from: <www.youtube.com/watch?v=BnVB2-GxOmQ> (00:35-00:49). Accessed on: Apr. 1, 2015.

TRACK 6

Page 24. Activity 6

Listen to conversation 1 again and complete the chart.

Conversation one

Keith: What's your name?
Jaq: I'm Jaq Mackenzie.
Keith: Jaq?
Jaq: Yeah.
Keith: J-A-Q?
Jaq: Yeah.
Keith: I like that.
Jaq: Thank you.
Keith: Where're you from, Jaq?
Jaq: I'm from Santa Monica, California.
Keith: And what do you do there?
Jaq: Ah, I go to school at Los Angeles County High School for the Arts.
Keith: Yeah?
Jaq: Yeah.

Extracted from: <www.youtube.com/watch?v=BnVB2-GxOmQ> (00:35-00:49). Accessed on: Apr. 1, 2015.

TRACK 7

Page 24. Activity 7

Now listen to conversation 2 and choose the correct alternatives.

Conversation two

Will: What's your name?
Sophie: Hello. Hi, I'm Sophie.
Will: Hi, Sophie. Where're you from?
Sophie: I'm from Wakefield.
Will: And how old are you?
Sophie: I'm seventeen.
Will: That's great.

Extracted from: <www.youtube.com/watch?v=i8OH-LSwomY> (04:00-04:14). Accessed on: May 12, 2016.

UNIT 2

TRACK 8

Page 34. Activity 1

Look at the pictures. Listen and underline what people say at different periods of the day.

a. Good morning, everyone!

b. Good afternoon, class.

c. Ah, good evening, my little ones.

Extracted from: *Escola de Rock* (00:52:12-00:52:13); *Harry Potter e a Pedra Filosofal* (00:54:20-00:54:23); *Os Aristogatas* (00:14:59-00:15:05).

TRACK 9

Page 35. Activity 3

Complete the chart with the words from the box. Then listen to two journalists listing the five coolest countries in the world and number them.

Presenter 1: And Americans are number five on a list of the world's coolest nationalities, Anderson, because of great inventions like rock'n'roll. Mongolians are number four.

Presenter 2: Mongolians?

Presenter 1: Yes, because they have a quiet mystery.

Presenter 2: All right, I go with that.

Presenter 1: O.K. Number three: Jamaicans, because of their dreadlocks.

Presenter 2: All right.

Presenter 1: Singaporeans are number two.

Presenter 2: What?

Presenter 1: Yeah, that's right.

Presenter 2: For coolest nationality, Singaporeans? Really? Well, I mean… I have nothing against Singaporeans, but…

Presenter 1: Because they're super computer literate. Would you like to take ah… a run at number one?

Presenter 2: Ahm… I will… I do… I… Yes, I'll tell you. Brazilians.

Presenter 1: I think you cheated, but I'll go with that. It is indeed. Congrats.

Presenter 2: Ah, I was right. Oh, well, they are… They're the coolest. That's true.

Extracted from: <www.youtube.com/watch?v=0rYTwuhCjkw> (00:01-00:48). Accessed on: May 12, 2016.

TRACK 10

Page 35. Pronunciation practice

Listen to the nationalities and write them in the correct column.

British	English	Scottish
Australian	Welsh	Northern Irish
Japanese	Brazilian	Canadian

TRACK 11

Page 37. Pronunciation practice

Circle the correct options according to what you hear.

a. No! Oh! Ooh! No! But, Jane, they're Italian!

b. We're French, and it's dinnertime.

c. You're in France, children.

Extracted from: *Tarzan & Jane* (00:17:05-00:17:07); *Ratatouille* (01:20:17-01:20:19); *Anastasia* (00:59:17-00:59:22).

TRACK 12

Page 41. Activity 3

Match the pictures to their corresponding sentences. Then listen and check.

1. Oh, Gru, se llama Antonio. Me llamo Margo.
2. Je m'appelle Piscine Molitor Patel, dit Pi.
3. Hallo, Philipp. Tag, mein Junge. Willkommen.
4. Ho due sorelle. Una si chiama Viviana e ha ventitré anni, e una si chiama Eleonora, e ne ha tredici.

Extracted from: *Meu Malvado Favorito 2* (00:46:42-00:46:45); *As Aventuras de Pi* (00:08:32-00:08:35); <www.dw.de/episode-01-a-visit-to-the-countryside/a-2438302> (00:02:58-00:03:04); <www.bbc.co.uk/languages/italian/talk/family/> (00:00:22-00:00:30). Accessed on: May 12, 2016.

TRACK 13

Page 42. Activity 4

Look at the photos and try to complete the sentences with the words from the box. Then listen and check.

a. Hi. My name's Birna. I'm an exchange student from Iceland in the United States, in New York.

b. Hi! My name's Alis, I'm 16 years old and I'm from Scotland.

c. My name's Matej Kasl and I'm from Czech Republic, in Europe.

d. My name is Ellienay Simony. I'm from Brazil and I am an academic English student.

Extracted from: <www.youtube.com/watch?v=jRBADAO_5vQ> (00:00-00:07); <www.youtube.com/watch?v=ZPppQT3yXz4> (00:00-00:04); <www.youtube.com/watch?v=UOQDvOggA7M> (00:02-00:06); <www.youtube.com/watch?v=ciiwhKiRw9Q> (00:00-00:05). Accessed on: May 12, 2016.

UNIT 3

TRACK 14

Page 63. Activity 3

Listen to Homer Simpson introducing his family. Check the alternatives that best complete the sentences.

Homer: It is, it is, but first let me introduce you to my family. My perfect family. This is my wife, Marge.

Marge: Hello!

Homer: And our beautiful baby. My daughter Lisa, IQ 156.

Lisa: Hi!

Homer: See? And my son Bart.

Extracted from: <seekcartoon.com/watch/26328-the-simpsons-season-8-episode-23-homers-enemy.html#.VQHYH47F98H> (11:00-11:14). Accessed on: Mar. 12, 2015.

TRACK 15

Page 63. Activity 4

Listen to Homer Simpson again and answer the questions.

Homer: It is, it is, but first let me introduce you to my family. My perfect family. This is my wife, Marge.

Marge: Hello!

Homer: And our beautiful baby. My daughter Lisa, IQ 156.
Lisa: Hi!
Homer: See? And my son Bart.

Extracted from: <seekcartoon.com/watch/26328-the-simpsons-season-8-episode-23-homers-enemy.html#.VQHYH47F98H> (11:00-11:14). Accessed on: Mar. 12, 2015.

UNIT 4

TRACK 16

Page 74. Activity 2

Look at the list of numbers below and write the missing ones. Then listen and check.

zero
one
two
three
four
five
six
seven
eight
nine
ten
eleven
twelve
thirteen
fourteen
fifteen
sixteen
seventeen
eighteen
nineteen
twenty

TRACK 17

Page 74. Activity 3

These are some of the school supplies students use the most. Listen and write their names. Then check the ones you use.

colored pencils
a glue stick
a notebook
a pen
pencils
a ruler
a mechanical pencil
an eraser

TRACK 18

Page 76. Pronunciation practice

Listen to the words and match them to the correct article. Then listen again and check.

a cartoon
a humanitarian
a university
an hour
an SMS
an umbrella

TRACK 19

Page 82. Activity 3

Listen to the conversations. Then answer the questions.

Conversation one

Teacher: I'd like to introduce a new student, Samantha Parkington, who comes to us from Mount Bedford, New York, which is quite a change. Isn't that right, Samantha?

Samantha: Yes.

Teacher: Maybe you'd like to tell us a little about your life in Mount Bedford.

Extracted from: <www.youtube.com/watch?v=mj-kGsicng> (00:41:47-00:42:04). Accessed on: May 14, 2016.

Conversation two

Teacher: All right, class. Listen up! We're getting a new student today. Make him feel at home. Go ahead. Introduce yourself.

Sōhei: I'm Sōhei. It's nice to meet you.

Extracted from: <www.youtube.com/watch?v=X_1PgHjFZM4> (01:12:07-01:12:18). Accessed on: Mar. 12, 2015.

UNIT 5

TRACK 20

Page 95. Activity 4

Complete with the missing numbers. Then listen and check.

twenty-one
twenty-two
twenty-three
twenty-four
twenty-five
twenty-six
twenty-seven
twenty-eight
twenty-nine
thirty
thirty-one
forty
fifty
sixty
seventy
eighty
ninety
one hundred (or a hundred)

TRACK 21

Page 102. Activity 3

Listen to a department store commercial and check the correct answers.

It's about to happen! Zayre is stocking up for a grand opening sale you won't wanna miss. Setting up special brand opening bargains everywhere you look. We are celebrating the opening of our new store at 115th Street and South Austin Street and every Zayre store in Chicago land is joining in. A great grand opening sale just when you need it. Just in time for spring. Just about to start in every Zayre store. It starts 10 am Sunday.

Extracted from: <www.youtube.com/watch?v=z-fSfUEUoxE> (00:00-00:30). Accessed on: May 14, 2016.

TRACK 22

Page 102. Activity 4

Listen to the commercial again and order the parts. Then listen once more and check.

It's about to happen! Zayre is stocking up for a grand opening sale you won't wanna miss. Setting up special brand opening bargains everywhere you look. We are celebrating the opening of our new store at 115th Street and South Austin Street and every Zayre store in Chicago land is joining in. A great grand opening sale just when you need it. Just in time for spring. Just about to start in every Zayre store. It starts 10 am Sunday.

Extracted from: <www.youtube.com/watch?v=z-fSfUEUoxE> (00:00-00:30). Accessed on: May 14, 2016.

UNIT 6

TRACK 23

Page 112. Activity 1

Unscramble the letters and form names of animals. Then listen and check.

a. bear
b. cow
c. elephant
d. horse
e. lion
f. tiger
g. hummingbird
h. cicada

TRACK 24

Page 115. Pronunciation practice

Listen to the pronunciation of the words below. Then choose the best answer to the question that follows.

the ant – the elephant – the tiger – the lion

TRACK 25

Page 116. Activity 7

Write the plural form of these animals' names in the correct column. Then listen and check.

-s	-es	-ies
monkeys	foxes	butterflies
frogs	platypuses	canaries

TRACK 26

Page 120. Activity 8

Listen to the song below and complete the verses. Use the words from the box.

Please give me the right just to be free
To grow up normally
To grow up happily
Please give me the choice just to live free
A voice unspoken
is talking straight to your heart
to your heart. (x 3)

Cramped up in cages
cryin' pain for ages
while the dawn is gone
the kill of life is done.

Give it a chance
eyes full of revenge
savage and cold
Now it's time to evolve (x 2)
Set me free (x 4)

I will never see the sunrise
I will never see it set
Never feel a kind touch
I will never be a pet

I will never feel love
For I will not be loved
As I'm led to my end
I wonder who would care...

Please give me the right just to be free
To grow up normally
To grow up happily
Please give me the choice just to live free
Please give me the right just to be free
(x 5)

Extracted from: <soundcloud.com/simon-dabbicco/be-kind-to-the-innocent-simon> (00:00-03:34). Accessed on: May 14, 2016.

UNIT 7

TRACK 27

Page 132. Activity 2

These are some popular Iranian foods and drinks. Match the pictures to their names. Then listen and check your answers.

1. tea
2. yogurt
3. soup
4. honey
5. jam
6. dessert

TRACK 28

Page 133. Activity 3

Look at the food color wheel and read about some of the benefits fruits and vegetables give us. Use the names of the colors to complete the texts. Then listen and check your answers.

a. Red fruits and vegetables help to prevent prostate, lung and stomach cancers. They're high in vitamin C. They are strawberries, apples and tomatoes.

b. Yellow and orange fruits and vegetables help to keep the skin and the eyes healthy. They're full of beta-carotene. They are peaches, corn, carrots and papayas.

c. White fruits and vegetables are rich in dietary fiber. They help to prevent high cholesterol and reduce the risk of stroke. They are bananas, cauliflower, potatoes and onions.

d. Green fruits and vegetables help to prevent heart diseases. They maintain the bones and teeth strong. They are limes, broccoli, green grapes and avocados.

e. Blue and purple fruits and vegetables are powerful antioxidants. They are eggplants, plums and blackberries.

Based on: <www.disabled-world.com/artman/publish/fruits-vegetables.shtml>. Accessed on: May 14, 2016.

TRACK 29

Page 140. Activity 3

Listen to a recipe of homemade lemonade and number the steps.

A cool glass of freshly squeezed lemonade is one of summer's sweetheart cooldowns and it is so easy to make. Here's how. In just three steps.

Step one: Squeeze the lemons – use a juicer to squeeze 10 lemons. Pour the juice into a large pitcher.

Step two: Add sugar. Measure one cup of sugar and pour into the pitcher. Stir until the sugar dissolves.

Step three: Dilute with water. Fill the pitcher ¾ full with cold water. The added benefit to homemade lemonade is that you can customize it to your liking. Taste and adjust the water and sugar until you get it as sweet or as tart as you like it. Pour the lemonade into a glass filled with ice and garnish it with a slice of lemon. Refreshing and easy. A cool glass of lemonade is just a squeeze away.

Extracted from: <www.youtube.com/watch?v=COx5BfOPsQs> (00:00-01:11).
Accessed on: May 14, 2016.

TRACK 30

Page 140. Activity 4

Listen again and answer the questions.
A cool glass of freshly squeezed lemonade is one of summer's sweetheart cooldowns and it is so easy to make. Here's how. In just three steps.

Step one: Squeeze the lemons – use a juicer to squeeze 10 lemons. Pour the juice into a large pitcher.

Step two: Add sugar. Measure one cup of sugar and pour into the pitcher. Stir until the sugar dissolves.

Step three: Dilute with water. Fill the pitcher ¾ full with cold water.
The added benefit to homemade lemonade is that you can customize it to your liking. Taste and adjust the water and sugar until you get it as sweet or as tart as you like it. Pour the lemonade into a glass filled with ice and garnish it with a slice of lemon. Refreshing and easy. A cool glass of lemonade is just a squeeze away.

Extracted from: <www.youtube.com/watch?v=COx5BfOPsQs> (00:00-01:11).
Accessed on: May 14, 2016.

UNIT 8

TRACK 31

Page 151. Activity 4

Label the pictures using the words from the box. Listen and check your answers. Underline the sports you would like to practice.

a. cycling	**c.** swimming	**e.** soccer
b. basketball	**d.** judo	**f.** tennis

TRACK 32

Page 158. Activity 3

Listen to an interview with Tommy Des Brisay, a Canadian Paralympic athlete with autism. Use the words from the box to complete the text. Then, listen to the interview again and check.
[...]

Reporter: Tommy Des Brisay loves to run and he runs a lot. Just about every day he is at the track, on a treadmill or outdoors trying to become even faster.

Des Brisay: I have been running for so long. Five years ago, on August 2nd, 2006.

Reporter: Des Brisay has autism. He suffers from a developmental disorder of the brain which impacts social and communication skills. He was seven years old when he uttered his first word. Do you get nervous when you run, when you compete?

Des Brisay: Not really. I'm not nervous. I'm... I'm too excited.
[...]

Extracted from: <www.youtube.com/watch?v=IqGIOKiiFMw> (00:20-01:02).
Accessed on: May 14, 2016.

TRACK 33

Page 158. Activity 4

Listen to the interview once again and check the correct answers.
[...]

Reporter: Tommy Des Brisay loves to run and he runs a lot. Just about every day he is at the track, on a treadmill or outdoors trying to become even faster.

Des Brisay: I have been running for so long. Five years ago, on August 2nd, 2006.

Reporter: Des Brisay has autism. He suffers from a developmental disorder of the brain which impacts social and communication skills. He was seven years old when he uttered his first word. Do you get nervous when you run, when you compete?

Des Brisay: Not really. I'm not nervous. I'm... I'm too excited.
[...]

Extracted from: <www.youtube.com/watch?v=IqGIOKiiFMw> (00:20-01:02).
Accessed on: May 14, 2016.

FURTHER PRACTICE 1
(UNITS 1 & 2)

TRACK 34

Page 166. Activity 6

Listen to the first part of the interview with Paul and Cristina and answer the questions.

Interviewer: Now, what's your name?

Paul: Paul.

Interviewer: Thank you. And what's your name?

Cristina: Cristina.

Interviewer: Thank you. Cristina, what's your surname?

Cristina: Romera.

Interviewer: How do you spell that?

Cristina: R – O – M – E – R – A.

Interviewer: Thank you. And, Paul, what's your surname?

Paul: Achatz.

Interviewer: How do you spell that?

Paul: A – C – H – A – T – Z.

Interviewer: Thank you.

Extracted from: <www.youtube.com/watch?v=MjIYSM27z_U> (00:15-00:42). Accessed on: May 16, 2016.

TRACK 35

Page 166. Activity 7

Listen to the second part of the interview and complete each gap with one word.

Interviewer: Paul, where do you come from?

Paul: From Austria.

Interviewer: Do you study English at school?

Paul: Yes.

Interviewer: Do you like it?

Paul: Yes, it's very funny and... yeah.

Interviewer: Thank you. Cristina, where do you come from?

Cristina: I come from Spain.

Extracted from: <www.youtube.com/watch?v=MjIYSM27z_U> (00:43-00:59). Accessed on: May 16, 2016.

TRACK 36

Page 166. Activity 8

Listen to Paul talking about his free time. What does he enjoy doing? Check the true sentences.

Interviewer: And what do you enjoy doing in your free time, Paul?

Paul: I play football with my friends and my neighbors outside, and... sometimes I'm watching TV and playing computer games, but the most time I'm outside.

Interviewer: Thank you. [...]

Extracted from: <www.youtube.com/watch?v=MjIYSM27z_U> (01:41-02:01). Accessed on: May 16, 2016.

TRACK 37

Page 166. Activity 9

Listen to Cristina talking about her family. Complete the sentence with words from the box.

Interviewer: [...] Cristina, tell us about your family.

Cristina: My family... I live with my parents and my little brother, and... I have... visits on the weekend of my aunt, my granny, my granddad, my uncles and my cousins.

Interviewer: Thank you.

Extracted from: <www.youtube.com/watch?v=MjIYSM27z_U> (02:02-02:23). Accessed on: May 16, 2016.

TRACK 38

Page 166. Activity 10

Listen to these movie extracts and underline the correct option according to what you hear.

a. A: Where's Selvam?

b. A: So, which one is it?

B: I'm from the ocean.

A: Ah, the ocean. The ocean? Aah! Aah! Aah!

c. A: We're not chickens, we're geese!

B: No!

d. A: It's gone.

B: They are savages. Tonight we die.

A: The feet... I told you...

Extracted from: *As Aventuras de Pi* (00:21:31-00:21:32); *Procurando Nemo* (00:26:43-00:26:50); *Os Aristogatas* (00:43:19-00:43:24); *Madagascar* (00:40:01-00:40:10).

FURTHER PRACTICE 2
(UNITS 3 & 4)

TRACK 39

Page 170. Activity 5

Read the text and complete it using the words from the box. Then listen and check your answers.

You have parents, and your parents have parents. These are your grandparents, who also have parents – your great-grandparents. Keep adding parents, keep adding "greats". [...] You have siblings, and so do your parents. These are your aunts and uncles. [...] Now down the tree, your siblings' children are your nieces and nephews, collectively, niblings, and you are their aunt or uncle. Their children are your grandnieces and nephews, and you are their grandaunt or uncle. [...]

Extracted from: <www.youtube.com/watch?v=PM79Epw_cp8> (00:05-00:14; 00:27-00:31; 00:47-00:58). Accessed on: May 16, 2016.

TRACK 40

Page 171. Activity 7

Listen to Lauren Chu talking about Chinese families and do the activities below.

Lauren: [greeting in Chinese] Hello, everyone. I'm going to show you some Chinese tradition and culture. Most Chinese families are made up of parents, one to two kids and sometimes elders. In China, both parents normally work. That is why some parents bring their retired parents to live with them, so that they can take care of their little children while they're at work.

Depending on their income, most Chinese families live in big or small apartments. Their homes mostly have a living room, a dining room, a kitchen, a balcony, a couple of bathrooms, a few bedrooms, a storeroom, all in one or sometimes two floors.

Extracted from: <www.youtube.com/watch?v=CbNwdEqZQJY> (00:03-00:48).
Accessed on: May 16, 2016.

TRACK 41

Page 171. Activity 8

Now listen to Lauren talking about homes in China again. What is there in most homes? Circle the items that she mentions.

Lauren: [greeting in Chinese] Hello, everyone. I'm going to show you some Chinese tradition and culture. Most Chinese families are made up of parents, one to two kids and sometimes elders. In China, both parents normally work. That is why some parents bring their retired parents to live with them, so that they can take care of their little children while they're at work.

Depending on their income, most Chinese families live in big or small apartments. Their homes mostly have a living room, a dining room, a kitchen, a balcony, a couple of bathrooms, a few bedrooms, a storeroom, all in one or sometimes two floors.

Extracted from: <www.youtube.com/watch?v=CbNwdEqZQJY> (00:03-00:48).
Accessed on: May 16, 2016.

FURTHER PRACTICE 3
(UNITS 5 & 6)

TRACK 42

Page 174. Activity 5

Listen to some interesting fun facts and match the name of the animal to the corresponding information.

A camel can drink up to 100 liters of water in just 10 minutes. That's an amazing 5 liters per 30 seconds.

Adult elephants' trunk is made up of more than a hundred thousand muscles and no bones.

Giraffes only sleep for around two hours each day and sometimes even less, as little as five or ten minutes.

A polar bear has an extremely well-developed sense of smell and it's able to detect a seal from over a mile away.

The fingerprints from a koala are so similar to human fingerprints that the slight differences can only be identified under a microscope.

Extracted from: <www.youtube.com/watch?v=wrGExDCACts>
(00:04-00:12; 00:21-00:27; 01:00-01:07; 01:40-01:45; 02:32-02:45).
Accessed on: Nov. 25, 2014.

FURTHER PRACTICE 4
(UNITS 7 & 8)

TRACK 43

Page 178. Activity 6

Listen to a girl talking about her favorite athlete. Underline the correct words in the sentences below according to what you hear.

My favorite athlete is my little sister Freya. She plays football. She has practiced football since she was seven years old. Now she is eleven years old and practices football five times a week, six hours and forty minutes. She also practices with my dad a lot of times and with her friends in recess and after school. When she grows up, she wants to become a professional football player for Iceland's national team.

Extracted from: <www.youtube.com/watch?v=eT3ZcJIMUCE> (00:00-00:28).
Accessed on: May 16, 2016.

GLOSSARY

A

abbreviation abreviação
ability (pl.: abilities) aptidão
able capaz
abroad no exterior, para o exterior
academic English student estudante acadêmico de inglês
access acesso
acrobat acrobata
act número (de circo)
action ação
actor ator
actress atriz
add adicionar
addressee destinatário
admire admirar
admit admitir
adopt adotar
adopted son filho adotivo
adult adulto
adult educational center centro educacional para adultos
advanced avançado
afraid com medo
again de novo
against contra
age idade
ages eras, muito tempo
air conditioner ar-condicionado
alphabet letter letra do alfabeto
amazing incrível
American norte-americano
amphibious anfíbio (adj.)
animal rights direitos dos animais
announce anunciar
annual flooding enchente anual
answer responder
antioxidant antioxidante
appealing atraente
appear aparecer
applaud aplaudir
apple maçã
area área
Argentinean argentino
Art, Arts Artes
article artigo
athlete atleta
athletic talent talento atlético
audience plateia
August agosto
aunt tia
Australian australiano
author autor
autism autismo
average média
aviary (pl.: aviaries) viveiro de aves
avocado abacate
avoid evitar
awarded premiado

B

backhand revés (tênis)
backwards para trás
bacon *bacon*
bakery padaria
balance on balls equilibrar-se sobre bolas
ban proibição
banana banana
bank banco
bargain pechincha
barrier barreira
basketball basquete
beach praia
beachbreaks praias, arrebentação (ondas do mar)
bear urso
beat vencer alguém
beautiful bonito
because of por causa de
bed cama
beginner iniciante
Belgium Bélgica
believe acreditar
below abaixo
belt faixa (em artes marciais)
best melhor
best friend melhor amigo
between entre
bicycle bicicleta
big grande

bike helmet capacete de ciclista
biological equilibrium equilíbrio biológico
bird pássaro
birth date data de nascimento
birth place local de nascimento
black negro
blackberry (pl.: blackberries) amora
blackboard quadro negro
blender liquidificador
blue azul
boat barco
body corpo
body message corpo da mensagem
boldly audaciosamente
bomb bombardear
bone osso
book livro
book cover capa de livro
book title título de livro
bookstore livraria
box quadro
boxcar vagão
Brazilian brasileiro
bread pão
break quebrar
breath respiração
British britânico
broccoli brócolis
brother irmão
buffalo (pl.: buffaloes) búfalo
building construção
bulky volumoso
bus ônibus
butterfly borboleta
bye tchau

C

cage jaula
calculator calculadora
calorie caloria
Canadian canadense
canary (pl.: canaries) canário
cancer câncer
care cuidado; importar-se
care for cuidar
career path plano de carreira
caring cuidado
carrot cenoura
cartoon cartum
cartoonist cartunista
cat gato
cauliflower couve-flor
celebrate comemorar
celebration comemoração
celebs (celebrities) celebridades
cell célula
cell phone telefone celular
certificate certidão
chair cadeira
chalkboard lousa de giz
challenge desafiar
chance chance
change trocar, mudar
characteristic característica
chart tabela
check checar, ticar
cheese queijo
child (pl.: children) criança
chimpanzee chimpanzé
choice escolha
cholesterol colesterol
choose escolher
church igreja
cicada cigarra
circle circular
circus (pl.: circuses) circo
citizen cidadão
classmate colega de classe
classroom sala de aula
clean water activist ativista pela água limpa
closing encerramento
clothing roupas
clown palhaço
coconut coco
cold frio
Colombian colombiano

color cor

colored pencils lápis de cor

column coluna

come vir

commercial comercial (de TV, rádio)

communication channel canal de comunicação

community (pl.: communities) comunidade

compete competir

complete completar

complete name nome completo

computer computador

computer visionary visionário da computação

concern preocupação

condensed milk leite condensado

consonant sound som de consoante

constant constante

constant confinement confinamento constante

context contexto

contrast contraste

cooking time tempo de preparo

corn milho

correct corrigir

corresponding correspondente

country (pl.: countries) país

country of birth país de nascimento

cousin primo, prima

covered coberto

cow vaca

cramped up apertado

create criar

creative criativo

cry chorar

culture cultura

curious curioso

current atual

cute fofo, bonitinho

cycling ciclismo

D

dairy laticínios

darker mais escuro

date data

date of birth data de nascimento

daughter filha

dawn amanhecer

decide decidir

declared declarado

deep profundo

deer (pl.: deer) veado

deny negar

department departamento

department store loja de departamentos

dependent dependente

describe descrever

description descrição

descriptive descritivo

desert deserto

desk carteira escolar

dessert sobremesa

destroy destruir

developmental disorder distúrbio de desenvolvimento

diagram diagrama

dialog, dialogue diálogo

dictionary (pl.: dictionaries) dicionário

diet dieta

dietary fiber fibra alimentar

dig cavar

dilute diluir

director diretor

disabled deficiente

discount desconto

dish (pl.: dishes) prato

dissolve dissolver

distance distância

distributed distribuído

draw desenhar

drawing desenho

drawing room sala de desenho

dream sonhar

drink beber; bebida

during durante

E

each cada

early cedo

earn ganhar

GLOSSARY

eating habits hábitos alimentares
education educação
eggplant berinjela
elderly idoso
elephant elefante
emerging reader leitor emergente
employ empregar
end terminar; fim
English inglês
equal rights direitos iguais
eraser borracha
everywhere por toda parte
evolve evoluir
example exemplo
excelent excelente
excerpt trecho
exchange student estudante de intercâmbio
excited empolgado
exciting empolgante
executive director diretor executivo
explore explorar
express expressar
extract extrair
extremely extremamente
eye olho

F

face encarar; rosto
fact files textos informativos
family (pl.: families) família
family member membro da família
family tree árvore genealógica
famous famoso
fan fã
fascinate fascinar
fat gordo, gordura
father pai
favorite favorito
feel sentir
feeling sentimento
feline felino
female feminino
fiber, fibre fibra
fill encher
filmmaker diretor de cinema
final final
find out descobrir
finger dedo (da mão)
first name primeiro nome
flightless bird ave que não voa
flipper nadadeira
floating health clinic clínica de saúde flutuante
floating school escola flutuante
flood inundação
flyer panfleto
follow seguir
food comida
foot pé
football prodigy prodígio futebolístico
forehead testa
forename primeiro nome
fork garfo
form forma
forwards para a frente
founded fundado
fox raposa
freedom liberdade
French francês
friendly amigável
frog sapo
from time to time às vezes
fruit fruta
full cheio
full name nome completo
fun divertido
fun fact fato curioso
furry peludo

G

gender gênero
geography Geografia
gestation gestação
giraffe girafa
give dar
glass copo
globe globo terrestre

gloves luvas
glue stick cola em bastão
go ahead ir adiante
go back voltar
goal objetivo
goggles óculos de natação
good afternoon boa tarde
good evening boa noite (quando chegamos)
good morning bom dia
good night boa noite (quando nos despedimos)
goodbye tchau
gorgeous lindo
grand grande
granddaughter neta
grandfather avô
grandmother avó
grandparents avós
grandson neto
grape uva
graph gráfico
great ótimo
green verde
greeting cumprimento
ground water água subterrânea
group grupo
grow up crescer
growing number número crescente
guess adivinhar
gym academia de ginástica

H

habitat hábitat
handsome bonito
handywork trabalho manual
happen acontecer
happily felizmente
have ter
have fun divertir-se
headline manchete
healthy saudável
hear ouvir
heart coração
heart disease doença do coração
hello olá
herbivorous herbívoro
hero (pl.: heroes) herói
high alto
high school ensino médio
hippo hipopótamo
history História
hold manter, segurar
homeless sem-teto
hometown cidade natal
honey querido, mel
horn chifre
horse cavalo
hospital hospital
hospitality hospitalidade
hot quente
hotel hotel
hour hora
hover planar
how about que tal
how are you? como vai?
human being ser humano
humanitarian humanitário
humble humilde
hummingbird colibri
humorous engraçado
hundreds of thousands centenas de milhares

I

ice cream sorvete
ice cube cubo de gelo
identify identificar
Identity Card Carteira de Identidade
image imagem
imaginary imaginário
impassable obstruído
imperative imperativo
in favor of a favor de
in time a tempo
incredibly por incrível que pareça
infer deduzir
influence influenciar

informality informalidade
ingredient ingrediente
innocent inocente
innovative inovador
inside interior
instructions instruções
intelligent inteligente
interest interesse
interview entrevista
introduce apresentar (alguém)
inundate inundar
invite convidar
IQ (intelligence quotient) QI (quociente de inteligência)
Iranian iraniano

J

jam geleia
Japanese japonês
join juntar
join in participar
judo judô
juice suco
juicer espremedor
July julho

K

keep manter
kid criança
kill matar
kind amável
kindergarten teacher professor de jardim de infância
kindness bondade, gentileza
knee pad joelheira
know saber

L

label rótulo
land terra, terreno
landless family família sem terra
languages spoken línguas faladas
large grande
last name último nome
leading member membro principal
leave deixar
led levado, conduzido
leg perna
leisure lazer
leisure and culture activist ativista pelo lazer e pela cultura
lemon limão-siciliano
lemonade limonada
leopard leopardo
lesson lição
let's vamos
letter letra
level nível
library (pl.: libraries) biblioteca
lie down deitar-se
life vida
lifespan expectativa de vida
like gostar
lime limão
lion leão
list listar
listen ouvir
liter, litre litro
live morar, viver
look olhar
lose perder
loud alto (volume de som)
love amor; amar, adorar
low-fat milk leite desnatado
lung pulmão

M

magazine revista
maintain manter
make fazer
mammal mamífero
man homem
mane juba
map mapa
martial arts artes marciais

masterpiece obra-prima
match relacionar
Math, Maths Matemática
May maio
meal refeição
meal bar barra de cereais, proteínas etc.
meaning significado
measure medir
mechanical pencil lapiseira
medical staff equipe médica
meet conhecer
mile milha
miss perder
missing information informação que falta
mix misturar
mixed misturado
mom mãe
money dinheiro
monkey macaco
monument monumento
mother mãe
mouse (pl.: mice) camundongo
movie filme
muscle massage massagem muscular
museum museu
must dever (verbo)

N

name nome
nationality (pl.: nationalities) nacionalidade
natural environment ambiente natural
nature natureza
near perto
nearby próximo, perto
necessary necessário
necessity (pl.: necessities) necessidade
need precisar
neighborhood bairro
nervous nervoso
never nunca
news notícias, novidades
nice bom
night vision visão noturna
noisy barulhento
non-flying não voador
North Pole polo norte
Northern Irish norte-irlandês
northwest noroeste
note anotação
notebook caderno
nothing nada
notoriety notoriedade
noun substantivo
number número; numerar
nutrient nutriente
nutrition label tabela nutricional

O

objective objetivo
occupation profissão
October outubro
official oficial
often com frequência
Olympics Olimpíadas
onion cebola
only único, somente
opening inauguração
opening sale liquidação de inauguração
operate operar
orange cor de laranja, laranja
order ordem
origin origem
outdoors ao ar livre
overview visão geral
own próprio

P

pain dor
pair par
papaya mamão
paralympic athlete atleta paraolímpico
parents pais
park parque
parrot papagaio
partner parceiro
pass passar
passion paixão

GLOSSARY

passionate fervoroso
pay attention prestar atenção
peace paz
peach (pl.: peaches) pêssego
peel descascar
pen caneta
pencil lápis
pencil case estojo de lápis
penguin pinguim
people (pl.); person (sing.) pessoas; pessoa
per serving por porção
performance performance
period período
pet animal de estimação
phenom fenômeno
photo foto
photo caption legenda de foto
Physical Education Educação Física
picture imagem, foto
piece pedaço
pitcher jarra
place lugar, casa; colocar
place of birth local de nascimento
platypus ornitorrinco
player jogador
please por favor
plum ameixa
plump rechonchudo
plural plural
poor pobre
popularity popularidade
population população
Portuguese português
position posição
post office correio
poster cartaz
potato (pl.: potatoes) batata
pour despejar
powerful forte, poderoso
preceded precedido
predator predador
prediction previsão
prefer preferir
preparation preparo
present apresentar
price tag etiqueta de preço
primitive primitivo
probably provavelmente
profile perfil
program, programme programa
project projeto
promising promissor
promote promover
promotion promoção
proper apropriado
properly apropriadamente
prostate próstata
provide dar, prover
public safety segurança pública
publishing house editora
punish punir
puppy filhote de cachorro
purple roxo
push incentivar
put pôr

Q

question pergunta

R

rage fúria
rainy season estação de chuvas
raise levantar
reach atingir, alcançar
read ler
realize perceber
recipe receita
recipient ganhador
recognize reconhecer
red vermelho
refer referir-se
register registro
relatives parentes
repeated repetido
represent representar
reproduce reproduzir
republic república

respected respeitado

rest descansar

restrict restringir

result resultado

revenge vingança

rich rico

ride a bicycle andar de bicicleta

rights direitos

rise subir

risk risco

river rio

road estrada

roar rugir

role papel, função

routine rotina

ruler régua

run correr

runner corredor (esportista)

S

sailor velejador

salt sal

sanitation saneamento básico

Santa Claus Papai Noel

saturate fat gordura saturada

sauce calda

savage selvagem

say dizer

scan ler por alto

school escola

school bus ônibus escolar

school calendar calendário escolar

school competition competição escolar

school grade ano escolar

school house escola (edifício)

school name nome da escola

school principal diretor da escola

school subject matéria escolar

school supplies material escolar

school team time escolar

schoolbag bolsa escolar

Science Ciências

scientific name nome científico

scoop colher de sorvete

score marcar ponto

Scottish escocês

screen tela

seal of approval selo de aprovação

second grade segundo ano (escolar)

sedentary sedentário

see you até logo

see you later até mais

sender remetente

sentence frase

serve servir

serving porção

set up organizar

share compartilhar

sheep (pl.: sheep) ovelha

sheer enorme

shingards caneleiras

short curto

show mostrar

shower banho, chuveirada

shy tímido

similar semelhante

singer cantor

sister irmã

size tamanho

skill habilidade

skin pele

skyscraper arranha-céu

slice fatiar; fatia

slip escorregar

small pequeno

smile sorriso

smoothie bebida de frutas, leite e gelo batidos

snow neve

so então

soccer, football futebol

soccer shoes chuteiras

social sociável

social attitudes iniciativas sociais

sodium sódio

solo concert show solo

GLOSSARY

solution solução
son filho
song canção
sound som
soup sopa
source fonte
South American sul-americano
Spain Espanha
special especial
spell soletrar
spelling grafia
spend passar
spoon colher
spot posição (em *ranking*)
spring primavera
squeeze espremer
staff member funcionário, membro da equipe
stand on your head plantar bananeira
stand up ficar de pé
start começar
step passo
stereo set aparelho de som
stir mexer (com colher)
stock up abastecer-se
stomach estômago
store loja
story história
straight diretamente
stranded isolado
strawberry (pl.: strawberries) morango
street car bonde
stroke derrame
strong impact impacto forte
student estudante
stumpy curto
success sucesso
sugar açúcar
sugar cube cubo de açúcar
summarize resumir
sunrise nascer do sol
supermarket supermercado
superstar superestrela
sure com certeza
surfer surfista
surname sobrenome
sustenance subsistência
swamp pântano
sweetened adoçado
swim nadar
swimmer nadador
swimming natação
swimming cap touca de natação

T

table mesa
tablet *tablet*
take notes tomar notas
talented talentoso
talk conversar
tea chá
teacher professor
teen adolescente
teenager adolescente
tennis tênis (esporte)
text message mensagem de texto
that aquele
think pensar
this este, esse
tie empate
tiger tigre
tightrope walker equilibrista (de corda bamba)
tiring cansativo
title título
toe dedo do pé
tomato (pl.: tomatoes) tomate
tooth (pl.: teeth) dente
top colocar em cima
topic tópico
touch toque
track pista de corrida
trailer *trailer*, reboque
train treinar
train station estação de trem
trans fat gordura *trans*

transport transportar

trapeze artist trapezista

travel viagens

treadmill esteira de corrida

tree árvore

trick truque

trophy troféu

truck caminhão

true verdadeiro

turn tornar; virar; vez

tusk presa (de elefante)

U

ultimate supremo, máximo

umbrella guarda-chuva

Unabridged Birth Certificate Certidão de Nascimento Completa

uncle tio

underline sublinhar

uniform uniforme

university (pl.: universities) universidade

untrue falso

up to até

upside down de ponta-cabeça

use usar

usually geralmente

V

vanilla baunilha

vegetables legumes

versatile versátil

veterinary care assistência veterinária

victory vitória

village vila

violate violar

vitamin vitamina

vocalize vocalizar

voice unspoken voz não dita

volleyball match partida de vôlei

voluntary voluntário

volunteer voluntário

W

wake up acordar

walk andar

wall parede

want querer

watch assistir

water água

weather tempo (meteorologia)

weight peso

welcome bem-vindo

Welsh galês

wheelchair cadeira de rodas

while enquanto

white branco

who quem

whose de quem

wife esposa

wild selvagem

wild, the a natureza

win ganhar

window janela

wing asa

wish desejar

within dentro

wolf (pl.: wolves) lobo

wonder perguntar a si mesmo

word palavra

world mundo

world champion campeão mundial

worldwide no mundo todo

wristband munhequeira

writer escritor

written text texto escrito

wrong errado

Y

year ano

yellow amarelo

yogurt iogurte

young jovem

Z

zoo zoológico

BIBLIOGRAPHY

ABREU-TARDELLI, L. S.; CRISTOVÃO, V. L. L. (Org.) *Linguagem e educação*: o ensino e aprendizagem de gêneros textuais. Campinas: Mercado de Letras, 2009.

BRASIL. *Lei de Diretrizes e Bases da Educação Nacional*. Brasília: Ministério da Educação, 1996.

______. *Parâmetros Curriculares Nacionais* – Língua estrangeira. Brasília: Ministério da Educação, 1998.

______. *Ensino Fundamental de nove anos* – Orientações gerais. Brasília: Ministério da Educação, Secretaria de Educação Básica, Departamento de Políticas de Educação Infantil e Ensino Fundamental, Coordenação Geral do Ensino Fundamental, 2004. Disponível em: <portal.mec.gov.br./seb/arquivos/pdf/Ensfund/noveanorienger.pdf>. Acessado em: 3 jan. 2015.

COPE, B.; KALANTZIS, M. Multiliteracies: The beginning of an idea. In: COPE, B.; KALANTZIS, M. (Ed.) *Multiliteracies*: literacy learning and the design of social futures. London: Routledge, 2000. p. 3-8.

CROSS, D. *Large Classes in Action*. Hertfordshire: Prentice Hall International, 1995.

DIONÍSIO, A. P.; MACHADO, A. R.; BEZERRA, M. A. (Org.) *Gêneros textuais & ensino*. São Paulo: Parábola, 2010.

FREIRE, P. *Pedagogia da autonomia*: saberes necessários à prática educativa. São Paulo: Paz e Terra, 1996.

GRELLET, F. *Developing reading skills*. Cambridge: Cambridge University Press, 1981.

HEIDE, A.; STILBORNE, L. *Guia do professor para a internet*: completo e fácil. Trad. Edson Furmankiewz. 2. ed. Porto Alegre: Artmed, 2000.

HOFFMANN, J. *Avaliar para promover*: as setas do caminho. Porto Alegre: Mediação, 2001.

LAPKOSKI, G. A. O. *Do texto ao sentido*: teoria e prática de leitura em língua inglesa. Curitiba: Ibpex, 2011.

MARCUSCHI, L. A. Gêneros textuais: definição e funcionalidade. In: MARTINEZ, P. *Didática de línguas estrangeiras*. São Paulo: Parábola, 2009.

MOITA-LOPES, L. P. Ensino de inglês como espaço de embates culturais e de políticas da diferença. In: GIMENEZ, T. et al. (Org.) *Perspectivas educacionais e o ensino de inglês na escola pública*. Pelotas: Educat, 2005.

______. *Oficina de linguística aplicada*. Campinas: Mercado de Letras, 2000.

RAIMES, A. *Techniques in teaching writing*. New York, Oxford: Oxford University Press, 1983.

RICHARDS, J. C.; RENANDYA, W. A. (Ed.) *Methodology in language teaching*: an anthology of current practice. New York: Cambridge University Press, 2002.

RODRIGUES, D. (Org.) *Inclusão e educação*: doze olhares sobre a educação inclusiva. São Paulo: Summus, 2006.

SOUZA, A. G. F. et al. *Leitura em língua inglesa*: uma abordagem instrumental. São Paulo: Disal, 2005.

TOMLINSON, B. *Developing materials for language teaching*. Londres: Continuum, 2003.

VYGOTSKY, L. S. *Pensamento e linguagem*. São Paulo: Martins Fontes, 1993.

WALESKO, A. M. H. *Compreensão oral em língua inglesa*. Curitiba: Ibpex, 2010.

TIME TO SHARE Jornadas

Workbook 6

Organizadora:

Editora Saraiva

Obra coletiva organizada e produzida pela Editora Saraiva

Editor responsável:

Vicente Martínez

Licenciado em Tradução/Interpretação pela Universidad Pontificia de Comillas (Madrid)

Editor de conteúdos didáticos

Coordenadora:

Gisele Aga

Licenciada em Letras pela FMU – Faculdades Metropolitanas Unidas

Professora de Inglês na rede particular de ensino e em cursos de idiomas

Coordenadora pedagógica em cursos de idiomas

Editora de conteúdos didáticos

Editora Saraiva

PRESENTATION

Caro estudante,

Este caderno foi elaborado com a finalidade de ajudá-lo a organizar seu conhecimento. Ao resolver as atividades propostas, você terá a oportunidade de buscar informações, utilizar a própria experiência e conhecimento prévio sobre os assuntos tratados, desenvolver habilidades, elaborar opiniões sobre assuntos da atualidade, refletir sobre atitudes e comportamentos e ampliar a sua visão do mundo.

As atividades estão distribuídas em oito unidades, correspondendo às unidades do livro para que possa retomar e ampliar os tópicos estudados. A cada unidade, você encontrará as seguintes seções: *Review the journey*, *Another look* e *Reading the world*.

- Em *Review the journey*, você irá aplicar os conceitos gramaticais apresentados na unidade.
- A seção *Another look* propõe uma leitura complementar (verbal ou não verbal) ligada a algum tema ou gênero trabalhado na unidade do livro. As atividades visam trabalhar aspectos que não foram abordados no livro ou que são tratados sob outro aspecto. Além disso, nas últimas atividades você será incentivado a refletir e se posicionar em relação ao assunto tratado na seção.
- Em *Reading the world*, você lerá textos com temáticas instigantes, como aspectos culturais de diversos países, novas tecnologias, entre outras. Ao final das atividades, você poderá contar com uma produção (oral ou escrita).

Esperamos que sua jornada por este caderno seja bastante produtiva e o auxilie a desenvolver a autonomia nos estudos.

Os editores

CONTENTS

UNIT 1

Hi! What's your name?

Review the journey

1. Complete the form with your personal information.

http://siteresources.worldbank.org/INTAFRICA/Resources/Basic_Information_Form.pdf

BASIC INFORMATION FORM

Personal Information

First Name: ______________________________

Last Name: ______________________________

City: ______________________________

State/Province: ______________________________

Postal Code: ______________________________

Country of Origin: ______________________________

Telephone Number: ______________________________

E-mail Address: ______________________________

Native Language(s): ______________________________

Other Language(s): ______________________________

Extracted from: <siteresources.worldbank.org/INTAFRICA/Resources/Basic_Information_Form.pdf>. Accessed on: Mar. 7, 2016.

Another look

1. Look at the text below and choose the correct answer. The text is

a. ☐ a letter. **b.** ☐ a personal profile.

2. Circle the elements you can find in the text.

photo | long sentences | personal information | songs

3. Read and answer: What's the main topic of the text?

a. ☐ Shakira's career. **b.** ☐ Shakira's biography. **c.** ☐ Shakira's possessions.

SHAKIRA

Quick Facts

MATT SAYLES/INVISION/AP/GLOW IMAGES

ALSO KNOWN AS	Shakira Isabel Mebarak Ripoll
NATIONALITY	Colombian
BORN ON	February 2, 1977
BIRTHDAY	2nd February
SUN SIGN	Aquarius
BORN IN	Barranquilla
FATHER	William Mebarak Chadid
MOTHER	Nidia del Carmen Ripoll Torrado
SPOUSE	Gerard Piqué
CHILDREN	Milan and Sasha Piqué Mebarak
FOUNDER/ CO-FOUNDER	Pies Descalzos Foundation, ALAS Foundation

- She is well-known for her philanthropy and charitable works. She founded the Pies Descalzos Foundation in 1997 which funds special schools all over Colombia for poor children.

Adapted from: <www.thefamouspeople.com/profiles/shakira-4125.php#kKp9j1eJjewbWI8Q.99>. Accessed on: Mar. 7, 2016.

4. Answer **T** (true) or **F** (false) according to the text.

a. ☐ Shakira is from South America.

b. ☐ She has only one child.

c. ☐ Her husband's first name is Piqué.

d. ☐ Her mother's surname is Nidia del Carmen.

5. Answer these questions.

a. What's her last name? ______________________

b. What's her country of birth? ______________________

c. What's her date of birth? ______________________

d. What's her place of birth? ______________________

6. Complete the information about Shakira.

Gender: ______________ **Forename:** ______________

Family: ______________________

____

____

7. Which sentence describes a philanthropist?

a. ☐ A person who does charitable work and helps people in need.

b. ☐ A person who is famous because of his/her artistic or athletic talent.

1. If you were a celebrity like Shakira, how would you help society? Why?

____

____

2. Does the community where you live need help from an entity such as Pies Descalzos Foundation? Why?

____

____

Reading the world

1. Look at the picture from the text below and answer: What is she wearing?

a. ☐ hat **b.** ☐ headscarf **c.** ☐ band

2. Find the missing words in the word search and complete the text.

The word *hijab* comes from the ____________ for veil, curtain or barrier. Nowadays this word refers to the ______________________ worn by ______________________ women. This traditional covering for the head is considered a ____________ of modesty.

ALAMY/FOTOARENA

H	I	E	Q	D	Y	B	F	X	J	O	V	A	V
R	I	V	A	R	A	B	I	C	A	N	V	Y	J
H	M	Q	V	N	S	P	B	O	L	A	D	L	P
G	U	Z	S	M	M	B	L	L	H	A	J	Q	L
D	S	N	J	W	V	L	R	U	B	W	A	R	I
A	L	V	C	L	X	I	S	Y	M	B	O	L	D
I	I	A	G	Q	U	W	L	N	F	O	V	T	Q
F	M	I	B	Q	G	J	U	C	C	R	Q	T	E
I	T	W	I	Q	N	Q	D	V	U	M	U	S	E
T	O	E	C	U	A	D	O	C	R	C	O	S	K
H	E	A	D	S	C	A	R	F	T	R	O	P	Y
E	Q	M	U	J	T	R	C	B	S	L	Y	O	V

3. Discuss with your colleagues: How do you think a woman who usually wears a hijab would feel if she could not wear it in another country?

____

____

UNIT 2 I'm from Bogotá

Review the journey

1. Write questions to given answers.

a. ____

Their names are Brad Pitt and Angelina Jolie.

b. ____

No, they aren't British. They are American.

c. ____

No, they aren't from Florida. She's from California and he's from Oklahoma.

2. Complete the conversations with the expressions from the box.

Good afternoon	Goodbye	Good evening	Good morning

a. **A:** ______________________________, kids.

B: Hi, Dad. It's 7 pm. Let's have dinner!

b. **A:** ______________________________, Paulo. It's 6 am. Time for breakfast!

B: No, Mom, 5 more minutes, please!

c. **A:** Bye, Adam. See you tomorrow.

B: ______________________________, Sophie!

d. **A:** ______________________________, class.

B: Ms. Jenkins, it's only 1:00 pm. Can we play for 10 more minutes?

A: Hmmm... Only 5 minutes and then right into the classroom!

Another look

1. Read the text conversation between Juan and his friends and underline the abbreviations you find.

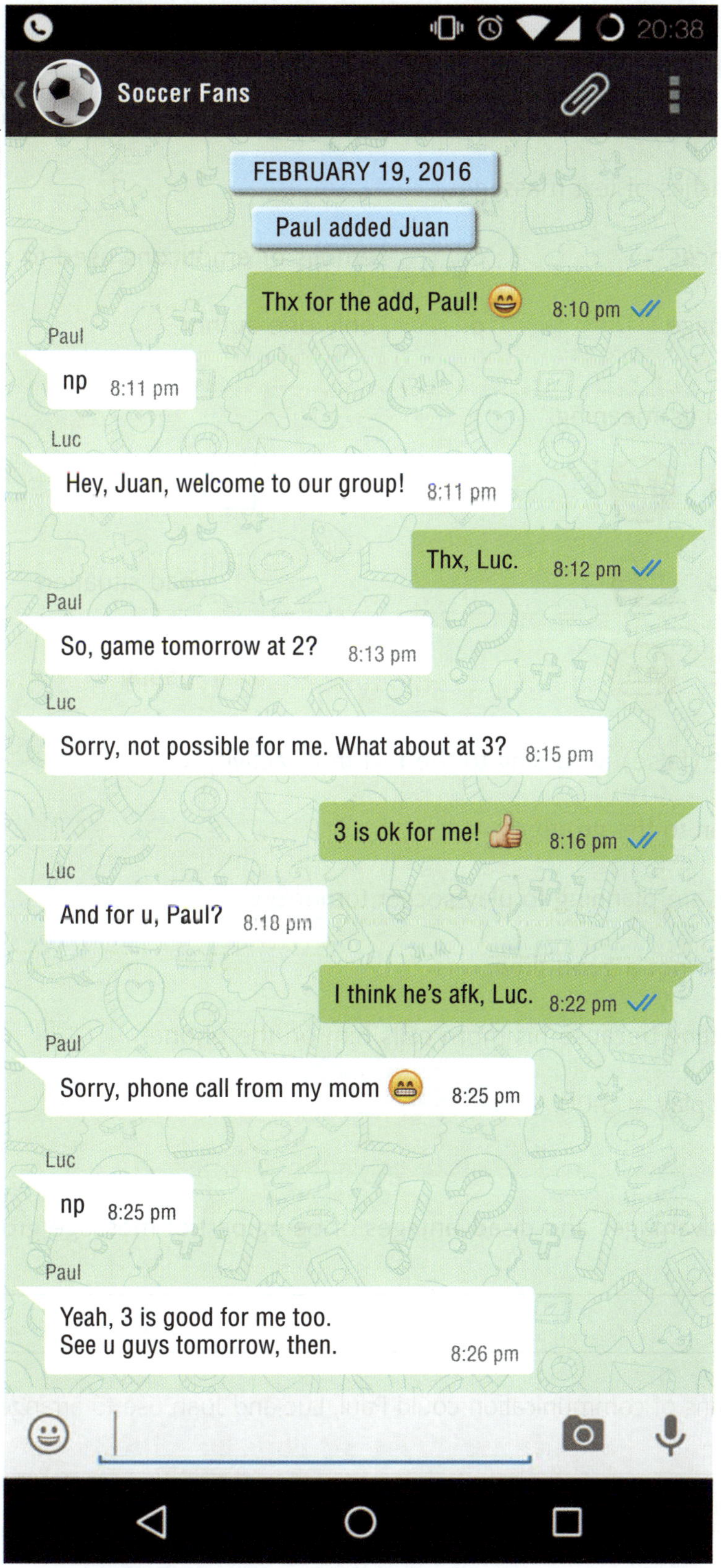

2. Match the abbreviation and its meaning.

a. u

b. thx

c. afk

d. np

☐ thanks

☐ you

☐ no problem

☐ away from keyboard

Away from keyboard: afastado(a) do teclado

3. Check the characteristics of text messages.

a. ☐ short sentences

b. ☐ formal language

c. ☐ emojis or emoticons used to express emotions

d. ☐ only one author

4. Match the emoji and its meaning.

a. 

b. 

c. 

☐ OK

☐ bad situation

☐ happy

5. Answer **T** (true) or **F** (false) according to the text from activity 1.

☐ Paul added Juan to the group.

☐ The three boys are planning to play soccer tomorrow.

☐ For Paul, 2:00 is not a good time.

☐ Paul stops chatting because his mom calls him on the phone.

☐ They decide to play at 3:00.

1. What are the advantages and disadvantages of being part of message groups?

____

____

2. What other means of communication could Paul, Luc and Juan use to arrange the game?

____

____

Reading the world

1. Look at the text. What is it?

a. ☐ An e-mail. **b.** ☐ An infographic.

2. Underline the elements of an infographic.

use of graphs | long sentences | numbers and statistics

3. Read the text and complete the following sentences with the mathematical symbols **>** (larger than) or **<** (smaller than).

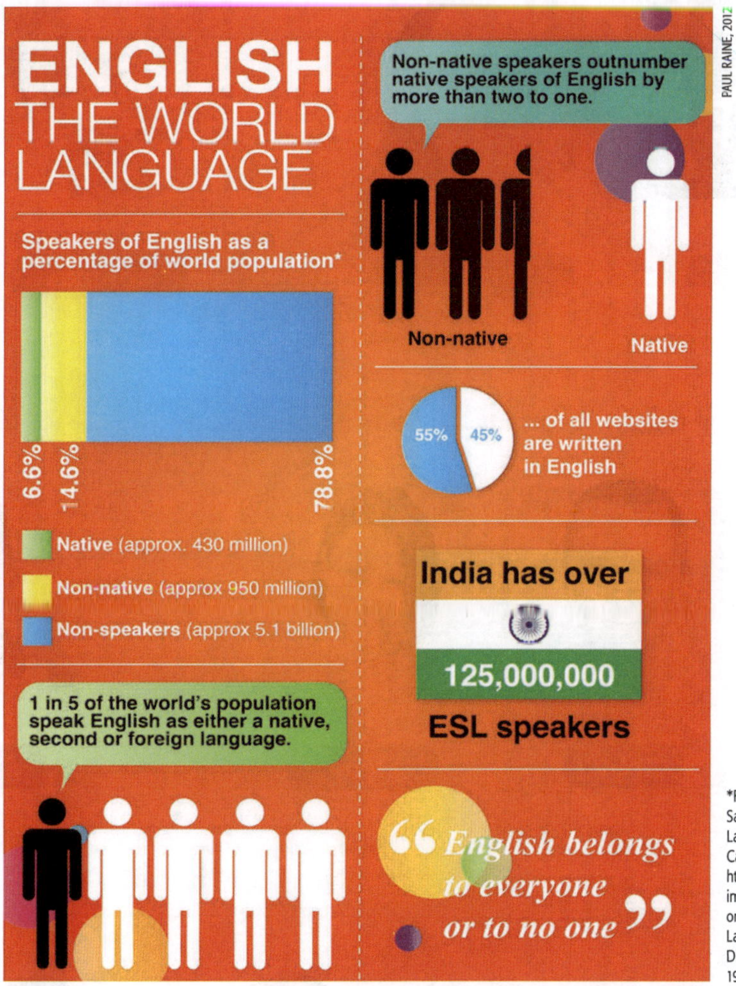

*Figures based on 2006 estimates | Sources: Saville-Troike, Muriel. Introducing Second Language Acquisition. Cambridge, UK: Cambridge UP, 2006 http://unesdoc.unesco.org/images/0018/00187016e.pdf | http://en.wikipedia.org/wiki/English_language | Wardhaugh, Ronald. Languages in Competiotion: Dominance, Diversity, and Decline. Oxford. UK: B. Blackwell, 1987. This infographic ©Paul Raine 2012.

a. number of English speakers ☐ number of non-English speakers

b. number of non-native speakers ☐ number of native speakers

c. number of websites in English ☐ number of websites in other languages

d. number of English speakers in India ☐ total population of India

UNIT 3

This is my family

Review the journey

1. Study the family tree and do the crossword puzzle. Then complete the sentences.

Across

2. Patty is Mark and Keila's __________.

4. Toby is Mark and Keila's __________.

8. Patty is Elena's __________.

9. Tomiko is Walter's __________.

10. Mark is Keila's __________.

11. Ralph is Elena's __________.

Down

1. Walter and Tomiko are Sammy's __________.

3. Sammy is Elena's __________.

5. Maya is Mark and Keila's __________.

6. Julie is Elena's __________.

7. Julie and Ralph are Maya's __________.

Another look

1. Look at the text below and answer the questions.

a. The text is

☐ an e-mail. ☐ a note.

b. The author of the text is

☐ Yuki's mother. ☐ Yuki.

2. Circle the elements of a note.

short text	formal language	addressee (Dear...)
descriptions	signature	

3. Read the text and underline all the transparent words.

THINKSTOCK/GETTY IMAGES

BIS

To Yuki

We've come to the final bento of your high school life. Thank you for eating each and every one. Through these bentos we were able to communicate more. I don't know when I'll have the opportunity to make a bento for you again, so I hope you really enjoy this one. Your high school life was lots of fun, wasn't it? There's only a little time left, so enjoy it with your friends.

Thank you. From Mom

Extracted from: <http://en.rocketnews24.com/2016/01/30/mothers-cute-note-in-final-bento-of-sons-high-school-life-gives-twitter-the-feels/>. Accessed on: May 10, 2016.

4. What is the main topic of the text?

a. ☐ A mother wants her son to eat well.

b. ☐ A mother wants to celebrate the end of high school with her son.

c. ☐ A mother and a son making plans for university.

5. According to the text write **T** (true) or **F** (false).

a. ☐ The mother's name is Yuki.

b. ☐ It's Yuki's last day in high school.

c. ☐ Yuki's mother will make Yuki another bento tomorrow.

d. ☐ Yuki's mother wants Yuki to have fun with her.

e. ☐ Yuki's mother put the note in the bento box.

6. Write **F** (fact) or **O** (opinion).

a. ☐ Yuki's mother prepared a bento box for him every day during high school.

b. ☐ Yuki's mother is a nice person.

c. ☐ Yuki is not going to school the next day.

d. ☐ Japanese kids eat well at school.

1. In the note you read on page 14, Yuki's mother says she could communicate more with him through the bento boxes she made. Do you exchange notes with your parents? When and why?

___

___

2. According to the note, Yuki always had homemade snacks. What are the advantages and disadvantages of this habit?

___

___

3. How do you think Yuki's mother felt while writing this note?

___

___

Reading the world

1. Read the title and subtitles of the text. What do you think it is about? Read the text and check your answer.

____

AROUND THE WORLD

George Adjei

My name is George Adjei. I am 11 years old and in the sixth grade. I live with my mother, grandmother, and older sister, in Accra, the capital. I love reading and playing soccer.

MSHEP2/ISTOCKPHOTO/GETTY IMAGES

Extracted from: <www.timeforkids.com/destination/ghana/day-in-life>. Accessed on: Mar. 17, 2016.

LAU YAN WAI/FLICKR RF/GETTY IMAGES

Karyn Tania Lee

My Name is Karyn Tania Lee. I live with my mom, dad, brother, and sister, in eastern Singapore. I am the oldest of three children.

Extracted from: <www.timeforkids.com/destination/singapore/day-in-life>. Accessed on: Mar. 17, 2016.

Brid Cannon

Hello! I'm Brid Cannon, and I'm 11. I live with my parents and siblings in Dunlewey, which is in northwest Ireland.

HOLGER LEUE/LONELY PLANET IMAGES/GETTY IMAGES

Extracted from: <www.timeforkids.com/destination/ireland/day-in-life>. Accessed on: Mar. 17, 2016.

RON LEVINE/GETTY IMAGES

Jackie Allen

Hi! My name is Jackie Allen. I am 11, and live with my parents and two brothers in Halifax, Nova Scotia, on the East Coast.

Extracted from: <www.timeforkids.com/destination/canada/day-in-life>. Accessed on: Mar. 17, 2016.

Renan Rodrigues Almeida

Hi! I'm Renan Rodrigues Almeida, and I'm 10. I live with my two brothers, two sisters and parents in a city near São Paulo.

MONKEY BUSINESS IMAGES/GETTY IMAGES

Extracted from: <www.timeforkids.com/destination/brazil/day-in-life>. Accessed on: Mar. 17, 2016.

2. Read the text again. Then answer the questions.

a. Who is from Ghana? ______________________________

b. Who is from Canada? ______________________________

c. Who is Brazilian? ______________________________

3. Complete the table based on the text.

Who...	George	Karyn	Brid	Jackie	Renan
is 11 years old?					
lives with both parents?					
has two brothers?					
lives with grandmother?					
has no sisters?					

4. Write a similar paragraph about you. You can glue your picture or make a drawing of yourself.

____
____
____
____
____
____
____
____

UNIT 4

Our school is awesome!

Review the journey

1. Unscramble the names of school supplies.

a. _ _ _ _ _(4) _ _(9)   _ _ _(6) _ _(10) _ _(7)   DOOLERC SIPCELN

b. _ _(13) _ _(3)   _ _(1) _ _ _   GULE SITKC

c. _ _ _ _ _ _ _(14) _   KEBNOOTO

d. _ _ _   EPN

e. _ _ _(5) _ _ _   REREAS

f. _ _ _ _ _ _   LICENP

g. _ _(8) _ _ _   LEURR

h. _(11) _ _ _(2) _ _ _ _ _ _   _ _ _ _(12) _ _   NMCICLAAHE PINCEL

2. What's the mystery sentence?

_(1) _(2) _(3) _(4) _(3)   _(5) _(4) _(3)   _(1) W _(3) _(6) _(1) Y

_(7) _(1) _(8) _(9) _(3) _(6) _(1) _(7)   _(10) _(6)   _(11) Y   _(12) _(13) _(5) _(7) _(7) _(4) _(14) _(14) _(11)

3. Look at the picture and answer the questions.

HAGAQUEZART ESTÚDIO

a. Where's the teacher?

____

b. Where is the schoolbag?

____

c. Is the whiteboard behind the clock?

____

d. Are there posters on the wall?

____

e. Is there a map next to the whiteboard?

____

4. Write five more sentences about the picture.

____

____

____

____

____

Another look

1. Look at the text below and answer the questions.

"I've prepared a few different options."

a. This text is a

☐ poster.

☐ cartoon.

b. It was extracted from

☐ a website.

☐ a newspaper.

2. These are common elements of a typical cartoon. Which are present in this one?

a. ☐ short text
b. ☐ image
c. ☐ color
d. ☐ humor
e. ☐ signature
f. ☐ speech bubbles

3. Read the text again and circle the author's name.

4. What is the main topic of the text?

a. ☐ Math is not easy for some students.

b. ☐ The teacher is very severe.

5. Study the visual elements of the text and choose the best alternative to complete the sentences.

a. The sentence at the bottom is

☐ what the teacher is saying. ☐ what the student is saying.

b. You know that because

☐ in the picture, the boy's mouth is open. ☐ it is indicated in the text.

c. You know that the text is what a person is saying because

☐ in the picture, the boy is pointing. ☐ the text is between quotation marks ("...").

d. The characters are

☐ in the classroom. ☐ at the library.

6. Answer **T** (true) or **F** (false) according to the text.

a. ☐ The student knows the correct answer.

b. ☐ The teacher is not behind a table.

c. ☐ The student is pointing to the correct alternative.

d. ☐ The correct alternative is between options 1 and 3.

7. Complete the paragraph with the words from the box according to the cartoon.

in front of	Math	next to (2x)	on (2x)	there is

This is a __________ class. The student is __________ the board. He is writing some operations ______ the board. The teacher is __________ the student. __________ maybe a window or another board ______ the wall ______ the big board.

1. Is the comic funny? Why?

____

____

2. According to the comic, the student has some trouble with Math. Do you think he does well in other subjects? What subjects are easier for you to study? Why do you think they are easier than the others?

____

____

3. The student tries an alternative solution to solve the problem. What do you think the teacher is going to answer? Why?

____

____

Reading the world

1. Discuss with your classmates: Are schools in Brazil similar to or different from schools abroad? Why?

2. Look at the text and answer the questions.

a. The text is a

☐ fact sheet. ☐ magazine article.

b. The pictures express

☐ diversity. ☐ equality.

3. Read the text below and answer: What is the main topic of the text?

a. ☐ Different habits in schools around the world. b. ☐ Different schools in special countries.

BIS

www.bitrebels.com/lifestyle/20-facts-education-around-world/

FASCINATING FACTS ABOUT EDUCATION AROUND THE WORLD

1. Of all the schools in the world, the largest is in India. It is called the City Montessori School and it has over 32,000 students.
2. China is the country where kids get most homework. Teenagers in Shanghai do their homework during 14 hours a week.
3. Canadian kids are taught a lot of their lessons in both French and English.
4. Children in Holland all start school on their fourth birthday so there's always someone new in class.
5. Even if it's a weekend or a holiday, Russian children always start school on "Knowledge Day", which is September 1st.
6. The smallest school in the world is in Turin, Italy, and has just one pupil.

ANNA HENLY/GETTY IMAGES

ANDIA/ALAMY/FOTOARENA

JOERG BOETHLING/ALAMY/FOTOARENA

ROSAIRENEBETANCOURT 3/ALAMY/FOTOARENA

Adapted from: <www.bitrebels.com/lifestyle/20-facts-education-around-world/>. Accessed on: May 13, 2016.

4. Match the numbers to what they refer to.

a. 1	☐	Number of hours a Chinese kid studies at home per week.
b. 2	☐	Age Dutch kids start school.
c. 4	☐	Number of students in an Italian school.
d. 9/1	☐	Number of students in an Indian school.
e. 14	☐	Number of languages in which students are taught in Canada.
f. 32,000	☐	First day of the school year in Russia.

5. Now answer about your school.

a. How many students are there?

There are ____.

b. How many hours of homework do you do per week?

I do ____ per week.

c. Do they teach foreign languages in your school? Which ones?

____

____

6. Which of the facts mentioned in the text did you find the most interesting? Why?

____

____

____

7. How would you feel in a school with 32,000 students? And how would you feel in a school where you were the only student?

____

____

____

UNIT 5

Places in town

Review the journey

1. Look at the picture and correct the statements.

a. There are four cars in the picture.

____

b. The department store is on Main St.

____

c. The skyscraper is behind the church.

____

d. The tree is in front of the houses.

____

2. Solve the riddles.

a. It's on Sunset Ave., between two stores. There's a bicycle in front of it. What is it?

____

b. It's on Ocean Rd. behind the supermarket. What is it?

____

c. They are on Third St. There are three of them. What are they?

____

3. Write questions for the answers.

a. ______________________________

It's on Ocean Rd., between Second and Third Streets.

b. ______________________________

No, there isn't a car in front of it, but there's a bus.

c. ______________________________

Yes, there are three.

d. ______________________________

Yes, there is. It's between the bookstore and the music store.

4. Write the addresses in full.

a. 125 Sunset Ave. *A hundred twenty-five Sunset Avenue*

b. 76 Ocean Rd. ______________________________

c. 36 Main St. ______________________________

d. 91 First St. ______________________________

e. 42 Sunset Ave. ______________________________

Another look

1. Scan the text and check the correct alternative.

a. The text is a

☐ DVD cover. ☐ flyer.

b. The image in the text has the objective of

☐ showing the store products. ☐ helping clients understand directions.

2. Underline the characteristics of a flyer.

It is transmitted on radio or TV.
There is a sentence which identifies the topic.
It publishes information about a store or a product.
There are long sentences.

3. Read the text and find the new address of the store.

___

4. The main objective of the text is to

a. ☐ advertise the products of the store.

b. ☐ advise clients of the new location of the store.

5. Find the information in the text.

a. Name of the store ______________________________

b. Name of the street ______________________________

c. Name of the city ______________________________

d. Postal code ______________________________

e. Telephone number ______________________________

f. Website ______________________________

6. Answer the questions.

a. Is there a car park near the store?

____

b. Is the store near High Street?

____

c. What is next to Regent Tailoring?

____

d. Where is Old George Mall?

____

e. Is there a cathedral near Regent Tailoring?

____

1. How is a flyer distributed? What are the advantages of this kind of advertising?

____

____

2. If you were a client of Regent Tailoring, what would you do with this flyer? Why?

____

____

Reading the world

1. Scan the text and check the correct alternative.

a. The readers are probably

- [ ] Salisbury residents.
- [ ] tourists visiting Salisbury.

b. The text was published in

- [ ] a website.
- [ ] a travel brochure

2. Read the text and underline the transparent words.

www.dayoutwiththekids.co.uk/things-to-do/salisbury

HISTORICAL AND EDUCATIONAL ATTRACTIONS NEAR SALISBURY

Salisbury Cathedral (< 1 mile)

Visit one of the finest medieval cathedrals in Britain, which has the tallest spire in England! Holds the world's best preserved copy of the *Magna Carta* and a medieval clock.

Stonehenge (8 miles)

Stands as a testimony to the people who built it, between 3000 BC and 1500 BC. An amazing feat of engineering and the most sophisticated stone circle in the world, it remains a mystery. Fantastic new visitor centre!

Old Wardour Castle (13 miles)

Explore the set of *Robin Hood*: Prince of Thieves via audio tour, with enchanting grotto and circular staircases, plus play and picnic space outside.

Magna Carta: documento de 1215 que criou limites para o poder dos soberanos

Adapted from: <www.dayoutwiththekids.co.uk/things-to-do/salisbury>. Accessed on: Mar. 25, 2016.

3. Read the text again and find the information below.

a. the name of a Robin Hood movie: ______________________________

b. the period of the construction of Stonehenge: ______________________________

c. a word that means a tall, triangular structure: ______________________________

4. Write the names of the attractions under the correct pictures.

LEON NEAL/AFP

DAVE PATTISON/ALAMY/FOTOARENA

THINKSTOCK/GETTY IMAGES

______________________ ______________________ ______________________

5. Answer **T** (true) or **F** (false) according to the text.

a. ☐ Salisbury Cathedral has a tall spire.

b. ☐ There's a modern clock in the cathedral.

c. ☐ Stonehenge is a stone circle.

d. ☐ Stonehenge is in a mysterious location.

e. ☐ Old Wardour Castle is thirty miles from Salisbury.

6. Answer the questions.

a. What two objects can visitors see in Salisbury Cathedral?

____

b. What's the distance from Salisbury to Stonehenge?

____

c. Is there an external area in Old Wardour Castle?

____

7. Which of the attractions mentioned in the text would you like to visit? Why?

____

____

8. Are there any historical attractions in your city or state? What are they?

____

____

UNIT 6

Be kind to the innocent

Review the journey

1. Complete the conversation with **a**, **an** or **the**.

Dana: Mom, can I have _______ pet?

Mom: Oh Dana, taking care of _______ pet is _______ big responsibility. Are you sure?

Dana: Yes, Mom. Let's go to _______ pet store, please!

Mom: No, Dana. We don't have to buy _______ pet. We can adopt _______ dog or _______ cat. I have _______ friend who helps a lot of animals. Her name is Luciana. She has some pictures, too. Let's see them!

Dana: Mom! Look at _______ dogs! They're beautiful!

Mom: Yes, but we have to choose one! Look at _______ white dog. Do you like it?

Dana: Hmm, I prefer _______ black one.

Mom: Hmmm, I think this is _______ old dog. It has white hairs!

Dana: I like it, Mom!

Mom: Maybe _______ baby dog would be better, Dana!

Dana: Maybe, but I want _______ intelligent dog! I already have _______ awesome name for it: Professor Black!

Mom: Haha. That's _______ interesting name, Dana. So you really like _______ black dog?

Dana: Yes, mom!

Mom: OK, so let me send _______ e-mail to my friend and we can get it on _______ weekend.

Dana: Thanks, Mom. I'm so happy!

THINKSTOCK/GETTY IMAGES

PEOPLEIMAGES/ISTOCKPHOTO/GETTY IMAGES

2. Write these sentences in the plural. Use the numbers in parentheses.

a. There's a platypus in the river. (12)

____

b. There's a butterfly in the garden. (3)

____

c. There's a deer in the park. (15)

____

d. There's a monkey on the tree. (4)

____

3. Label the pictures.

a.

THINKSTOCK/GETTY IMAGES

two lions

c.

ERIC NATHAN/ALAMY/FOTOARENA

____

e.

ROBERTA OLENICK/ALL CANADA PHOTOS/GETTY IMAGES

____

b.

WENDY SHATTIL AND BOB ROZINSKI/OXFORD

____

d.

BLICKWINKEL/ALAMY/FOTOARENA

____

f.

KEN WELSH/AGE FOTOSTOCK/EASYPIX BRASIL

____

4. Solve the riddles.

a. It's very big. It has very big ears and a very long nose. What is it?

____

b. It's a bird. It likes cold places. It's black and white. What is it?

____

c. It's an insect. It plays "music". What is it?

____

Another look

1. Look at the text and check the correct alternative.

a. The text is a

- [ ] magazine article.
- [ ] fact file.

b. It was published at

- [ ] a website.
- [ ] an encyclopedia.

2. Circle the elements of this text genre.

images | moral lesson | narrative | scientific information | topics

3. Read the text to answer the following questions.

BIS

http://kids.nationalgeographic.com/animals/sloth

SLOTH

WORLDSWILDLIFEWONDERS/SHUTTERSTOCK.COM

Overview

It's a good thing sloths don't have to go to school. They'd never make it on time. These tree-dwellers sleep up to 20 hours a day!

Sloths live in the tropical forests of Central and South America. They can be 2 to 2.5 feet (0.6 to 0.8 meters) long and, depending on species, weigh from 8 to 17 pounds (3.6 to 7.7 kilograms).

They rarely come down from the trees. About once every week, they descend to go to the bathroom.

Scientific name
Bradypus variegatus

Family name
Bradypodidae

Classification
Mammal

Life span
10 years

Diet
Herbivore

Endangered status
LEAST CONCERN

Range

NATIONAL GEOGRAPHIC CREATIVE

Adapted from: <http://kids.nationalgeogralphic.com/animals/sloth>. Accessed on: Mar. 21, 2016.

a. What's the main objective of the text?

☐ To show different opinions about the sloth.

☐ To give information about the sloth.

b. Look at the picture and describe the sloth.

____

c. Look at the map and name three countries where the sloth lives.

____

4. Write **T** (true) or **F** (false) according to the text.

a. ☐ Sloths are sub-tropical animals.

b. ☐ They live in trees.

c. ☐ The sloth's diet consists of plants.

d. ☐ It's a very endangered species.

e. ☐ It lives for about 10 years.

f. ☐ On the map, the area where the sloth is common is colored green.

5. Match the numbers to what they refer.

a. 20 ☐ a sloth's **length** in feet

b. 2-2.5 ☐ number of hours a sloth sleeps per day

c. 8-17 ☐ a sloth's maximum **age**

d. 10 ☐ a sloth's **weight** in pounds

length: comprimento
weight: peso
age: idade

1. The animal mentioned in the text is called *preguiça* in Portuguese and its equivalent in English, **sloth**. Based on what you read about it, is this an appropriate name for this animal? Why?

____

____

2. Do you think a sloth would adapt as a pet? Justify your answer.

____

____

Reading the world

1. Answer the questions.

a. Where's New Zealand?

☐ South America. ☐ Europe. ☐ Oceania.

b. What are the official languages of New Zealand?

☐ English and French. ☐ English and Maori. ☐ French and Spanish.

2. Read the text and write the subtitles in the correct places.

Interesting New Zealand History | New Zealand Geography | New Zealand Nature

www.coolkidfacts.com/new-zealand-facts-for-kids/

NEW ZEALAND FACTS

CHAMELEONSEYE/SHUTTERSTOCK.COM

1. ______________________________

A. The Maori people, known as New Zealand's native people, arrived by canoe from islands in Polynesia near Tahiti around 1,000 A.D.

B. New Zealand was founded in 1642 by Dutch explorer Abel Tasman.

C. In 1769, British Captain James Cook and his crew came to the islands and they settled there.

2. ______________________________

A. This country has two main islands, the North and South Islands and these are separated by the Cook Strait.

B. It is small at 269,055 km^2. It is about the same size as the UK. Now the UK has 63 million people living there, and New Zealand only has about 4 million.

C. There are over 50 volcanoes, some of which can still erupt.

D. The capital city of New Zealand is Wellington; however, the largest city is actually Auckland, where most people live.

3. ______________________________

A. Unbelievably nearly all the land animals are birds and most of them can't fly anymore.

B. This is a frightening fact! In the last 1,000 years, half of all animals on the islands are now extinct.

C. New Zealand is home to one of the world's heaviest insects. It's called the weta. It weighs 70 grams. That is very heavy for an insect; it weighs three times more than a mouse and looks like a giant cockroach.

D. The only parrot that can't fly, the kakapo, is found here too. They really do have some interesting creatures on this awesome island.

BIS

Adapted from: <www.coolkidfacts.com/new-zealand-facts-for-kids/>. Accessed on: Mar. 23, 2016.

3. Answer the following questions.

a. Where are the Maori originally from?

____

b. Is New Zealand big or small?

____

c. What is different about the birds in New Zealand?

____

d. Is Auckland the capital?

____

4. Find the words in the text to complete the crossword puzzle. Then answer the question.

Last name of the British explorer
Natives of New Zealand
A very big insect
Nationality of the settlers
Most New Zealand birds can't do this
The kakapo is a kind of
The founder's nationality
The capital
Volcanoes do this

What's New Zealand's typical fruit? ______________________________

5. Do you know the kiwi? It is a native New Zealand animal. Do a short research about it and write its life span, diet, species and classification. You can write it as a fact file, like the one on page 32.

____

____

____

____

____

____

____

UNIT 7

A healthy life

Review the journey

1. Complete the text with the names of foods.

ILUSTRAÇÕES: SIMONE ZIASCH

FOLLOW MYPLATE GUIDELINES

According to the USDA, a healthy plate should be composed like so:

> **USDA:** Departamento de Agricultura dos Estados Unidos (United States Department of Agriculture)

- 30% grains (at least half of them should be whole, unprocessed grains);
- 30% vegetables (try ____________ , ____________ , snap peas, ____________ , sweet ____________ , spinach, and green beans);
- 20% fruits (____________ , a cup of ____________ , ____________  slices, cut-up ____________ );
- 20% protein (lean proteins are best);
- a small helping of dairy (try a cup of skim or 1% ____________ , a stick of low-fat string ____________ , or low-fat ____________ ).

Adapted from: <http://titleboxingclub.com/family-fitness/teach-your-kids-about-good-nutrition/>. Accessed on: Mar. 25, 2016.

2. Do the crossword puzzle.

THINKSTOCK/GETTY IMAGES

Guacamole.

Across

3. It's a green citrus fruit. We use it to make juice and to season salads.

4. It's a red fruit that we eat in salads.

6. It's a small purple berry, but there is another color in its name.

Down

1. It's a purple vegetable. It's very common in Italian cuisine.

2. It's a purple fruit. It's similar to a peach.

5. In Brazil, we eat it with sugar. In Mexico, they make guacamole with it

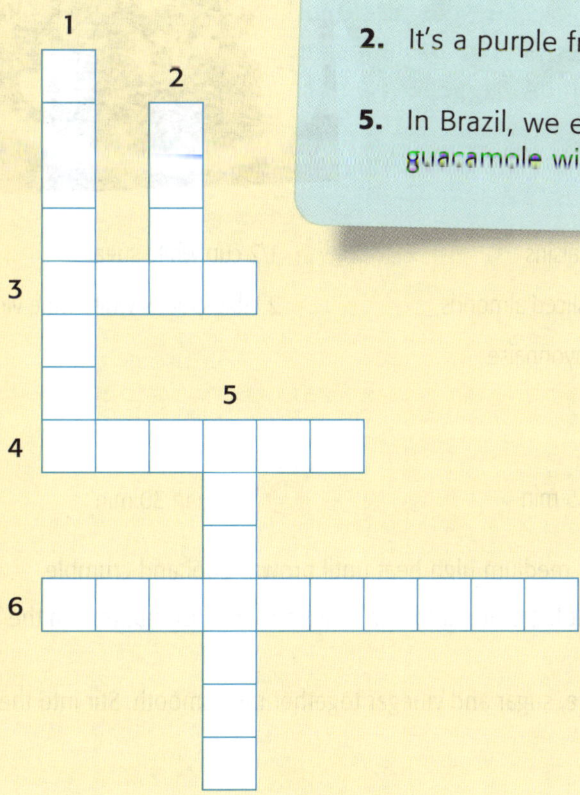

Another look

1. Look at the text below and choose the correct alternative to complete the sentence.

a. The text is

- [ ] an instruction manual.
- [ ] a recipe.

b. The picture illustrates

- [ ] the final result of the process.
- [ ] the steps of the process.

2. Underline the elements of this text genre.

contains two parts	contains a lot of adjectives
presents formal language	second part has step-by-step instructions
first part is in form of a list	presents verbs in the imperative form

3. Read the text and circle the quantities of the ingredients you need.

BIS

FRESH BROCCOLI SALAD

9 servings

374 cals

MILOSR/SHUTTERSTOCK.COM

Ingredients

- 2 heads fresh broccoli
- 1 red onion
- 1/2 pound bacon
- 3/4 cup raisins
- 3/4 cup sliced almonds
- 1 cup mayonnaise
- 1/2 cup white sugar
- 2 tablespoons white wine vinegar

Directions

Prep 15 min — Cook 15 min — Ready in 30 min

1. Place bacon in a deep skillet and cook over medium high heat until brown. Cool and crumble.
2. Cut the broccoli into bite-size pieces and cut the onion into thin bite-size slices. Combine with the bacon, raisins, your favorite nuts and mix well.
3. To prepare the dressing, mix the mayonnaise, sugar and vinegar together until smooth. Stir into the salad, let chill and serve.

Adapted from: <http://allrecipes.com/recipe/14280/fresh-broccoli-salad/>. Accessed on: Mar. 26, 2016.

4. Label the pictures with the words from the box.

bacon crumble	deep skillet	dressing	raisins	red onions	white wine vinegar

a.

THINKSTOCK/GETTY IMAGES

____

c.

MARIYANA M/SHUTTERSTOCK.COM

____

e.

THINKSTOCK/GETTY IMAGES

____

b.

THINKSTOCK/GETTY IMAGES

____

d.

THINKSTOCK/GETTY IMAGES

____

f.

THINKSTOCK/GETTY IMAGES

____

5. Answer the questions with numbers.

a. What's the total time necessary to prepare the salad?

____

b. How many portions does the recipe make?

____

c. How many calories do nine servings of the salad have?

____

d. How many ingredients do you need for the dressing?

____

1. Considering the ingredients and calories per serving, do you think this is a healthy dish? Why?

____

Reading the world

1. Look at the text. It is

a. ☐ a poster. b. ☐ an infographic.

2. Read the text and circle the foods that you like.

FOTOGRAFIAS: THINKSTOCK/GETTY IMAGES

Based on: <http://rentalcars24h.com.blog/what-does-the-world-eat-for-breakfast>. Accessed on: Jul. 12, 2016

3. The main objective of the text is

a. ☐ to show different breakfast habits in different countries.

b. ☐ to show breakfast recipes from around the world.

4. Read the descriptions and find the name of the food in the text.

a. ____________________ is popular in many Asian countries. It consists of cooked rice and some vegetables, meat or eggs.

b. ______________________ is made with fava beans and served with oil, onion and other spices.

c. ______________________ is the combination of stock made with cooked sardines and miso paste.

d. ________________ is a vegetable stew with lentils, popular in South Indian and Sri Lankan cuisines.

e. ________________ is a dark brown paste extracted from various vegetables. People eat it on toast or bread.

5. Write your name and what you have for breakfast. Then, draw or paste pictures of the food items.

__________________'s
(your name)
TYPICAL BREAKFAST

____

____

____

____

____

6. Is the Brazilian breakfast presented in the infographic similar to yours? If not, why do you think there is a difference?

____

____

____

UNIT
8 Can you play soccer?

Review the journey

1. Look at the pictures and write sentences using **can** or **can't**.

a.

ARTHUR TILLEY/GETTY IMAGES

Marion and Stuart

____

b.

CHERYL MAEDER/GETTY IMAGES

Greg

____

c.

MAX TOPCHII/SHUTTERSTOCK.COM

Hayley

____

d.

INTI ST CLAIR/GETTY IMAGES

Julia and Tamara

____

e.

BRAND X/GETTY IMAGES

Ned and Bob

____

f.

PHOTO BY JASON WEDDINGTON/FLICKR RF/GETTY IMAGES

Neil

____

2. Use the words from the box to label the pictures.

cleats	gloves	goggles	helmet	knee pads
racquet	shin guards	swim cap	wristband	

a. 

THINKSTOCK/GETTY IMAGES

____

d. 

TORSAK THAMMACHOTE/SHUTTERSTOCK.COM

____

g. 

HAPPY STOCK PHOTO/SHUTTERSTOCK.COM

____

b. 

THINKSTOCK/GETTY IMAGES

____

e. 

THINKSTOCK/GETTY IMAGES

____

h. 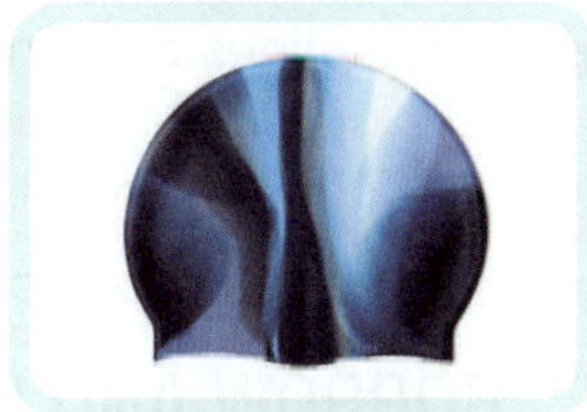

THINKSTOCK/GETTY IMAGES

____

c. 

THINKSTOCK/GETTY IMAGES

____

f. 

THINKSTOCK/GETTY IMAGES

____

i. 

THINKSTOCK/GETTY IMAGES

____

3. Solve the riddles.

a. It's a martial art. People wear kimonos. The athletes have belts in different colors according to their rank. What sport is it?

____

b. It's a water sport. You need a board and waves. What sport is it?

____

c. It's a team sport. There are five players on each side. The ball is heavy and orange. What sport is it?

____

4. Write your own riddle.

____

____

Another look

1. Look at the short texts in activity 3 and choose the best option to complete the sentence.

The texts are

a. ☐ headlines. **b.** ☐ commercials.

2. Check the characteristics of headlines.

a. ☐ They summarize the article.

b. ☐ They are complete sentences.

c. ☐ They usually use verbs in the simple present.

d. ☐ They attract the reader's attention.

3. Read the headlines and underline who or what they are about.

a. NEW APP LETS USERS BORROW AND SHARE DOGS

b. MISO SOUP DELIVERS DEEP WEEKNIGHT FLAVOR

c. NEYMAR BRILLIANCE PUTS SEAL ON BARCELONA'S 3-0 WIN OVER VILLARREAL

d. ZIKA OUTBREAK: WHAT YOU NEED TO KNOW

4. Match the headlines in activity 3 to the beginning of the corresponding articles.

☐ The infection is suspected of leading to thousands of babies being born with underdeveloped brains.

Some areas have declared a state of emergency, doctors have described it as "a pandemic in progress" and some are even advising women in affected countries to delay getting pregnant.

Adapted from: <www.bbc.com/news/health-35370848>. Accessed on: Mar. 27, 2016.

☐ Here is a recipe for a fast meal: Put one teaspoon of miso in a mug and dissolve with a tiny bit of hot water to make a sort of loose paste. Add a squeeze of lime juice and fill the mug to the top with hot water from the kettle. Stir. You have just made the simplest form of miso soup, and a pretty tasty one.

Adapted from: <www.nytimes.com/2016/03/23/dining/miso-soup.html?ref=dining&_r=0>. Accessed on: Mar. 27, 2016.

☐

Neymar scored twice and Luis Suárez added another to again lead Barcelona to a 3-0 win over Villarreal that lifted the defending champions to the top of the Spanish league.

Barcelona needed an hour of insistent attacks until Neymar broke through before Suárez added a penalty in the 70th.

Adapted from: <www.theguardian.com/football/2015/nov/08/neymar-barcelona-villarreal-match-report>. Accessed on: Mar. 27, 2016.

☐

In a new twist on the sharing economy, you can now enjoy man's best friend for just a short time. Thanks to a new mobile app, dog lovers who aren't ready to commit or are unable to own a dog, can borrow a pup for a short time or even overnight.

The service is called *Bark'N'Borrow*, and works similarly to Uber and Airbnb.

Adapted from: <www.voanews.com/content/mht-new-app-lets-users-borrow-share-dogs-barknborrow/3253001.html>. Accessed on: Mar. 27, 2016.

5. Read the beginning of the articles again. Write **T** (true), **F** (false) or **NM** (not mentioned).

a. ☐ Zika is more common in South than in North America.

b. ☐ Some doctors are advising women to delay pregnancy.

c. ☐ Miso soup is simple and it tastes good.

d. ☐ Miso soup is the most popular dish in Asia.

e. ☐ Neymar scored all the goals in the game.

f. ☐ One of the goals came from a penalty.

g. ☐ People use the new app to adopt dogs.

h. ☐ The new app is very popular among young people.

1. Which headline called your attention the most?

____

____

2. Which of the news articles would you like to read the complete version? Justify your answer.

____

____

Reading the world

1. Look at the text and choose the best option to complete the sentences.

a. The audience of the text is probably

☐ from India. ☐ not from India.

b. The words after the numbers are

☐ names of sports. ☐ provinces of India.

2. Read the text and find the most popular sport in India.

____

SPORTS IN INDIA

LONELY PLANET IMAGES/GETTY IMAGES

The history of sports in India is very ancient and dates back to the Vedic era. Chess, wrestling, polo, archery and hockey are some of the games believed to have originated in India.

Following are some of the games played in India.

1 Gilli-Danda

It is a sport played using one small stick called "gilli" and one long stick called "danda".

2 Kancha

It is played using marbles called "kancha". The festival of "Makar Sankranti" is marked with competitions of this sport.

3 Badminton

Badminton is a very popular sport in India. Badminton is supposed to have originated in India 2,000 years ago.

4 Cricket

Cricket is the most popular sport in India.

5 Cycling

This history of cycling in India dates back to 1938.

Vedic era: período da história da Índia entre 1500 e 500 a.C.

6 **Golf**

Golf is an emerging sport in India. It is more popular in wealthier classes. There are numerous golf courses all over the country.

7 **Ice hockey**

Ice hockey in India is mainly played in the Himalayan region. In winter season the game is extremely popular. However, the game is limited to cold winter months of December, January and February.

8 **Rugby**

Like other sports founded in England and introduced during the British Raj such as cricket, rugby union has a long history in India. The first recorded match was played on Christmas day 1872, at CFC in Calcutta.

9 **Volleyball**

Volleyball is a sport played all over India, both in urban as well as rural India. It is a popular recreation sport.

Adapted from: <www.facts-about-india.com/sports-in-india.php>. Accessed on: Mar. 28, 2016.

3. Write the sports mentioned in the text next to their corresponding images.

a. 

UNIQUELY INDIA/PHOTOSINDIA/GETTY IMAGES

____

b. 

YOGESH S. MORE/AGE FOTOSTOCK/AGB PHOTO

____

c. 

YOGESH S. MORE/AGE FOTOSTOCK/AGB PHOTO

____

4. Answer the questions.

a. Which are the ball sports on the list?

____

b. What part of India is near the Himalayas, the north or the south?

____

5. Write a similar list for Brazil in your notebook. Include five sports.

Connecting ideas

UNIT 1

- **www.shakira.com/home**
  Shakira's official website
- **www.fundacionpiesdescalzos.com/en/**
  Pies Descalzos Foundation
- **www.youtube.com/watch?v=WoKE1-oxkOM**
  Sob o véu do Islã – movie teaser

UNIT 2

- **www.unhcr.org/en-us/special-envoy-angelina-jolie-pitt.html**
  Angelina Jolie's webpage at the United Nations Refugee Agency
- **www.avant-pr.com/pr/the-language-of-emoji/**
  The language of emoji
- **www.xavier.edu/emoji/**
  Emoji as a second language
- **www.bbc.com/future/story/20151012-will-emoji-become-a-new-language**
  Will emoji become a new language?

UNIT 3

- **www.familyecho.com/**
  Free Online Family Tree Maker
- **www.bbc.com/news/world-africa-13433790**
  Ghana – country profile
- **http://kids.nationalgeographic.com/explore/countries/canada/#canada-playing-hockey.jpg**
  Canada – country profile

UNIT 4

- **www.youtube.com/watch?v=at2gAjtsgtk**
  Scenes from schools around the world
- **www.youtube.com/watch?v=MxBfqd639BE**
  Journeys to school
- **www.youtube.com/watch?v=qcmINpEN5FY**
  Biggest school in the world
- **www.cmseducation.org/home.htm**
  City Montessori School official website
- **http://rbth.com/articles/2012/08/01/russia_celebrates_day_of_knowledge_holiday_17823.html**
  Russia celebrates 'Day of Knowledge'

UNIT 5

- **www.salisburycathedral.org.uk/**
  Salisbury Cathedral
- **www.stonehenge.co.uk/**
  Stonehenge
- **www.english-heritage.org.uk/visit/places/old-wardour-castle/**
  Old Wardour Castle

UNIT 6

- **www.theslothinstitutecostarica.org/**
  The Sloth Institute
- **www.youtube.com/watch?v=KjuDYUPWCSk**
  Meet the Sloths
- **www.youtube.com/watch?v=E4-x5bFtgiA**
  Cute Animals: A Tiny Orphaned Sloth Named Velcro
- **www.youtube.com/watch?v=B9b2lVo584o**
  New Zealand
- **www.youtube.com/watch?v=Kh1UrZP8SNk**
  'The Hobbit' cast talk about New Zealand

UNIT 7

- **www.youtube.com/watch?v=i5lnQLsNqJk**
  Authentic Mexican Guacamole Recipe
- **www.youtube.com/watch?v=YdrH-TObXX0**
  Best Guacamole Recipe
- **www.youtube.com/watch?v=vt41Okmwl2w**
  Avocado Guacamole Recipe

UNIT 8

- **https://indiantraditionalgames.wordpress.com/**
  Research and instructions on how to play traditional Indian games
- **www.britishcouncil.org/sites/default/files/international_inspiration_traditional_games_resources_full_set_part1.pdf**
  Traditional games from different countries around the world (part 1)
- **www.britishcouncil.org/sites/default/files/international_inspiration_traditional_games_resources_full_set_part2.pdf**
  Traditional games from different countries around the world (part 2)